W9-AEB-806

WOODWORKING TECHNIQUES

THE COMPLETE GUIDE

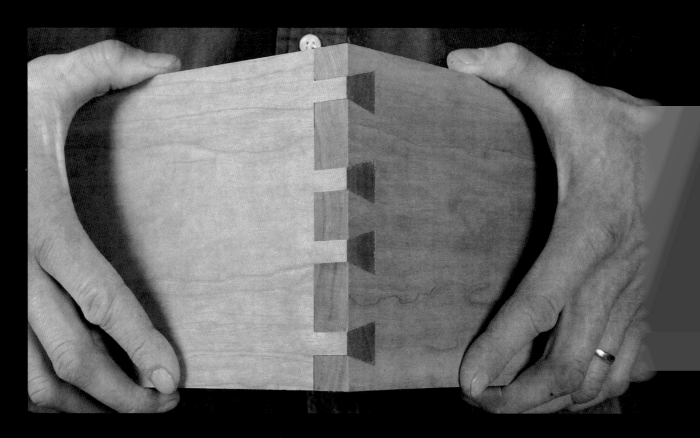

MINNETONKA, MINNESOTA

WOODWORKING TECHNIQUES
THE COMPLETE GUIDE

Printed in 2009.

All rights reserved. No part of this publication may be reproduced, stored in an electronic retrieval system or transmitted in any form or by any means (electronic, mechanical, photocopying, recording or otherwise) without the prior written permission of the copyright owner.

Tom Carpenter
Creative Director

Jen Weaverling
Managing Editor

Julie Cisler
Senior Book Designer

Alan Geho
Principal Photographer

Special Thanks to: Terry Casey, Janice Cauley and Bruce Kieffer.

The author wishes to thank the following sources for graciously providing locations for photography or supplying lumber and tools used in this book:

Blacklick Hardwoods, Bosch Tool Corporation, DeWalt Power Tools, General International Machinery, Laguna Tools, The Original Saw Company, Ridge Carbide Tool Company, RIDGID Tools, The Home Depot and WoodWerks.

3 4 5 6 / 15 14 13 12 11 10 09
© 2006 Handyman Club of America
ISBN 10: 1-58159-294-9
ISBN 13: 978-1-58159-294-8

Handyman Club of America
12301 Whitewater Drive
Minnetonka, MN 55343
www.handymanclub.com

ABOUT THE AUTHOR

Chris Marshall, a self-proclaimed tool addict, has been working wood since childhood. A former member of the editorial staff at *HANDY* magazine and book editor for the Handyman Club of America, Chris has authored books on table saws as well as trim carpentry and cabinetry, and has edited numerous volumes on woodworking and home improvement topics.

He is currently a full-time freelance writer, and serves as Field Editor for *Woodworker's Journal* magazine, for which he writes woodworking project stories and tool reviews. He also writes on a variety of shop, woodworking and home improvement topics from his home in Sunbury, Ohio.

TABLE OF CONTENTS

INTRODUCTION

If you're an active do-it-your-selfer, you've probably installed trimwork, built a few cabinets and constructed the occasional deck or fence. During countless trips to the home center, chances are you've spent some time in the tool section browsing over woodworking tools. If all those shiny new routers and saws conjure up fond memories of high school shop class, maybe you've toyed with the idea of getting into woodworking more seriously. What's holding you back?

It's time to take the woodworker inside of you more seriously.

Truth be told, "real" woodworking isn't all that different from the work you're already doing with wood. Planning out a project, selecting materials, measuring and marking, cutting parts and fastening them together are all solid building blocks for woodworking. Granted, you'll have new techniques to learn and probably a few more tools to buy, but building handsome furniture is well within your skills. With the right guidance and plenty of practice, you could build that grandfather clock, heirloom baby cradle or rocking chair you've always dreamed of. Wouldn't it be fun to make the dining table your whole family will marvel at next Thanksgiving?

Woodworking Techniques: The Complete Guide will help you take the plunge. It is a must-have addition to any woodworking library. The chapters are organized to help you follow the logical process of woodworking, so you can develop good habits and workflow right from the start. Hundreds of photographs and carefully written text will guide you to success every step of the way.

Chapter One introduces you to many sources for finding and buying lumber and sheet goods. If you thought red oak and pine are the only real choices you have for projects, think again! Learn how to select

Create raised panels on a router table, pages 223-225.

Cut coves on a table saw, pages 160-161.

the best stock and buy smart so every project starts off right.

Most woodworkers would rather be building projects than tuning up their tools, but maintenance is absolutely essential to doing precise work. Chapter Two will show you what you need to know to tweak your machines for tiptop performance and long life. You'll make discoveries that most owners' manuals fail to tell you, which will help you realize full value from your tool investment.

Speaking of investment, you already know that lumber is expensive, and prices will only continue to go up. The less of it you waste, the more you have to build with. Chapter Three will show you how to turn rough lumber into flat, smooth and square workpieces while minimizing what goes into the scrap bin. You'll also find storage tips for preserving your lumber until you need it.

Then discover how to lay out parts efficiently in Chapter Four. It's an important and essential step in the woodworking process, and the words and pictures show you how to do it right.

Chapter Five focuses on essential machining techniques. Here, we put each major woodworking machine under the magnifying glass. The content is organized so you can turn to sections for the machines you own rather than wading through a sea of general information. If you have a radial arm saw and want to cut dadoes with it, you'll find the details quickly and easily.

Finally, Chapters Six and Seven show you strategies for assembling and finishing projects without stress. If you plan ahead and prepare properly, there's no need to start sweating when you open the glue bottle! You'll also learn savvy sanding and staining techniques, as well as how to apply the "blue ribbon" finish your projects deserve.

There's never been a better time to be a woodworker—and there's no time like the present to get started. *Woodworking Techniques: The Complete Guide* will open new doors and possibilities for you. Enjoy the journey!

ONE

SELECTING LUMBER AND SHEET GOODS

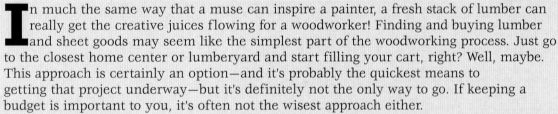

In much the same way that a muse can inspire a painter, a fresh stack of lumber can really get the creative juices flowing for a woodworker! Finding and buying lumber and sheet goods may seem like the simplest part of the woodworking process. Just go to the closest home center or lumberyard and start filling your cart, right? Well, maybe. This approach is certainly an option—and it's probably the quickest means to getting that project underway—but it's definitely not the only way to go. If keeping a budget is important to you, it's often not the wisest approach either.

In a book dedicated to woodworking techniques, this chapter will show you that there's a certain amount of know-how and process involved with locating, choosing and estimating the amount of lumber you need. Selecting and shopping carefully will help ensure that you find the type and quality of lumber that suits your project as well as your pocketbook. Developing a patient and measured approach to buying lumber usually pays dividends in the end. You'll be happier with the lumber you buy, and your projects can take full advantage of a wide range of lumber species with their own special characteristics. This chapter will help you find answers to the following important questions you should ask every time you need to find lumber for a new project:

1) Where can I find what I need?

2) How is lumber graded and sized?

3) How do I figure out how much to buy?

4) What should I look for in the lumber I buy to get the most from it?

Sources For Lumber

As the popularity of woodworking continues to grow, and the information age ushers in new technologies that make shopping easier, there are many options for buying lumber these days. Here are five alternatives to consider when your lumber supplies start to dwindle or you need to stock up for a new project:

Home Centers And Lumberyards

If you are just getting your feet wet in woodworking, the logical place to shop for lumber may seem to be the local contractor's lumberyard or home center. Depending on where you live and the range of tools you own, buying lumber from these two sources can make sense. Generally, you won't have to drive far to find a home center or lumberyard, and the folks at these places won't expect you have a base level of knowledge about shopping for wood. You're free to pick and choose what you want on your own. A large home center or lumberyard will have two or three hardwood species for you to pick from—usually oak, poplar and cherry or maple, as well as a few softwoods like pine and cedar. These may be all

Common home center lumber species (from top to bottom in photo) may include pine, oak, Douglas fir, cedar, poplar and maple. Options will vary depending on where you live.

the species options you need for the work you do.

Aside from the benefit of availability, lumber from the contractor's yard or home center can also be appealing because it's planed and jointed smooth on both faces and edges. The industry term for this degree of surfacing is "S4S," which stands for Surfaced Four Sides. S4S lumber is ideal if you don't own a thickness planer or jointer. Investing $600 or more in these surfacing machines may not make sense for you if you only build two or three projects a year, so paying a higher price for pre-surfaced lumber may be worth it. Provided the S4S lumber you buy is flat, it's ready to turn into projects. Another advantage to S4S lumber is that what you see on the surface is what you get—and the lumber is selected from premium-quality boards. With surfaced lumber, it's easy to identify surface cracks, pitch pockets, discolored areas in the wood and other defects when you pick

Home centers and the local lumberyard offer a few options for plywood, hardwood and softwood lumber, but the tradeoff for convenient shopping is usually limited selection.

One challenge to using roughsawn lumber is that small blemishes and sapwood can be difficult to spot beneath the unsurfaced faces, as these sections of the same board show. However, limited surfacing will save you money.

Lumber from the home center or lumberyard will be surfaced on both faces and edges for convenience. This may be helpful if you don't own a jointer or planer to do the surfacing work yourself.

your boards at the store. You can also see grain and figure for matching purposes. Unsurfaced lumber can hide these defects until they're exposed during the surfacing stage.

Despite the conveniences, there are drawbacks to home center lumber. When the lumber mill does all the surfacing work for you, it comes at a price. S4S lumber will cost more than unsurfaced lumber—sometimes considerably more. Depending on supply and demand, you may pay twice as much for S4S as the same board in the rough. Another issue to keep in mind is that even though the surfaces of S4S lumber may be pristine and smooth, the lumber may be far from flat. That's because the double-sided planers used by the lumber mill do little to flatten the boards.

Specialty Suppliers And Woodworking Stores

If you live in a large metropolitan area, there may be a few specialty yards for woodworking lumber. Woodworking stores that sell machinery and tools will often sell woodworking lumber as well. Check your local Yellow Pages or do an Internet search to find them. Not all of these places sell to the general public, but

those that do could offer a wealth of new wood species, sizes and grading options for you to choose from. Suddenly your alternatives for oak could expand from S4S red oak at $3/4$ in. to red, white or English oak in oversized thicknesses, lengths and special cuts. You may even be able to buy that oak from the same log in sequential pieces so the grain patterns match. A woodworking store may also carry unique plywoods with face veneers you won't find anywhere else.

A specialty supplier that sells in volume generally won't sell S4S lumber.

Most woodworking stores sell a variety of lumber species including exotics. Boards are usually pre-surfaced so you can match them for grain and color consistency. Expect to pay more than you would for roughsawn lumber.

Unlike a home center or typical lumberyard, where boards are milled into uniform widths and lengths, you'll find a wide selection of species and sizes at a specialty yard.

when the green lumber was cut from the log and dried. You'll need a planer and jointer to process your roughsawn stock, but the lumber is thicker to start with so you can remove minor surface imperfections and correct warping when you surface it.

A woodworking store may sell S2S or S4S lumber in a variety of species, cuts and sizes, but you'll pay higher prices than buying directly from a specialty yard. Again, as with home center lumber, a woodworking store has to charge more to offer lumber with additional surfacing already done for you.

Buying from a specialty yard won't provide the same creature comforts as aisle shopping at a home center or woodworking store. A busy yard may not have the staff to provide much personal service. Be prepared to be pointed in the general direction of the stock you need and then left to your own search. You'll probably also have to sort through the stacks yourself once you find what you need. Exercise common courtesy by restacking the lumber you pull off

Depending on demand, the yard may offer S2S surfacing as an option, where both faces are planed smooth. You may also be able to have your boards straight-line ripped along one edge, called "SLR1E." One flat edge makes the lumber easier to process at home. Both surfacing treatments come at an additional cost, and usually the service is only available if you buy more than a minimal amount. Typically, the majority of what you'll find at a specialty yard is roughsawn lumber. Board faces and edges still have the saw marks that were left

Hardwoods are sold in three surfacing options. "S4S" lumber (top in photo) is surfaced on both faces and long edges. "S2S" (center) will have two surfaced faces, but one or both edges may still be rough. "Roughsawn" (bottom) has no surface planing on the faces or edges.

A specialty yard may sell air-dried or kiln-dried lumber. Here, a stack of air-dried lumber has scrap "stickers" inserted between the boards to promote air circulation and prevent mold growth.

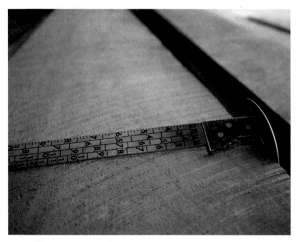

Roughsawn lumber is sold by the board foot. A specialized ruler with pre-marked computations makes calculating the volume of each piece fast and easy.

Hardwood is graded by the percentage of allowable defects it contains. This bundle of cherry is marked "FAS," which stands for "Firsts and Seconds," the clearest grade that's often available.

the pile. Keep your car clear of truck loading zones and forklift areas. What a specialty yard lacks in curb appeal or customer service it will probably make up for in variety and discounted pricing. If you are a wood lover at heart, a specialty yard can provide that "kid in the candy store" experience you won't soon forget.

Grade differences are usually easy to spot. Notice the knots, wane and sapwood on the #1 Common board (right) as compared to the clear FAS board (left). More defects are allowable on lower grades of hardwood lumber.

Internet Lumber Vendors

Check the listings section in the back of most woodworking magazines and you'll find numerous lumber suppliers you could try from all parts of the United States and even abroad. All it takes is a quick Internet search for whatever lumber species you want, and you'll have numerous sources at your fingertips. The Internet has truly opened the global doors to lumber buying—even on the small, home-shop scale. You don't have to live anywhere near the best supplier of mesquite or lacewood to obtain these woods, provided you have a computer and web access.

As far as advantages go, buying from lumber suppliers in other areas allows you to find dealers that specialize in woods from their geographic locale. If you want premium tiger striped cherry or quartersawn white oak with showy flakes, there's probably an Appalachian lumber retailer that still buys from local mills. Need some clear redwood? Try a vendor in the Pacific Northwest or California. Suppliers focus their inventory on any number of niche areas as well: reclaimed lumber, instrument-grade woods, unusual burls or oversized stock and exotic veneered plywood, to name just a few. Shopping by cyberspace offers you the widest spectrum of lumber choices, and you can browse from the convenience of your computer.

One limitation to buying from these suppliers is that you don't have the luxury of hand-selecting your boards. Reputable vendors will usually guarantee the quality of their inventory and offer return policies meant to build confidence. However, in most cases you'll still have to buy "sight unseen." Sometimes a vendor will actually photograph individual pieces of particularly valuable or rare lumber so you can see the exact board you are buying, but not always.

When placing your order, avoid online buying. Many suppliers won't even give you the "shopping cart" option on their websites for most of their inventory. You'll need to call to obtain current pricing or to request a price sheet, and calling is a good idea anyway. Try to speak with the person who will actually pull the boards for you—many yards are small enough to make this feasible. Be as specific as possible about what you're looking for. If the top on your dining room table project won't work unless each board is at least 6 ft. long and 8 in. wide, spell this out clearly with the yard representative. Do what you can

to minimize your own surprises when the truck delivers your order. Extensive communication with the supplier is the key to success when purchasing lumber by mail order.

Another factor that impacts buying lumber remotely is the cost you'll pay for shipping. Lumber is heavier than most commodities we buy— short of woodworking machinery— and shipping charges can be significant. If your supplier is located on the far side of a mountain range from where you live, or if the cost of fuel is particularly high, you may pay a surcharge for extra trucking costs. Have the yard tabulate the packaging and shipping costs you'll pay for your order so you can factor that into your project budget. It's a real and unavoidable cost to you. One way to help reduce your overall costs is to convince your woodworking friends to place a group order and do what you can to buy in volume.

Be sure to find out whether the truck that brings your wood will deliver directly to your home. If you have back trouble or other physical limitations, request that the truck have a lift gate. Otherwise, you may have to help the driver unload your order, board by board. Some freight companies will only deliver the wood as far as a local terminal, and you'll have to pick it up there. It's another unpleasant surprise that's easy to avoid by asking before you buy.

Internet Auctions

A third way to buy lumber is to win it at auction. If you're lucky, you could end up paying rock-bottom prices for good-quality material. However, buying lumber this way means you'll face some of the same issues as when shopping from an Internet lumber dealer. You can't put your hands on the actual wood you're bidding on, and you'll probably have to pay for shipping and packaging costs unless you make the drive to pick up your winnings. Unlike a reputable lumber dealer, the source you're buying from probably won't

The Internet has opened a wellspring of options for buying lumber. Most specialty yards and wholesalers have websites that provide information about their inventory. You can also buy lumber through Web auction sites such as eBay.

offer a guarantee on the quality of lumber you win. In fact, the "seller" may not be a lumber dealer at all or even know much about what's being sold. If there's a photograph depicting what's up for auction, be careful that it actually shows what you'll buy if you win. Ultimately, let common sense be your guide. Look for sellers with positive feedback ratings in their seller's posted record. Search for earlier lumber sales in the comments area left by other buyers. E-mail or call the seller with any and all of your questions, including applicable shipping charges. If some aspect of the auction seems unclear or the least bit unscrupulous, don't make a bid. When it comes to Internet auctions, buyer beware.

Another option to locate hard-to-find lumber, plywood or exotics is the classified section of woodworking magazines. Call to obtain a price list and shipping information.

Urban Lumber, Low-Volume Sawyers Or Your Backyard

Depending on how specific your lumber needs are, you may not have to look far and wide to find great lumber affordably. One option that's gaining popularity among woodworkers is buying city trees that are felled to make way for urban development or to clear storm damage. If you have mature hardwood trees on your property, they could become woodworking lumber as well. Either way, harvesting your own lumber is definitely labor intensive and requires long-term commitment. You'll need to find a local sawyer with a portable lumber mill that can saw the log into boards for you. Usually, this is a relatively inexpensive service, and you might be able to pay a portion of the cost to the sawyer in what the tree yields. Once you've got your green lumber cut, you'll need to stack and dry it correctly to avoid distortion, splits and mold growth. You'll need to tend to this lumber throughout the drying period by occasionally rotating the stack and watching for signs of decay. Drying time can take a year or longer. When done properly, air-dried lumber can yield wonderful project wood. If not managed carefully, you could be left with a bunch of board-size firewood. Seek the advice of others who have dried their own lumber, or find books on the subject to learn all you can before taking a chainsaw to that old sycamore tree.

If you live in a rural area or wooded state, there may be a small-volume private sawmill or hobbyist wood cutter close by with lumber to sell. Finding these places and people may be a word-of-mouth discovery, as many weekend woodcutters don't advertise. Check with a local woodworking guild, the message board at a woodworking store or talk with firewood suppliers in your area to find those hole-in-the-wall sources for lumber. It could be well worth the effort.

A portable sawmill can turn that backyard tree into a viable source of project lumber. This stack of walnut, for instance, all came from one neighborhood tree, which yielded boards as wide as 14 inches.

How Is Lumber Sized And Graded?

If you're a lumberyard shopper, you already know that the actual measurements of surfaced lumber don't match the nominal (named) size. In other words, a 1 x 6 isn't an inch thick and six inches wide. Actual dimensions are $3/4$ in. by $5^1/2$ in. Nominal sizing refers to the "named" size of the boards before they were dried and milled to final dimensions. See the chart on the next page for a quick reference guide to actual board sizing. You'll need to take this information into account when estimating the sizes of lumber you need to buy for a project. Standardized board sizing can have an impact on how you design your project. If you don't have the means to glue up your own panels from narrower pieces of lumber, you'll have to design your project based on the board widths available.

The system of lumber sizing is entirely different if you buy wood from a specialty yard. Here, lumber thickness is designated by a "quarter-ing" system of measurement. Typically, the thinnest lumber you'll find is $4/4$ thick, which translates into "four quarter" inches, or about 1-inch thickness. The actual thickness of $4/4$ lumber varies by about $1/8$ in., depending on the supplier. Surfaced (S2S) $4/4$ lumber is usually milled to about $13/16$ in., while roughsawn $4/4$ lumber will be closer to an actual inch. Either way, $4/4$ material will always be thick enough to plane down to $3/4$. That's the intention. The extra thickness is helpful for jointing the board faces flat.

Once you know the basics, a little math is all it takes to figure out the rough thickness of other quartered sizes. A $5/4$ board is roughly five quarter inches, or $1^1/4$ in. thick. A $6/4$ board is six quarter inches, or $1^1/2$ in. thick, and so on. Common quarter thicknesses are $4/4$, $5/4$, $6/4$, $8/4$, $10/4$ and $12/4$. A supplier may not stock all these thicknesses for each species or grade. Ask for a pricing sheet to check the available inventory.

There are other differences you'll need to know about between buying dimension lumber from a home center and quartered lumber at a specialty yard. At the home center, you buy the board by the piece or by the lineal foot. A piece of quartered lumber will be sold by volume, which is measured in "board feet." A board foot is equivalent to 144 cubic inches, determined by multiplying a board's thickness times its width times its length. So, one board foot, hypothetically, is a piece measuring 1 in. thick, 12 in. wide and 12 in. long (1 x 12 x 12 = 144). By the same token, a board foot could also be a piece measuring 2 in. thick by 8 in. wide by 9 in. long (2 x 8 x 9 = 144). The primary reason why specialty lumber is sold by volume is that it allows specialty lumber to be sold in random widths and lengths instead of standard sizes. This maximizes the yield of lumber from the log. Short or narrow pieces don't have to be rejected because they don't meet a minimum size.

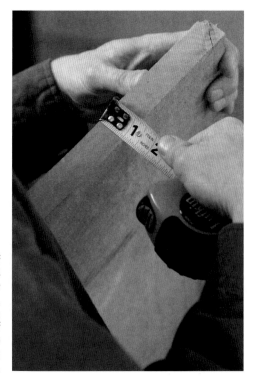

This piece of roughsawn 4/4 lumber is slightly more than 1 in. thick. The extra thickness is helpful if you need to remove distortions during the surfacing stage.

What this means for the shopper is that you'll find a much wider assortment of board sizes at a specialty yard, based on what's available from the mill. At a given time, you may not be able to buy cherry that's wider than 10 in. in 8 ft. lengths, but there may be plenty of stock that's 7 to 9 in. wide and 12 ft. long. Inventories vary constantly, and you pay by the board foot, whatever the board proportions may be. To figure out how much you'll actually pay for a board, you'll need to determine how many board feet the piece contains. Take the thickness to the nearest greater inch, and multiply by the width and length in inches, then divide by 144. A 4/4 piece of cherry measuring 10 in. wide by 8 ft. long calculates as follows: 1 x 10 x 96 = 960. 960 cubic inches divided by 144 = 6.67 board feet. If the yard is charging $4.50 per board foot for cherry, you'll pay $30 ($4.50 x 6.67) plus applicable sales tax for this board.

Another issue to consider is lumber grading. Specialty hardwoods are graded by standards established by the National Hardwood Lumber Association. Grading is based on the percentage of clear lumber a board has. From clearest to most knotty, the system is delineated as follows:

Hardwood Grading

- Clear Face Cuttings: Highest grade

- Firsts and Seconds (FAS) or Selects and Better

- No. 1 Common

- No. 2 Common

- No. 3 Common

- Sound Cuttings

- No. 2B Common

- No. 3B Common

- Sound Wormy

NOMINAL LUMBER SIZES

NOMINAL SIZING	ACTUAL DIMENSION
1 x 2	¾ x 1½
1 x 3	¾ x 2½
1 x 4	¾ x 3½
1 x 6	¾ x 5½
1 x 8	¾ x 7¼
1 x 10	¾ x 9¼
1 x 12	¾ x 11¼

Within this system, Firsts and Seconds will be nearly free of knots and large surface imperfections, while No. 2 Common will have knots but still a fair amount of clear wood. The percentage of clear wood can range from as much as 83.5% to as little as 25%, depending on the grade. Most suppliers don't have the warehouse space to store more than a few grades of any given lumber species. Typically, a yard will stock FAS, No. 1 Common and possibly No. 2 Common. Clear Face Cuttings is a grade usually reserved for premium, highly figured lumber. As you might expect, the higher the grade, the more you'll pay per board foot.

Keep in mind, however, that you may be able to buy a lower grade and still get clear areas of lumber large enough to meet your needs for a specific project. The

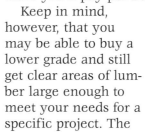

Lumber is sold by volume in the quartering system of measurement. In this photo, all three pieces of wood have a volume of one board foot. Notice the dramatic difference in physical proportions!

only way to know is to cull the inventory at the yard and bring your tape measure and cutting list along.

Cuts Of Lumber

Lumber is sawn from a log in a couple different ways to maximize yield, avoid defects in the log or to make the most of interesting grain patterns. The lumber you buy at a home center or typical contractor's yard is usually plain-sawn. The log is simply cut through the diameter, from one side of the log to the other. Sometimes, depending on the purpose of the lumber or to avoid major defects, a mill may rotate the log a quarter turn midway through to cut

around the center pith area of the log. Plain-sawing produces boards with grain patterns that can vary widely. The direction of the growth ring pattern on the end of the boards can vary from nearly parallel to almost perpendicular to board faces. You'll find a range of face grain patterns, from the common cathedral-shaped concentric ovals to more straight lines in quartersawn areas of the board.

Quartersawing, a second milling method, involves splitting the log into four pie-shaped wedges and slicing boards so the growth rings are at a right angle, or nearly so, to the board face. This method is a less efficient way to mill a log, and it results in more waste, but the perpendicular orientation of the rings creates lumber that is more dimensionally stable than plain-sawn lumber. Certain species of trees such as oak, cherry and sycamore reveal beautiful medullary ray patterns when boards are cut this way. This is the "flake" or "ray" pattern you see on Mission style furniture. You'll pay more for quartersawn lumber, but it makes some of the best lumber for woodworking projects.

Growth rings on a piece of quartersawn Douglas fir lumber run nearly perpendicular to the board face (left). Plain-sawn lumber (right) will have growth rings that run parallel to the board face.

Quartersawing some species of lumber, including this white oak (left), can reveal spectacular medullary ray patterns that aren't apparent on plain-sawn white oak (right).

A related cut to quartersawing is rift-sawing, which basically means the growth rings are at roughly a 45° angle to the board face. Quartersawn lumber often has rift-sawn areas in it, depending on the circumference of the log. Rift-sawn lumber provides the same benefits as quartersawn lumber but with a slightly different face grain pattern. The rays and flakes will be much smaller or entirely absent, and the grain pattern tends to be uniform and parallel.

A specialty yard may also offer flitch-sawn wood. This means the log was cut and stacked sequentially to retain the original ordering of the boards. Buying flitch-sawn lumber gives you a much better chance to match the grain pattern, figure and coloration of your lumber. Color match is usually the best reason to buy flitch-sawn wood, followed by grain consistency and then figure.

Plywood

Plywood and other sheet materials like melamine and medium-density fiberboard certainly have their place in woodworking. Generally, the main reason to use plywood is that its composition offers better dimensional stability than solid wood. Plywood does not shrink and expand with changes in humidity like solid wood. Plywood may warp when exposed to high levels of humidity, but its length and width will not change. It's also a convenient material to use when you need to make large panels. You could glue up individual boards to make a cabinet back or drawer bottom, but a single piece of sheet material will do the same job with much less effort.

For fine projects, you'll probably want to use plywood with a high-quality wood face veneer. Hardwood and softwood veneered plywood have their own elaborate grading systems, but knowing the various grades is less important than recognizing what will look best on your final project. Try to match the plywood veneer to the type of solid lumber you're using for the rest of a project. A cherry bookcase, for instance, benefits by having a back panel made of cherry veneered plywood. Matching the veneer to the wood provides more consistent grain and figure, and you'll get a better color match between the solid wood and the plywood when you finish it.

You may not know that there are far more veneer options for plywood than what your local home center or lumberyard stocks (usually birch or oak veneer only). In fact, you can buy plywood with veneer to match virtually any common woodworking lumber. Walnut, quartersawn or rift-sawn oak, maple, hickory, ash, mahogany, and clear pine are all easy plywood veneers to find. Again, an Internet search will reveal many specialty plywood sources around the country. If you can't find a particularly unusual face veneer, you may be able to have the

Plywood is available in dozens of veneers if you buy it from specialty suppliers and woodworking stores. You can also have it custom made with face veneer that matches virtually any project wood.

supplier make up the sheets for you by special order. Specialty suppliers can also make up sheets with the same grade or species of veneer on both sides, if you need it. It will cost significantly more per sheet for this service.

Construction grades of plywood with wild, undulating grain patterns on the outer faces don't look anything like solid wood. The face veneer is rotary cut, produced by spinning the log and shearing off the veneer in a continuous sheet around the tree's circumference. Rotary-cut plywood may be suitable for a painted project, but it's distracting and unsightly for clear-finished projects. Cabinet-grade plywoods will have "bookmatched" or "slipmatched" outer veneers instead of rotary-cut veneer. Here, the veneer is made by slicing paper-thin sheets off the log in the same manner as boards are cut from the log. The benefit is that the plywood face grain looks more like pieces of real lumber laid side by side, with a repeating or mirror image pattern to the grain.

Cabinet-quality plywood can have several different cores. Home centers typically stock the type with layers of lower-grade veneers making up the center. It's easy to tell the difference

One consideration to keep in mind when choosing plywood for a project is the appearance of the face veneer. Bookmatched face veneer (left) looks more like real board lumber than rotary-cut face veneer (right), which has an irregular, almost surreal grain pattern.

then you'll run across lumber-core plywood, but it's relatively uncommon these days. As far as workability is concerned, MDF-core plywood is heavier than the other options, and it's more prone to splitting when driving fasteners into the edges. However, all three core types provide good dimensional stability and are easy to machine. Depending on your options for sources and your budget, you may need to settle for whichever plywood your supplier carries.

Other sheet materials are also handy to use for woodworking. Medium-density fiberboard, commonly known by the acronym MDF, is made of tiny wood fibers and glue compressed under great pressure. MDF doesn't take stain well or look like wood, but it's an excellent material for making jigs or as a substrate under wood veneer. It also accepts paint well. Be aware that MDF is extremely heavy, and the edges are relatively easy to damage. MDF has no grain structure or layered plys to give it stiffness, so be sure to provide adequate support when using MDF for shelving. Otherwise, it will sag. You can find MDF in 1/2- and 3/4-in. thicknesses at most lumberyards and home centers. MDF is also made in 1/4- and 1-in. thicknesses, but these are usually special-order sizes.

between the "good" plywood and the rest of the construction plywood on the shelf: aside from the attractive face veneer, the core will have a few more internal ply layers and usually there will be few or no voids between the layers. High-quality plywood may also have a composite of wood plys sandwiched between layers of particleboard, or the core may simply be a single layer of MDF. Every now and

Plywood is manufactured with various core compositions of wood veneer, lumber and MDF. Generally, more ply layers yield more stable plywood. Aside from counting the layers, it's difficult to evaluate the core quality based on its composition.

Other sheet good options for your woodworking projects can include (from top to bottom) medium-density fiberboard, melamine-coated particleboard and hardboard.

You probably already use hardboard—another common sheet material—for making drawer bottoms. Hardboard is darker than MDF and is usually available in 1/8- and 1/4-in. thicknesses at the home center. Aside from its use for drawer construction, hardboard is helpful to have on hand for making router templates.

Melamine is another useful sheet material to keep on hand. It has a particleboard core and faces made of colored, thermofused plastic. Melamine board is a good option for making cabinet carcases because you don't have to paint them. Home centers usually stock 3/4-in. white melamine, and you can order it in gray, black, tan and other colors. The surfaces are easy to clean and fairly durable, although melamine won't offer the same surface durability as countertop laminate. Sagging is a problem with melamine if you don't

support it sufficiently, and nails and screws will pull out more easily in melamine than MDF or plywood.

How Much Wood Should I Buy?

The only thing worse than wasting lumber is finding out midway through a project that you haven't bought enough. At the very least, you'll have to run to the lumberyard or home center to buy more, which is inconvenient. The problem is more irritating if you have to order more wood from a distant supplier and wait a couple weeks for it to arrive. Either way, a few lessons in estimating materials can save you time, frustration and inconvenience.

The key to figuring out how much lumber you need for a project is to

The best way to calculate the amount of lumber you need for a project is to start with a set of detailed drawings and a material list. Factor in an extra 20 to 30% to allow for natural defects and waste.

start with a reliable set of drawings. Drawings not only provide a way to work through your aesthetic and functional concerns about a project, but they also provide the raw dimensional data for estimating lumber. This book will not teach you how to design a project or create working drawings. Other project and design books can teach you that important skill. Or, try a computer aided software program to create your drawings. Most CAD programs are reasonably priced and are easy to use, once you get the hang of them. Some will even build a material list for you based on the dimensions of the parts in the project.

Try to develop your project drawings thoroughly so you can iron out as many of the details as possible. An easy project may only take a few sketches and dimensions to provide all the information you need, but most projects require multiple views, some detail drawings of joinery and a good bit of noodling. Before estimating what you need to buy, be sure you are happy with what you plan to build and confident about constructing it. It's cheaper to spend more time on your drawings than it is to waste lumber on building errors and oversights.

Once you've got a complete set of drawings, label all the parts and jot down a material list. Your material list should include part names, quantities, finished dimensions and type of material each part will be made of. If a part has joinery on the ends, don't forget to add on the extra material required to make the joints. If a rail has two 1½-in. tenons on the ends, the material list dimension for the rail should include the extra 3 in. of tenon length.

With your material list in hand, there are a couple ways to estimate what to buy. One approach is to calculate the number of board feet in each part and then add up the total number of board feet. Tally up board footage requirements for all the part thicknesses in the project.

This method will give you a rough idea of what you'll need once you've cut, jointed and planed away your waste. It won't help you determine how long or wide each board needs to be in order to yield the parts required. It also doesn't factor in the inevitable defects, miscuts or test pieces you'll need to make. To account for the "fudge factor," buy at least 20 to 30 percent more lumber than your estimate. It may seem like an astonishing amount of extra wood to buy, but you'll be surprised how often the overage provides just the right amount in the end. If there's a lot of wood left over, save it for the next project. It sure beats running short!

Another way to approach estimating is to sketch some boards in sizes that are commonly available, then draw your project parts on the "virtual" boards. This way, you'll not only be able to figure out rough board footage but also determine some logical ways to organize the parts on your stock to minimize waste. It's more challenging to use this method when buying rough-sawn stock, since rough lumber is sold in random widths and lengths. But, typically, most inventories will contain boards that are at least 6 in. wide and 6 to 8 ft. long. This estimating method won't help you determine waste percentages, because a sketched board still isn't the real thing. So, add in another 20 to 30 percent more wood, just to be safe.

It's easy to estimate plywood and other sheet goods if you create a cutting diagram for each sheet. The size of a typical sheet of plywood is 4 ft. x 8 ft. Draw sheets to scale, and sketch the parts on the sheets. Be sure to take saw kerfs and edge trimming into account when drawing your diagrams. You'll lose about ⅛ in. of material with each saw cut. Melamine and MDF generally come about an inch oversized in length and width to allow for edge trimming.

Avoiding Surprises When Buying Lumber

If you buy your lumber from a distant source, you know that asking good questions and being specific about what you want are ways to prevent surprises when the truck arrives. Let's presume that you are buying from a source close to home and you can pick what you buy. Here are a few tips to keep in mind as you sort through the stacks:

1. Ask About Wood Dryness

Suppliers will either dry their own inventory or buy it already dry from the mill. Usually, a price sheet will indicate whether the stock is air dried or kiln (oven) dried. Usually it doesn't matter which way the wood is dried.

However, if you plan on steam- or dry-bending parts of a project, buy air-dried stock. Kiln-drying can make wood more brittle. Some experts also argue that air-dried wood is more colorful than kiln-dried wood.

Despite the drying method, what's more important is that the wood is sufficiently dry when you buy it. Furniture lumber should have no more than 6 to 10 percent moisture content. Wetter lumber is more prone to warping. The yard manager should be able to tell you what moisture level the lumber is at. Most yards won't prove it to you by taking a moisture reading in your presence, so you'll have to take their word for it when you buy. Generally, you can trust what you hear, but it never hurts to take your own reading at home with a moisture meter (see tint box, this page), just to be sure. If the moisture content is too high, you'll have to dry the wood further or return it.

MOISTURE METERS

A moisture meter takes the guesswork out of determining moisture content in a board. These instruments are fairly expensive, with prices ranging from about $70 to as much as $200, but they may be worth the investment if you buy lumber from many different sources. The meter will come with a cross-reference chart for evaluating different species, or it may recalibrate itself automatically. To take a reading, first crosscut about 2 in. off the end of the board and press the meter's probes into the board's sawn edge. The meter's reading will tell you moisture content. Always take readings from a freshly cut end; wood dries from the ends inward. Old ends are often drier than the middle of the board, and they'll give you an inaccurate reading.

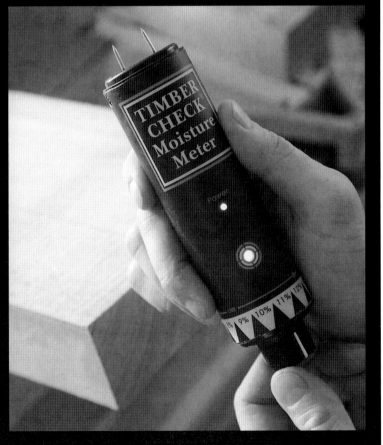

2. Take Your Time, And Bring Your Tools

Hand-selecting your lumber can be a little daunting, especially if you have several grades to choose from. It can also be unnerving if a yard worker is watching you pick through things or waiting for you to finish. Just remember, lumber is expensive. What you buy is what you end up with. Bring your material list along and carefully check your selection of boards against your estimate. It helps to have a calculator and tape measure handy to check your quantities again—especially if the inventory doesn't include boards with the proportions you need.

3. Look Carefully

Give each promising piece of lumber you find a good going-over. Sight along one edge to check for bowing or warping, then sight down the face to check for cupping and twist. Look closely for defects. Does

Be sure to bring along your project material list, a calculator and a tape measure when shopping at a specialty yard. You may need to make some compromises and re-evaluate your quantities based on the stock available when you shop.

Whenever you buy lumber, take your time and evaluate each piece carefully. Check for distortions, wane, splits and knots and sapwood areas. Prudent shopping will help avoid those unpleasant surprises later on.

the board have splits in the ends or elsewhere? End checks are easy to cut away, but splits in the center could be a sign of excessive internal stresses in the wood or poor kiln-drying methods. Look for surface checks too. They can be caused by poor drying, poor storage, stale stock (too long on the shelf) or inferior lumber. Does the board have obvious light and dark areas? Light regions usually are sapwood, which is sometimes desirable and sometimes not. If you don't want mismatched coloration, avoid pieces with sapwood. Keep an eye out for worm holes or even hidden nails, especially if you buy "backyard" or reclaimed lumber.

4. Remember Your Tooling Limitations

A 14-in.-wide piece of black walnut is a wonderful rarity to find, but you can't fit it through a 13-in. planer without ripping it first. Ripping and regluing is an entirely acceptable means of dealing with wide material but it's tough to do well if you don't have a jointer. Likewise, a 12/4 plank of oak can be resawn to yield several pieces of thinner, matched stock, but do you have a bandsaw and blade that are up to the task? Buy stock that is reasonable to work with using the tools you have.

5. Ask About "Shorts" And Common Lumber

It doesn't take 10-ft. boards to make a nightstand or jewelry box. If you're making a small project, ask if the yard carries "shorts," which are boards in lengths of 4 to 6 ft. Shorts are often sold at a discounted price, and they may be FAS or Select quality—just a bit shorter than ordinary. Keep in mind that common grades of lumber may also be an option, if you only need to make short parts. Lower grades of lumber will mean more knots to cut around, but the clear material in between may offer all the length you need.

TOOL TUNE-UP AND MAINTENANCE

For most of us, shop time is precious and usually too short. The promise of spending a Saturday afternoon turning a fresh stack of lumber into a project is probably more appealing than adjusting your band saw or sharpening a set of chisels. However, that old overworked adage about "an ounce of prevention" couldn't be more fitting when it comes to the care and upkeep of woodworking machines, and the reasoning is easy to see. From the standpoint of investment, properly adjusted, cleaned and lubricated tools will last longer than neglected tools. Well-tuned machines will also help your work more efficiently: you'll get more done at the end of the day when your table saw cuts accurately each time and the jointer actually produces flat surfaces. Wood certainly isn't getting cheaper as resources diminish, so tools that perform correctly can also help reduce the number of botched workpieces that end up in the scrap bin. And, just as a sharp knife is safer to use than a dull one, a well-tuned machine prevents accidents that come from misuse or malfunction.

Maintaining your tools also has intuitive value. By keeping cast iron pristine, your blades clean and sharp and those gears meshing smoothly, it shows that you take yourself seriously as a woodworker. The shop is an organized place, and your tools are the instruments that help improve your skills. You can approach each project confidently, calmly and with full anticipation of completing it successfully.

This chapter will help guide you through the tune-up and maintenance procedure for keeping your home shop woodworking machines in tiptop shape. Of course, not every power tool requires regular maintenance. Can you remember the last time you had to tune up your circular saw or power drill? But, other machinery with more moving parts, fences and reference surfaces should receive routine attention, so we'll focus on these. We'll also cover a few sharpening techniques for chisels and plane irons as well as how to clean and inspect your saw blades and router bits. Use the overviews presented here as supplemental material to the reference manuals that come with your power tools. Follow the maintenance procedures recommended by the manufacturer first. From there, this chapter can help direct you to other aspects of maintenance and tuning that some tool manuals fail to provide.

When To Tune And Maintain Tools

The good news about tool maintenance is that it really isn't as time-consuming as it might seem, provided you work systematically and tend to your tools as soon as you detect a problem. Most machines kept in decent repair can be lubricated and tuned up in a few hours or less. If you buy quality machinery that holds its adjustments, your maintenance time may amount to little more than an occasional cleaning and light lubrication.

The frequency with which you need to maintain your machines depends on a number of factors. The most critical time for general adjustment and tuning should happen when you first buy the tool. Don't expect that the manufacturer has done a thorough job of tuning your new machine at the factory—although reputable manufacturers usually do exercise high standards of quality control. Approach a new tool with the mindset that it needs a thor-

ough "going over" before it's ready for use. This is especially true for tools that require lots of initial assembly before use. Also, if you've just invested in a new table saw, jointer or other shop tool with cast iron, check the iron surfaces carefully for flatness. Even after cast iron is ground flat, it can still warp if stresses in the castings weren't completely relieved before it received final machining. If the castings are warped, return the machine immediately for another one with flatter surfaces.

If you've just purchased a used tool, be sure to carefully inspect and tune it up before use so you can establish a baseline of knowledge about it. Likewise, be sure to thoroughly tune your shop machines after moving them from one location to another or if your tools have been stored for a significant period of time. Lubricants evaporate, grease hardens and rust insidiously finds its way onto metal.

Maybe your woodworking "hobby" actually borders on light-duty production work instead of an occasional weekend project. Machines that are heavily used will obviously require more maintenance. If your tools aren't connected to dust collection equipment, they'll need regular cleanings to remove accumulated dust and debris. Naturally, you should tune up these tools more often than those you seldom use.

Keep in mind that lighter-duty, budget priced tools or machines that are made to be portable will require more frequent tune-up than heavy stationary machinery. Their castings will be thinner and the gearing and control systems will be more delicate. Tools lugged from the shop to the trunk to the jobsite and back again are more prone to fall out of adjustment. Set aside some time each week or month to tune up light-duty or heavily used tools. If you don't tune up your tools frequently, it may even help to keep a maintenance log so you can record when you last tended to each machine.

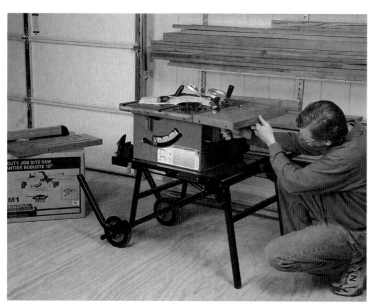

Straight out of the shipping carton, you'll need to give a new machine a thorough tune up to ensure top performance. Other important occasions for tune ups include buying used machinery or after dismantling and moving your machines to new locations.

You'll need a fair number of tools, lubricants and cleaners to perform thorough tune-ups on your woodworking machines. However, none are expensive or hard to find.

Tools You'll Need For Tune-Ups

Caring for woodworking machines won't require a big investment of tune-up tools to get the job done. You'll need the ordinary collection of metric and imperial sockets and wrenches, Allen wrenches, screwdrivers, and an accurate engineer's square or combination square. A plastic drafting triangle or metal set-up triangle can also be helpful for dialing in blade tilt settings.

Aside from these ordinary shop hand tools, you should also invest in a decent 4-ft. metal straightedge that's warranted for flatness to within a few thousandths of an inch over its length. Many woodworking supply catalogs offer these straightedges for reasonable prices (you can find them for less than $50). It's impossible to verify a flat surface without a reliable straightedge, and the one you use for tune-ups shouldn't be the same one you use to mark off a sheet of plywood. Buy a set of shim-style feeler gauges, available at any auto parts store, and a dial calipers. Dial calipers with scales that read in fractions are useful for both tool maintenance and for measuring part thicknesses. For extremely precise tuning, a dial indicator equipped with a magnetic base can also be helpful. You can find a serviceable dial and base for less than $50.

You'll also need various cleaners and lubricants to keep your machines working properly. Buy a can of "dry" emulsifying spray lube sold at auto parts stores or bike shops. These spray products are helpful for lubricating moving chains, shafts and gears that also come in contact with sawdust and wood chips. A dry lube won't attract contaminants that can gum up machine parts like ordinary machine grease. Or, use paste furniture wax instead of dry lube as an alternative; it won't attract contaminants either. White lithium grease, sold in spray or solid forms, works well for lubricating chains and gears that are protected inside sealed cases.

To clean wood pitch and dried grease from metal parts, use mineral spirits or turpentine as solvents and a synthetic scrub pad or an old toothbrush. Household 409-brand cleaner works well too, but make sure to dry the metal thoroughly afterwards so it won't rust. Although WD-40 makes a good cleaning agent and light lubricant, it contains silicone. Keep if off of machine tables and fence surfaces where it could soak into bare wood and prevent wood finishes from adhering properly. Whatever cleaning solvents you use, it's a good idea to protect your hands from harsh cleaners with disposable gloves.

When cleaning tool parts with aerosol solvents, be careful to control the overspray so it doesn't soak into electrical components or closed bearings. The solvent could ignite or dissolve the grease from bearings and cause them to seize up. Also, use degreasers sparingly or not at all when cleaning rubber bandsaw tires, planer feed rollers or other plastic surfaces that could be damaged by chemicals. Soapy water and a bit of extra scrubbing will usually do the trick without damaging rubber or plastic.

CARING FOR CAST IRON

Cast iron is arguably the best material for tabletops, undercarriages and fences on woodworking machinery. The trouble is, it will rust in the presence of even the slightest bit of moisture unless you protect it. A damp basement shop, a few drops of sweat or a soggy breeze through the shop on a rainy day are all it takes to turn a shiny tabletop tan with oxidation. If your tool surfaces already have some light rust, it's relatively easy to remove with naval jelly or spray-on rust dissolvers and a scrub pad. Use coarse steel wool or fine-grit wet/dry sandpaper and mineral spirits to remove pitted or accumulated rust. Once you've thoroughly removed the rust, apply a coat of furniture paste wax or a metal protective spray to seal the iron. Then buff the surface smooth.

Keeping cast-iron surfaces clean and in tiptop shape involves applying an occasional coat of paste wax or dry lubricant spray. When rust spots form, remove them promptly with naval jelly or other rust removing spray.

Apply rust remover to the table surface, allow a few minutes for it to dissolve the rust, then scrub with a gray synthetic scrub pad or fine-grit steel wool. Wipe the surface clean.

Polish a freshly cleaned tabletop with a coat of paste wax to help seal out moisture and improve smoothness.

TUNING UP A TABLE SAW

If you were to tally up the number of hours you use each of your wood-working machines, you probably use the table saw more than any other tool. It stands to reason then that a table saw deserves regular cleaning and occasional adjustment. Some of the checks and adjustments overviewed in this section will mainly apply if you are setting up a saw for the first time or if you're uncrating the saw after moving to a new location. If you're simply tuning up your saw, skip past the sections on inspecting the tabletop to other adjustment, cleaning and lubrication procedures.

One way to think of table saw tune-up systematically is to start from the top and work down. You'll hit each of the major target areas for adjustment in a sensible sequence of steps. Here are the major components to address: 1) Tabletop and extension wings; 2) Blade alignment to the miter slots; 3) Rip fence alignment; 4) Adjusting the blade tilt stops; 5) Adjusting the splitter and miter gauge and 6) General cleaning and lubrication.

Inspecting The Tabletop And Extension Wings

A table saw's cutting accuracy depends on a number of factors, including the flatness of the tabletop and extension wings. The goal here is that the center table and wings form a continuous flat plane. Tables and extension wings made of cast iron generally provide a flatter surface than tabletops made of other

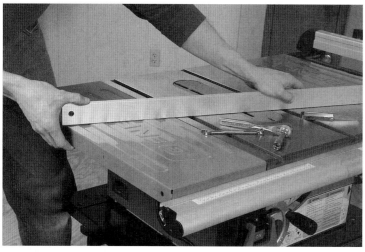

Check your saw table for flatness using a metal straightedge and an automotive feeler gauge. Check the table across its width, length and from corner to corner. It should be flat to within .005 in.

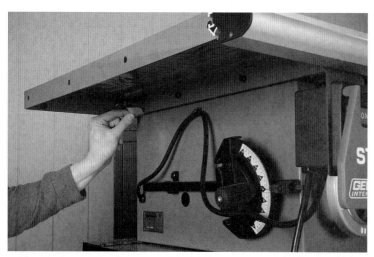

If the center table of the saw isn't flat, loosen the tabletop mounting bolts and insert a few shims between the casting and the saw base in the low area. Retighten the bolts and inspect for flatness again with a long straightedge.

materials. Pressed steel extension wings are particularly difficult to flatten completely, but there are some steps you can take to make them as flat as possible.

To examine your tabletop for flatness, hold a reliable 4-ft. straightedge across the table and extension wings crossways. Check the tabletop at the front and back edges as well as diagonally. Look for gaps under the straightedge, especially over the extension wings and where the wings meet the center table. If you have a cast-iron top and wings, use an automotive feeler gauge to check for gaps that may be too small to see. A deviation of .003 to .005 over the length of the table is acceptable. If your saw has pressed steel wings, it may be difficult to adjust them uniformly flat. The thin metal tends to twist, and the bends at the corners can also introduce distortion.

If you find gaps in the center table area, it's usually a sign that the table casting is warped, either due to poor machining, internal stresses in the metal or because the casting isn't meeting the saw base evenly. If your saw has an aluminum tabletop rather than one made of iron, it's also more prone to slight distortions. Sometimes moving your saw to a flatter area of the shop floor will remedy a sagging or twisted tabletop. If it doesn't, try slipping a few thicknesses of office paper or a piece of pop can metal between the saw base and table where the parts bolt together. Shim the low areas only. Add one shim at a time and retighten the tabletop bolts to check your progress.

Often, the extension wings will sag below the table or tip upward when you tighten the attachment bolts. To raise sagging extension wings, insert paper or pop can shims underneath the wings where they bolt to the center table. To lower extension wings that crown, install the shims on top instead of below, then trim the shims flush with the table surface. Be sure to check that the joints between the

Insert metal or paper shims between the extension wings and center table to raise or lower the wings. Retighten the mounting bolts and check the tabletop for flatness with a straightedge.

center table and the wings are flush when you tighten the wings in place. If shims don't solve the problem, you may be able to use the fence rails as anchor points for the wings. Pull the wings up or down until they line up with the table properly, then tighten the fence rail attachment bolts.

Once the tabletop and wings are flat, sweep your hand over the entire table surface and feel for any tiny burrs that may be present. Even a tiny burr can scratch your workpieces. Remove burrs by rubbing lightly with a fine-grit sharpening stone.

Finally, adjust your saw's throatplate so its edges are flush with the surrounding table surface. Most throatplates will have four to six Allen screws threaded around the edges for bringing the plate flush with the tabletop. Check your adjustments with a short straightedge. The plate should meet the table evenly all around to prevent workpieces from catching on the edges of the throatplate or the edges of its opening.

Remove any burrs in the tabletop casting by rubbing gently with a fine-grit sharpening stone.

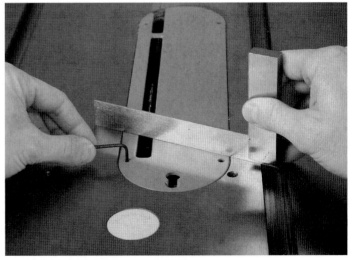

Adjust the throatplate so it's flush with the tabletop using the throatplate adjustment screws. Check your progress with a short straightedge.

Aligning The Blade And Miter Slots

One of the most important adjustments you can make to your table saw is to properly align the blade with the miter slots. When the blade is skewed to the miter slots, crosscutting accuracy will be lost; instead of cutting straight, workpieces will shift one way or the other along the miter gauge as they follow the angled plane of the blade. The bigger problem, however, is that the blade will usually be skewed to the rip fence as well as the miter slots. If the blade and fence form a funnel that narrows at the back of the blade, workpieces can become wedged during rip cuts, which can lead to burning, rough cuts and possibly a kickback—a dangerous situation where the blade lifts and throws the wood back in the direction of the operator. We'll use the miter slots to set rip fence parallelism in the next section, so it's important to align the blade and miter slots first.

The process of aligning the blade and miter slots involves shifting the position of the arbor assembly under the table until the saw blade aligns with the miter slots. Table saws vary in terms of how this arbor assembly attaches to the saw. On benchtop and contractor's style table saws, the arbor assembly fastens to the underside of the table. On cabinet table saws, the arbor assembly bolts to the saw base instead. Most consumer table saws have arbor assemblies that bolt to the table, so we'll use this style as our

example for making the blade and miter slot adjustment shown here. Refer to your saw's owner's manual to locate the bolts that hold the arbor assembly in place.

There are several methods for making this adjustment accurately. Some procedures involve using a dial calipers and taking readings off of a single tooth on the blade. If you have a heavy-duty table saw with a cast-iron arbor and table, it's reasonable to expect the saw to achieve and maintain this level of precise tuning. For ordinary home woodworking table saws, where a high degree of precision is less realistic, we'll use a simpler method that provides acceptable alignment quickly and easily.

To make the adjustment, you'll need to use a quality saw blade with flat faces, a long piece of hardwood that fits snugly in the miter slots, a metal straightedge and a combination square. First, check your saw blade against the rule of a combination square to be sure the blade body is flat—not all blades are. Thicker blades tend to be flatter than thin-kerf blades. Inspect the blade across its diameter, looking for gaps. Take a series of these readings all around the blade. Install it in the saw as usual, and slip the hardwood piece into a miter slot. Then raise the blade to full height and rest a 4-ft. straightedge against the blade body. Keep the straightedge against the blade body and not the carbide teeth.

Check for blade and slot alignment by pressing the head of a combination square against the straightedge and extending the square's blade until the end just touches the hardwood strip. Lock the square. Make this check at the front of the saw, then move the square to the back to see if the square's blade still touches the wood strip. If it comes up short or long, the blade and miter slot are not aligned. Make this initial check several times before shifting the arbor, just to be sure you are getting consistent readings with your straightedge setup.

In order to use a saw blade for the arbor alignment procedure, it's crucial that the blade body is absolutely flat. Check for flatness all around the blade by shifting the rule.

Extend the blade of a combination square until it touches the wood strip in the miter slot. Lock the square to hold the blade setting. Take this reading near the front of the saw table.

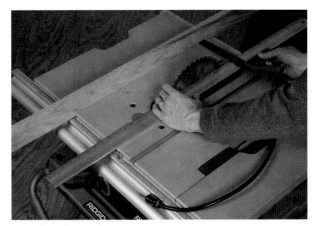

Move the square to the rear of the saw table and see if the square's blade still touches the wood strip. If it doesn't, the saw blade and miter slots are out of alignment. You'll need to adjust the arbor assembly.

The advantage to this straightedge method is that any skew that exists between the blade and miter slot will increase the farther away from the blade you measure. Even a slight misalignment will be obvious if you take your measurements from the front and back edges of the saw table.

Shift the arbor position by loosening three of the four arbor mounting bolts just enough to allow for arbor movement. Move the arbor as needed to bring it into alignment with the miter slot. Be aware that the slightest change in arbor position is probably all you'll need to make here; sometimes a tap or two with your knuckles is sufficient. Loosen the combination square and reset its blade to take more readings off the straightedge and hardwood strip. When the front and back readings match, you'll know the blade and miter slot are in alignment. Retighten the arbor mounting bolts.

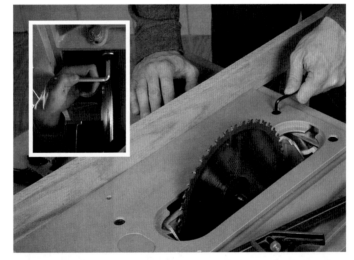

To adjust the arbor assembly, loosen three of the four arbor mounting bolts. These may be accessible from the top of the saw table or beneath the casting (see inset photo), depending on the type of saw you have.

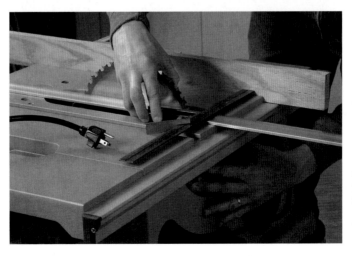

Shift the arbor assembly left or right slightly and recheck for blade alignment using the square and wood strip setup. A minor shift one way or the other may be all that's required to align it.

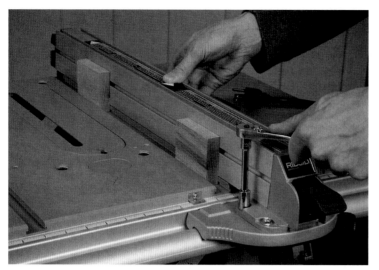

The rip fence beam should touch two scrap blocks set in the miter slots if it's lined up properly. Loosen the beam mounting bolts on the clamp and shift the beam to align it, then retighten the bolts.

Aligning The Rip Fence

Now that your miter slots and blade are in alignment, you can use the miter slots to align the rip fence to the blade. Insert a pair of scrapwood blocks in the miter slot near the front and back of the saw table. The blocks should fit the miter slot snugly. Slide the rip fence until it just touches one or both blocks. If the fence touches both blocks at once, you'll know that it's parallel to the miter slots and needs no further adjustment. If it touches only one

block, the fence beam is out of alignment with the miter slots and, secondarily, the blade. Refer to your owner's manual to find the bolts that fasten the fence beam to the fence clamp. On most rip fences, they're located along the top of the fence beam. Loosen them until you can move the fence beam, and press the beam against the wood blocks. Retighten the bolts. If your rip fence has a one-piece fence beam and clamp, align the rip fence with the wood blocks by tightening adjuster bolts on the fence clamp.

It's also important to check your fence for squareness with the saw table. Clamp down the fence as usual and hold an engineer's square against the beam and table. Your saw may have adjuster bolts to square the beam. If it doesn't, fasten an auxiliary scrap facing to the fence beam and slip shims behind it to adjust for squareness. Leave this facing on your fence permanently. You'll probably find this auxiliary fence facing to be beneficial for dadoing operations, attaching featherboards or supporting tall workpieces.

If your saw's rip fence can't be adjusted for squareness to the table, you might be able to insert a few metal or paper shims behind the facing to make this adjustment.

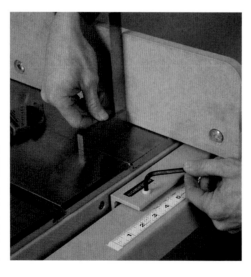

Adjust the saw's rip fence for squareness to the table, if possible. Some fences, such as the one shown here, have adjustment screws designed for this purpose.

Adjusting Blade Tilt Stops

All table saws have stops for setting the blade at 90° and 45° tilt angles. Adjuster bolts control the stopping action, and their locations vary from saw to saw. Some newer saws, like the one shown here, have adjuster bolts that are recessed into the saw table for easy access. Others will be tucked up underneath the saw table and on the arbor castings. Check your owner's manual to find the stops on your saw. Raise the saw blade to full height, and use an engineer's or combination square held against the blade body to fine-tune the 90° setting. A drafting triangle is a good reference aid for adjusting the 45° stop. Snug up the adjuster bolts to hold the blade settings, then make some test cuts and check the angles against a combination square.

With the saw blade fully raised, use a small triangle to check the blade for squareness to the table. Tilt the blade to 45° and check this angle as well. Adjust the blade tilt stops accordingly to hold these settings.

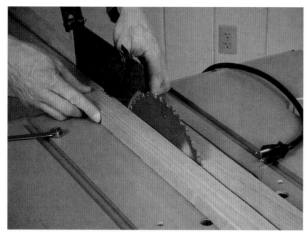

Two flat wood scraps held against the saw blade will tell you if the splitter is properly aligned. Neither scrap should touch the splitter.

Adjust the splitter left or right until it lines up behind the blade. If the splitter isn't flat, remove it and gently bend it into shape.

Adjusting The Splitter And Miter Gauge

The final tabletop adjustment to make involves aligning the splitter behind the saw blade. The splitter prevents the saw kerf from closing up on a workpiece as it passes the blade, which can cause binding or a blade kickback. Use a pair of straight scraps or straightedges to check for splitter alignment. Hold the scraps against both faces of the blade and so

Use a combination square held against the bar and fence on your miter gauge to adjust it for square. Tighten the knob securely.

they straddle the splitter. If the splitter is aligned correctly with the blade, there should be small gaps between the splitter and test scraps on both sides. If the splitter touches one or the other, check your owner's manual for the correct adjustment procedure. Some splitters have adjustable attachment bolts that reposition the splitter, or you may have to add shims to shift its position. If the splitter is bent, remove it from the saw and bend it gently back to shape on a flat worksurface.

It's also a good idea to check your miter gauge fence for square before you use it. Even though all miter gauges have a protractor scale to determine angle settings, it's not always accurate. For normal, square crosscutting, it's important that the miter gauge fence is perpendicular to the bar that fits in the miter slot. Hold a combination square against the bar and fence as shown here to set the fence to exactly 90°. Tighten the lock knob. If your miter gauge has a flip stop for 90°, adjust the setscrew until it just makes contact with the flip stop but doesn't distort it, and tighten the locknut to hold the screw in place. Set the miter gauge's 45° flip stop the same way, checking the fence angle with a combination square. Make some test cuts to test your miter gauge settings.

Checking Drive Belts

If your saw has drive belts, check them periodically for wear and proper tensioning. Belts will stretch over time, and they can slip on the pulley or pulleys unless you take up the excess slack. On a cabinet saw, belt tension can be adjusted by repositioning the motor on its mount. Check for tension by pressing on all the belts at once. They should deflect about ½ in. or less.

On contractor's saws with motors that hang behind the saw, the weight of the motor maintains bolt tension. If your contractor's saw seems to vibrate excessively as it runs, the belt may not be tracking properly in its pulleys. Remove the guard and use a long straightedge to see if the arbor and motor pulley sheaves line up. If they don't, loosen the Allen screw that holds the motor pulley in place and slide the pulley on the motor shaft to realign it with the arbor pulley. Or, loosen the four motor mounting bolts slightly and move the motor one way or the other until the pulleys line up. If the mounting bolts don't

Check the drive belt tension on a cabinet saw by pressing against the belts. Tighten them if they deflect more than ½ in.

have lockwashers, adding them can help keep the motor from shifting out of place again.

Another effective way to reduce vibration on a contractor's saw is to replace the standard drive belt with a link-style belt. Link belts are more flexible than V-belts so they spin more evenly. Most woodworking supply catalogs sell link belts by the foot, and they'll fit any brand of contractor's saw.

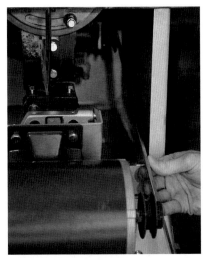

Check the pulley alignment on a contractor's saw with a long straightedge held against the arbor and motor pulley sheaves. The sheaves should rest flush against the straightedge in order for the drive belt to spin smoothly.

Loosen the motor pulley and slide it in or out on the motor shaft to line it up with the arbor pulley. Alternately, you can adjust the motor position on its mounts.

Segmented-link drive belts are an improvement over conventional V-belts for dampening vibration on a contractor's saw. They can be assembled in any length to fit all saws, and many woodworking suppliers sell them.

General Lubrication

A table saw's blade elevation and tilt movement should be smooth, and the handwheels should turn easily. If the action is sticky, the gears seem to bind or the wheels squeak, the culprit is probably dried grease or sawdust caking the worm and spline gears. Use a scrub brush and mineral spirits to dissolve the old grease and remove wood debris from the gear surfaces. Then apply paste wax to the gears. The wax will act as a lubricant without attracting dust and wood resin. If your saw has an arbor assembly that rides on curve-shaped trunnions, apply a little wax to these surfaces to provide smoother blade movement.

Scrub the worm and spline gears with a toothbrush to remove old grease and accumulated sawdust. Mineral spirits will help dissolve stubborn debris.

Lubricate gear teeth and other surfaces of the arbor assembly that slide with paste furniture wax. Do not use grease, which only attracts more gunk.

MEASURING ARBOR RUNOUT

A good quality table saw that's well maintained and equipped with a stiff, flat blade will usually make clean, smooth cuts. If you have an older, well-worn saw, or if the saw cuts unevenly no matter what blade you use, it may suffer from excessive runout. Runout means the motor shaft, arbor or blade isn't spinning in a true orbit. Worn motor bearings will introduce extra play as the motor shaft spins. It's also possible that the arbor shaft is bent or the flange that supports the saw blade is dirty. Portable saws with universal motors will tend to have more runout than heavier duty saws.

To check for runout, first clean the arbor flange carefully, then set the dial indicator's plunger arm lightly against the milled surface of the flange with the instrument fixed to a magnetic base on the saw table. Rotate the dial until the pointer reads zero. Then turn the arbor slowly by hand to inspect the range of runout. If the runout exceeds .001, consider having the motor or arbor shaft serviced by a reputable machine shop or a tool service center. The motor bearings may need to be replaced or the arbor trued. If the saw is new and the runout is excessive, return it as defective.

Check the arbor flange for runout by turning it slowly against a dial indicator mounted on a magnetic base. Runout should not exceed .001 in.

TUNING UP A BANDSAW

In order for your bandsaw to cut properly, the blade needs to spin smoothly on the saw's flywheels and in a single plane. The blade guides help keep the blade on track, but the wheels also need to be in alignment with one another. When the blade doesn't track correctly on its wheels, it can wear the blade guides and rubber tires prematurely. Blades that track poorly also tend to break more often and can even come off the wheels in extreme cases. Many factors influence blade tracking, and some you can remedy by careful tuning or repair. Heavy-duty, full-sized bandsaws tend to track better than light-duty machines, but even a budget-priced saw can be improved with careful tuning. If your bandsaw has an aluminum frame, the casting may not offer enough stiffness to keep wide blades tracking properly when under tension. If tuning up your saw doesn't improve the tracking, try switching to a narrower blade.

Routine Cleaning And Lubrication

Begin your bandsaw tune-up by removing the blade and vacuuming out the interior of the machine, especially where sawdust collects around the upper and lower blade guides. Use a synthetic bristle brush or scub pad to remove wood pitch and grime from the flywheel tires. Check your owner's manual to see if you can use a solvent, like mineral spirits, to help soften and remove the build-up. Or, use warm, soapy water. Once the tires are clean, inspect them for uneven wear. Most bandsaw tires have a slight crown to their shape. Replace the tires if the blade has created grooves in them over time. Your manual may recommend a method for using sandpaper to restore a "crown" to the tire surface. This will help extend the serviceable life of the tires and improve performance. However, if blade tracking is a routine problem or the tires are really worn, reshaping them won't help much.

Occasionally, it's a good idea to remove the upper flywheel and

Clean accumulated debris off of rubber bandsaw tires with a synthetic scrub pad and mineral spirits or soapy water. Check for cleaning recommendations in your saw owner's manual first.

Remove the upper flywheel and lubricate the sliding areas of the casting with paste wax. Raise the casting first to expose as much of the contact area as possible.

A dab of paste wax on the threads of the flywheel adjustment screw will help it turn smoothly when tensioning the flywheel. Do not use grease.

Spray the flywheel shaft with a light coating of dry lubricant. It will ensure that the flywheel is easy to remove again in the future.

clean and lubricate the moving parts of the tensioning system behind it. On stationary bandsaws, the flywheel mounts on a casting that moves up and down. With the wheel removed, raise this wheel mount to its highest setting by turning the blade-tensioning handwheel. Apply wax or a dry spray lube on the ways of the casting where it slides on the mating fixed casting. Lubricate the threaded shaft as well. Apply a light coating of wax or a metal protective spray to the wheel shaft to inhibit rust, then reinstall the flywheel and blade. Apply dry lube or wax to the blade guard post so it moves up and down easily.

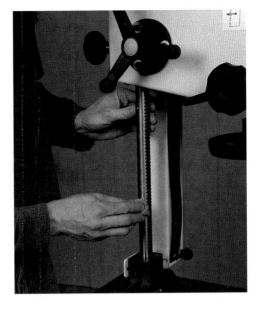

Seal and lubricate the blade guide post with paste wax or dry lube to help it slide smoothly and to prevent rust.

Tracking And Tensioning The Blade

Follow the procedure in your owner's manual for tensioning the blade. Turn the blade-tensioning wheel until an indicator scale on the saw reaches the correct pressure for the blade width you're using. This is an approximation of actual tension at best, but it's a good starting point. Experience with your band saw will teach you how much tension to apply, based on the blade size and type and the material you're cutting.

Most manufacturers recommend that the blade tracks along the center of both wheels as it spins, but the ability of your saw to do this will depend on the stiffness of the saw frame, the condition of the flywheel tensioning system and the general level of performance possible with your particular

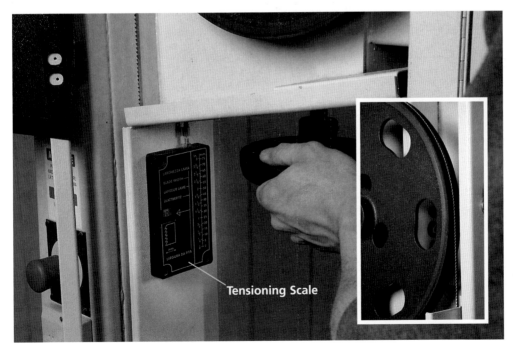

Tensioning Scale

Apply tension to the blade, using the saw's tensioning scale as a general guide. Experience will teach you whether the blade will require more or less tension from this point. Be sure the blade is tracking along the crown of the tire before tightening it (see inset).

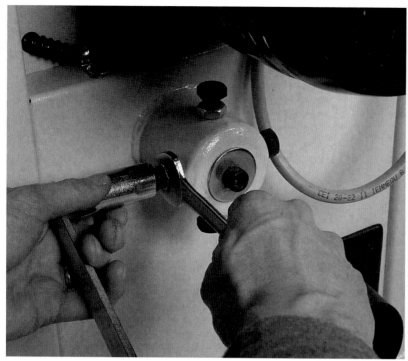

Larger bandsaws usually will have tracking adjustment bolts for the lower flywheel (left), but all bandsaws will have a tracking knob or wheel for the upper flywheel (right). Adjust this system and turn the flywheels by hand to be sure the blade tracks on the flywheels properly.

Use a combination or other large square to check the blade for squareness to the saw table. Adjust the table tilting system, if necessary.

saw. Your saw may or may not have adjuster bolts for changing the tracking on the lower flywheel, but all bandsaws will have an adjustment lever or handwheel for adjusting tracking of the upper flywheel. Turn the flywheel by hand as you adjust the tracking lever or wheel to monitor changes in the way the blade shifts on the wheel. You need to first back off all the blade guides prior to adjusting the tracking.

Once the blade is tracking correctly, hold an engineer's or combination square against the blade and saw table to check for square. Make this inspection both alongside the blade as well as in back. Adjust the table on its trunnions until it is square to the side of the blade. If the blade spine isn't square with the table, you may be able to bring the blade into alignment by readjusting the tracking.

Adjusting The Blade Guides

Blade guide styles vary from one saw to the next (see page 44). Saws may have bearings, ceramic blocks, solid cool block material or a combination of bearings and blocks. Regardless of which guides your saw has, the adjustment process is the same. Start by opening up the side guides and retracting the rear thrust guide or bearing enough to allow for general adjustment. Loosen the guide assembly bolts slightly and move the entire assembly forward until the side guides meet the blade just behind its gullets, as shown at right (see inset photo). Tighten the blade guide assembly bolts.

Double up a piece of paper to serve as a shim, and wrap it around the back of the blade in front of the thrust bearing. Move the thrust bearing forward until it just touches the shim. The shim will create a slight gap between the blade and the guide. Tighten the thrust bearing adjustment screw. When properly adjusted, the thrust bearing should not touch the blade

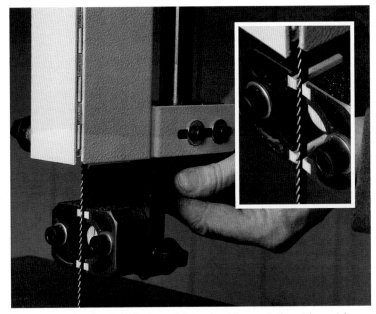

Loosen and slide the blade guide assembly until the side guides line up just behind the blade gullets. Tighten the assembly.

unless the blade is making a cut. If the thrust bearing touches the blade constantly, it will wear out prematurely.

Use the shim as a spacer for adjusting the side guides as well. When you tighten the side guide locking screws, be sure the guides don't creep forward so they make

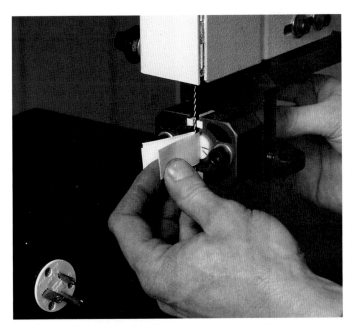

Wrap a doubled-up strip of paper around the blade to create the proper spacing between the blade and the thrust bearing or bushing behind it. Slide the thrust bearing or bushing forward until it just touches the paper, and lock it in place.

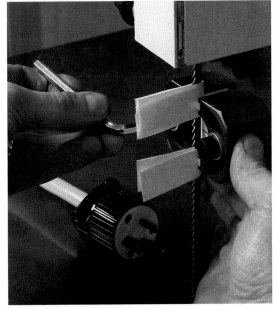

Adjust the side guides next to the blade using paper shims as spacers. The side guides should not rub the blade unless it's cutting something. Tighten the guide bolts.

contact with the blade teeth. To check your adjustments, remove the paper and rotate the flywheel slowly by hand. The blade should pass easily through the guides. If it rubs, the side guides are too close. Readjust them.

BLADE GUIDE STYLES

Band saw manufacturers use various styles of blade guides. Typically, the side guides are made of self-lubricating solid blocks or sealed bearings, and the thrust support behind the blade is a sealed bearing. However, one manufacturer uses a proprietary system of ceramic blocks and a ceramic puck for the thrust support instead of a bearing.

Regardless of the style, blade guides prevent the blade from deflecting as it cuts. They also keep it tracking properly on the fly wheels.

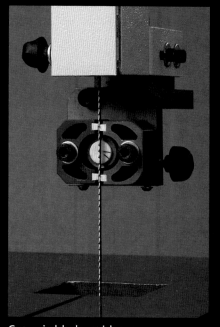

Ceramic blade guides.

Sealed bearing blade guides.

Inspecting And Smoothing The Blade Weld

Smoothing the back edges of new bandsaw blades can help improve cutting performance when sawing tight curves. It also reduces the wear and tear on your saw's thrust bearing. To soften the edges of the blade spine, set a sharpening stone on the saw table and press it lightly against one of the back corners of the blade. Turn the flywheel by hand through a few complete revolutions. Be careful not to press so hard that you shift the blade out of position on the guides. Move the stone to the other edge of the spine and repeat the process.

It's also a good idea to inspect the weld of any new bandsaw blade before you start using it. Look for a bright grind spot along the blade to

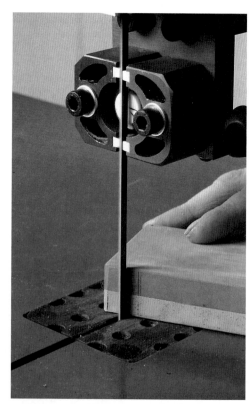

Hold a sharpening stone gently against the back of a spinning bandsaw blade to ease the sharp corners. It will help improve performance and reduce wear and tear on the thrust bearing.

find the weld. Make a visual inspection of the weld and feel it with your fingers. Sometimes the brazing won't be ground completely smooth on the sides or spine. Even a tiny bit of extra brazing can catch on the guides and cause trouble. Remove any defects with a sharpening stone or small fine-tooth file, but be careful not to nick the adjacent teeth. It's easy to accidentally dull the points if you aren't careful.

HOW TO COIL A BANDSAW BLADE

Here's how to coil your bandsaw blades for convenient storage. Be sure to wear gloves and eye protection, and follow the four-step procedure shown here.

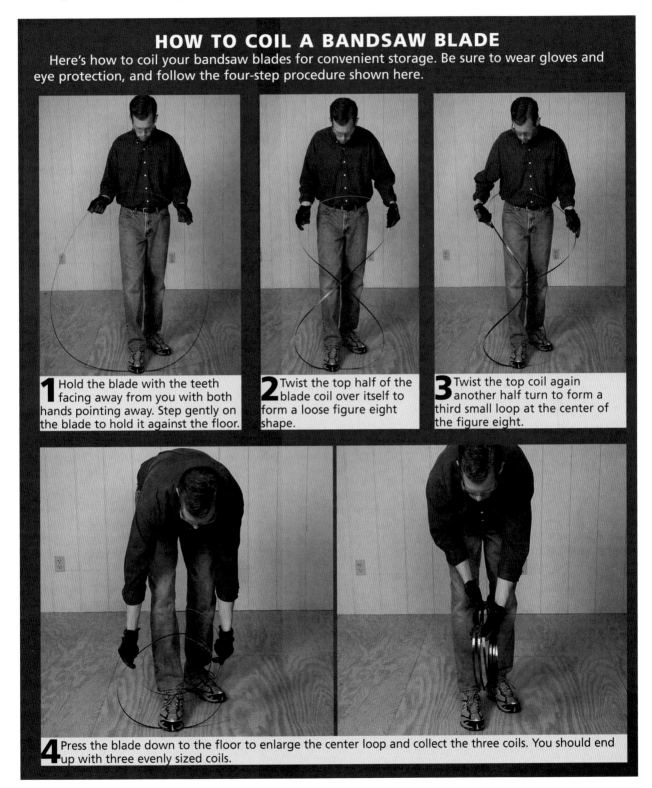

1 Hold the blade with the teeth facing away from you with both hands pointing away. Step gently on the blade to hold it against the floor.

2 Twist the top half of the blade coil over itself to form a loose figure eight shape.

3 Twist the top coil again another half turn to form a third small loop at the center of the figure eight.

4 Press the blade down to the floor to enlarge the center loop and collect the three coils. You should end up with three evenly sized coils.

Adjusting The Rip Fence

If workpieces tend to move away from the fence when making rip cuts, the condition is called drift. It's a common problem that usually results from a dull or unevenly worn blade or a misaligned rip fence. Most bandsaw rip fences can be adjusted to eliminate drift. Here's an easy way to do it.

Use a flat-edged scrap around 4 in. wide and 2 to 3 ft. long. Draw a line lengthwise along the board, and make a rip cut along this line without using the fence. Cut about halfway along the line, then hold the board in place and shut off the saw. Without moving the board, draw a pencil line across the saw table using the board as a straightedge. Remove the board. The line represents the blade's drift angle. In order to compensate for drift, you'll need to set your rip fence to line up with the reference line. Loosen the bolts that hold the fence beam to the clamp head and slide the fence next to the pencil line. Align the fence beam with the drift line, and retighten the fence bolts. Check the adjustment by using the fence to cut the test board the rest of the way. The board should follow along the fence with the blade tracking the cutting line. If it doesn't, shift the fence beam slightly and recheck with another test cut. If rip fence adjustments don't seem to do the trick, install a fresh blade in your saw to see if this helps.

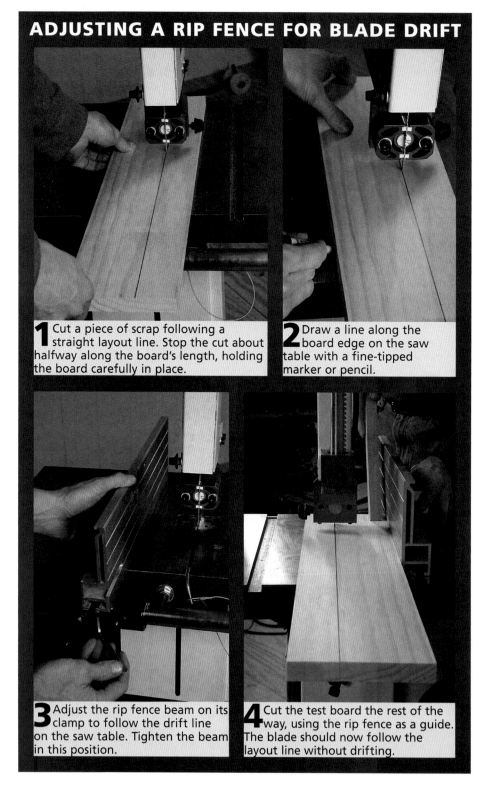

ADJUSTING A RIP FENCE FOR BLADE DRIFT

1 Cut a piece of scrap following a straight layout line. Stop the cut about halfway along the board's length, holding the board carefully in place.

2 Draw a line along the board edge on the saw table with a fine-tipped marker or pencil.

3 Adjust the rip fence beam on its clamp to follow the drift line on the saw table. Tighten the beam in this position.

4 Cut the test board the rest of the way, using the rip fence as a guide. The blade should now follow the layout line without drifting.

BENCHTOP PLANER

Benchtop planers are relatively simple machines. The motor spins a cylindrical cutterhead equipped with two or three knives that plane the top face of the lumber. Feed rollers on either side of the cutterhead pull workpieces through the machine against the direction of the cutterhead's rotation. The general cutting quality of your planer will depend primarily on how sharp the knives are, whether the wood has a flat face against the planer's bed and how smoothly and easily the wood moves past the knives.

A common problem with most planers is snipe, or the tendency of the cutterhead to make slightly deeper cuts on the ends of the board. Snipe appears as shallow dished out areas about two inches in from the ends of your planed lumber. Usually, a tiny bit of snipe is unavoidable, and it's fairly easy to sand out. You can often reduce severe snipe (deeper than about $1/64$ in.) by adjusting the infeed and outfeed tables on your machine so they are flush with the planer bed.

Sometimes a planer's cutterhead can become misaligned with the planer bed, which results in workpieces that taper from one edge of the board to the other. The cutterhead must be parallel with the planer bed in order to cut uniformly. There's an easy way to check for parallelism, outlined on page 51. On some planers, you can realign the cutterhead by adjusting the chain and sprockets that raise and lower it, and the manual may show you how to do this. Or, take the planer to a tool service center for adjustment. If your planer is new and the cutterhead is not aligned properly with the bed, return it.

As far as care and maintenance of a planer goes, most of the work involves removing debris and resin deposits (pitch) from inside the machine. Accumulated grime will make the cutterhead harder to raise and lower. Pitch-coated feed rollers will lose their grip on the wood when you feed it through, and chips that get stuck to the feed rollers can actually dent your workpieces. Planers should also receive light lubrication to keep moving parts working smoothly. Occasionally, you'll have to replace the knives, and most benchtop planers have disposable knives that require no special adjustment once they're installed. Change the knives when the planer begins to make ragged cuts or when the knives get knicked.

Cleaning The Planer Bed And Feed Rollers

Over time, you'll notice that the mirror finish on your planer's bed will become streaked with wood resin and smudges of grime. Bits of sand or grit from the lumber will also leave tiny nicks and scratches in the bed surface. To service the planer bed, raise the cutterhead to its highest position, then use mineral spirits and a synthetic scrub pad to clean the polished surface. Be sure to unplug the machine before reaching inside, and use caution to avoid brushing your hands or wrists against the sharp knives located above the bed. Once the bed is clean, inspect it closely for nicks and scratches. You may not be able to see tiny nicks, but they'll be easy to feel with your fingers. Remove any nicks by rubbing them

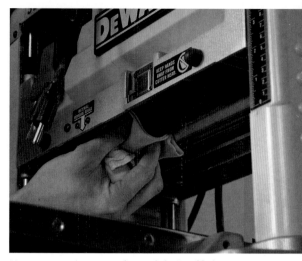

Use soapy water to clean debris off the two rubber feed rollers inside the planer. Be sure the machine is unplugged, and use extreme caution when working close to the cutterhead.

out gently with a fine-grit sharpening stone. Then apply a coat of paste wax to the bed, and buff it smooth.

The next order of business involves cleaning the rubber feed rollers. Feed rollers are constantly exposed to dirt and debris coming off the cutterhead, especially if you don't connect your planer to a dust collector. Unless you clean the rollers from time to time, they may begin to slip or leave small dents in the wood. Use a scrub pad and soapy water to wipe off as much of each roller as you can reach.

You won't be able to clean the entire circumference of the feed rollers without rotating them. To do this, turn the machine on and off briefly to expose the rest of the feed roller surfaces. Be sure to keep your hands clear of the machine's interior when doing this. Unplug the planer again before cleaning off the rest of the feed roller surfaces. **CAUTION:** *Be extremely careful when wiping down the feed rollers and working near the knives. Unless you've changed knives before, they're actually quite hard to see up underneath the dark interior of the machine. It's a good idea to wear leather work gloves as a safety precaution.*

Clean the planer bed with mineral spirits, then follow with a coat of paste wax to help keep workpieces moving smoothly through the machine.

Lubricating The Cutterhead Elevation System

The cutterheads on benchtop planers move up and down on four steel posts. The polished posts are easy to identify near the inside corners of the planer housing. You'll also see one or two threaded rods that raise and lower the motor. Clean the posts and rods by wiping them with mineral spirits. If your planer is new, it's a good idea to replace the factory grease on the posts and rods with a light coating of paste wax or a dry spray lubricant. Otherwise, grease will trap wood dust and chips and turn into a thick paste, which will gum up the elevation system.

Your planer probably also has two drive chains: one to raise the cutterhead and the other to turn the feed rollers. If one or both chains are exposed to wood debris, wipe them down to remove the grease and use a dry lubricant spray—not oil or grease—to lubricate the chains again. If the chains are sealed inside cases, you can use ordinary lithium grease to lubricate these chains. Lubricate sealed chains on an annual basis, but check exposed chains more often or before and after a period of heavy use.

Clean the four cutterhead elevation posts with a soft cloth and mineral spirits. Then apply a light coating of dry spray lubricant or paste wax.

Clean and lubricate the threaded rods that move the cutterhead with dry lubricant spray or a light coating of WD-40.

Clean and lubricate the bottom chain that raises and lowers the cutterhead. Use a dry lubricant spray instead of grease.

Remember to lubricate chains inside sealed cases, such as the feed roller chain on this planer. Either spray lube or ordinary grease is appropriate, since the chain isn't exposed to planing debris.

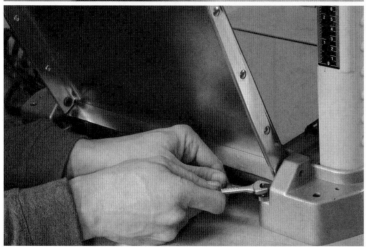

Changing Knives

Your owner's manual should explain the process of changing knives on your machine, but the steps are similar for most planers. You'll need to remove a dust diverter chute behind the motor to gain access to the cutterhead. Each knife fits in a slot in the cutterhead, and a series of small bolts and a steel gib bar hold the knives in place. If your planer has indexed knives, the knives will have slots that fit over

Hold a straightedge across the infeed and outfeed tables to inspect them for flatness with the planer bed. Raise or lower the tables to bring them flush with the planer bed using the table adjuster bolts.

Adjusting The Infeed And Outfeed Tables

One way to reduce snipe is to make sure the infeed and outfeed extension tables are flush with the planer bed. The adjuster bolts for the tables are usually located next to the table hinges. Or, your planer may have recessed Allen bolts that are threaded right into the tables. Hold a long straightedge flush against both tables and the planer bed to check for overall flatness. Thread the bolts in or out a little at a time until the bed and tables are flush, then retighten the locknuts that secure the adjuster bolts.

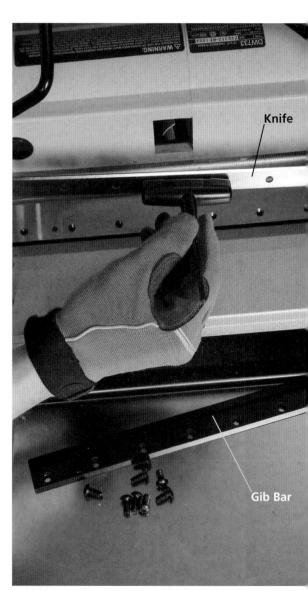

Knife

Gib Bar

Changing each knife on a benchtop planer involves removing a metal gib bar and lifting the knife off the cutterhead. Some planers come with a magnetic knife-changing wrench to make the process safer.

small tabs on the cutterhead to position them automatically. Many planers have double-edged knives. Mark the worn edge of each knife with a felt-tipped marker before removing it from the cutterhead so you won't confuse the fresh edge from the worn one. Always wear gloves when changing planer knives; new knives are razor sharp.

Many benchtop planers have disposable, double-edged knives with slots that fit over indexed pins to make them easier to position on the cutterhead.

Testing For Cutterhead Parallelism

A planer's cutterhead must be parallel with the bed in order to plane uniformly. To check for parallelism, you'll need two matching strips of flat scrap wood about 16 in. long. Position one strip along each edge of the planer bed, to simulate planing a wide board, and set the machine to take a light cut off of both test pieces. Feed the test strips through the planer as usual, then use a dial calipers to measure the thickness of both strips. You'll know the cutterhead is parallel to the planer bed if the thicknesses match. If the strips vary in thickness by more than a few thousandths of an inch, check your owner's manual to see if the cutterhead can be adjusted. Or, take your planer to an authorized tool service center to have this work done for you.

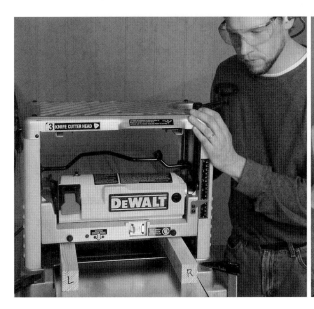

To inspect a planer for cutterhead parallelism, run two strips of matching scrap wood through the planer, with the strips placed along the edges of the planer bed. Measure the thickness of both strips with a dial calipers. The thicknesses should match.

TUNING UP A JOINTER

A jointer's primary function is to flatten the edges and faces of work-pieces. A flat face and edge are so fundamental to woodworking that a "nearly" accurate jointer simply won't suffice. The key to creating these critical reference surfaces is having a jointer with perfectly parallel table surfaces and a flat reliable fence. To some degree, accuracy needs to be built into your jointer when it leaves the factory, but there are a few things you can do to improve the performance of your machine.

Checking And Aligning Tables

If you've just purchased a new or used jointer, it's important to check the infeed and outfeed table surfaces for general flatness. The tables must also create a flat plane when they are leveled to one another. To inspect your tables, start by loosening the lock knob that holds the infeed table in place, and raise it until it is flush with the outfeed table. Unplug the machine and rotate the cutterhead so none of the knives are exposed in the slot between the tables. Turn the cutterhead by moving the drive belt or turning it with a scrap of wood; don't rotate the cutterhead with your fingers.

Using a reliable 3- to 4-ft. straightedge, inspect the flatness of your jointer tables. Lay the straightedge across both tables, diagonally, and look for gaps underneath. Then shift the straightedge parallel with both tables and check for gaps along the front and back edges of the table. There may be a slight sag near the cutterhead area, and provided this gap is smaller than .003 when measured with a feeler gauge, it isn't problematic. More typically, jointer tables will tend to sag at the outboard ends, farthest from the cutterhead.

Jointer tables slide along half-dovetail shaped ways milled into the machine's center casting. The ways enable the jointer tables to slide up and down in one plane of motion. Each table has a thin metal gib bar that fits into these ways, with bolts that press the gib against the table. The gib serves to take up extra slack between the two castings while still allowing the tables to slide up and down. Over time and repeated movement of the tables, the gib bars will begin to wear, allowing more play in the ways. If your jointer tables sag outward from the center casting, you might be able to raise them back into proper alignment by tightening the gib bolts slightly. Refer to your owner's manual to locate these bolts. There are typically two gib bolts per table located along the center casting near the ways.

The goal is to snug up the bolts just enough to press the gib bar firmly against the tables again. Usually, tightening the top gib bolt closest to the cutterhead will lift the ends of the jointer tables. Tighten the bolts a

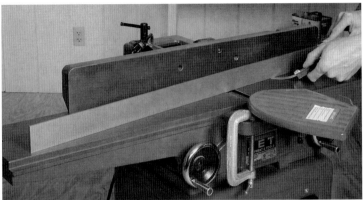

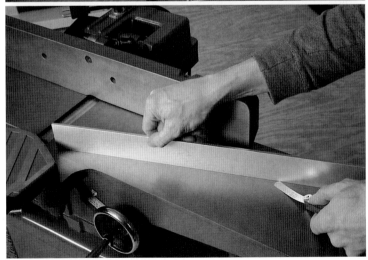

Check jointer tables for flatness in three ways: lengthwise and parallel to both tables, diagonally across both tables and diagonally across the infeed and outfeed tables individually. For the first two tests, raise the infeed table first so it's flush with the outfeed table.

little at a time, and inspect for flatness again. Be careful not to overtighten the gib bolts, or you'll actually make the problem worse by binding the tables against the ways and restricting movement.

Finally, check each jointer table for warp by measuring diagonally across the surface with the straightedge. If a table shows a gap when measured diagonally, it may have a slight twist in the casting. You may be able to have a warped table ground flat at a machine shop to correct the twist. There's no way to adjust the machine to correct a warped casting other than to have the table reground.

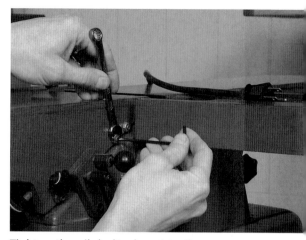

Tighten the gib bolts closest to the cutterhead a little at a time to raise tables that sag on the outboard ends.

Clean debris off the threads of the elevation crankshafts with a toothbrush.

Cleaning And Lubrication

Both jointer tables should crank smoothly up and down. If the tables seem to bind as they move, look for a threaded rod underneath each table that connects to the elevation handwheel. Chances are, wood debris and grease is caked on these threads and inhibiting the table movement, or some rust may have developed here if you don't move the table much.

Clean the threads with a toothbrush and mineral spirits, and remove any rust with a rust dissolving spray. Lightly lubricate the threads with wax or a dry spray lube. Spray a little lubricant into the bushings where the handwheels pass through the castings. Try to raise and lower the tables again to see if they move more smoothly. If the action is still difficult, spray lubricant into the dovetail ways to soften the grease inside them. If that doesn't help, you'll need to remove the tables, clean the surfaces of the ways more extensively and apply new grease to these areas.

One way to improve the sliding action of the tables is to spray lubricant into the ways to soften the grease. Raise and lower the tables several times to spread the lubricant around.

Check the drive pulley for tightness on the cutterhead shaft, and inspect the drive belt for signs of wear. Tighten the belt if necessary so it deflects no more than ½ in.

Spread a thin layer of wax on the casting that supports the jointer's fence so the fence slides back and forth easily.

Check Pulley And Belt

Loosen the attachment bolt or bolts that hold the jointer's fence on the center casting and lift the fence assembly off the jointer. This should expose the top cutterhead pulley and the drive belt or belts. Check the pulley to be sure it's tight on the shaft. If you detect any movement on the shaft, use an Allen wrench to tighten the bolt that holds the pulley in place. Check the condition of the drive belt or belts for wear, and spread paste wax on the flat area of the casting where the fence mounts to the machine.

Setting The Fence

Your owner's manual will acquaint you with the various stop bolts and adjusters on your jointer's fence. Reinstall the fence on the jointer and use an engineer's square to check the fence for squareness to the table. If it isn't square, loosen the locking and stop bolts slightly, and tip the fence to realign it. Then retighten the stop bolts and fence clamp.

It's important to square the jointer's fence carefully to the tables. Tighten the fence locking clamp, and adjust the 90° stop bolts that will hold the fence in place.

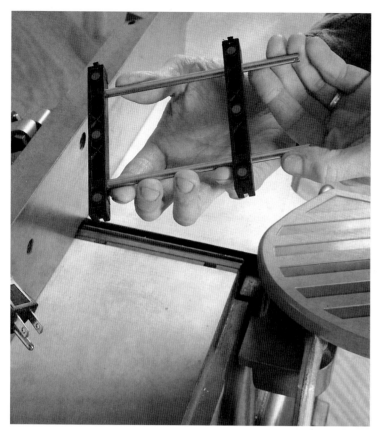

A magnetic jig makes it much easier to set conventional jointer knives accurately.

Changing Jointer Knives

If you use your jointer fairly regularly but not every day, the knives will keep an edge for a surprisingly long time. However, they'll eventually get dull or nicked. You'll know it's time to change out the knives with a fresh set when rough spots or little ridges begin to appear along a jointed surface. Dull knives will also make workpieces harder to feed over the machine, and the cutting action will make more noise.

The process of changing jointer knives involves loosening a series of gib bolts that hold a gib bar against each knife in an oversized slot in the cutterhead. Removing the knives is easy, but installing them correctly poses more of a challenge. This is because the knives are suspended off

the bottom of the cutterhead grooves by the gibs. You'll need to elevate each knife off the bottom of its groove, hold it in position and retighten the gib bolts without the knife slipping out of place. It's an exacting and sometimes frustrating job unless you use a knife-setting jig, like the one shown at left. The jig consists of a pair of parallel bars that slide on two metal rods. The bars are fitted with strong magnets. By setting the jig on the jointer table and over the cutterhead, the magnets lift and hold the knives at the correct height so you can tighten the gib bolts again. For more details on how to change the knives with the magnetic jig, follow the instructions that come with the jig.

TIP

When evaluating table flatness or changing jointer knives, use a small clamp to hold the guard open and out of your way. Be sure the jointer remains unplugged the entire time the guard is retracted and the knives are exposed.

Making fence adjustments and inspecting the tables is easier if you use a C-clamp to hold the guard in a retracted position. Don't overtighten the clamp.

Once you've reinstalled the knives, loosen the stop knob that holds the outfeed table in place, and raise it until it lines up with the highest point of the cutting arc made by the knives. Use a straightedge to find this point, called the "top dead center." The outfeed table must align exactly with the knives to provide proper support as workpieces pass over the cutterhead. Once you locate top dead center, lock the outfeed table in place. Then lower the infeed table about 1/32 inch below the outfeed table to set the cutting depth. You can use the depth setting scale on your machine or check the depth of cut with a straight-edge and a .03-in. feeler gauge. Of course, your jointer can be set for deeper cuts if you wish, but 1/32 in. cutting depth will create smooth, clean surfaces on your workpieces without taxing the machine. A shallow cutting depth will also produce better results on wood with irregular or reversing grain.

SETTING JOINTER KNIVES

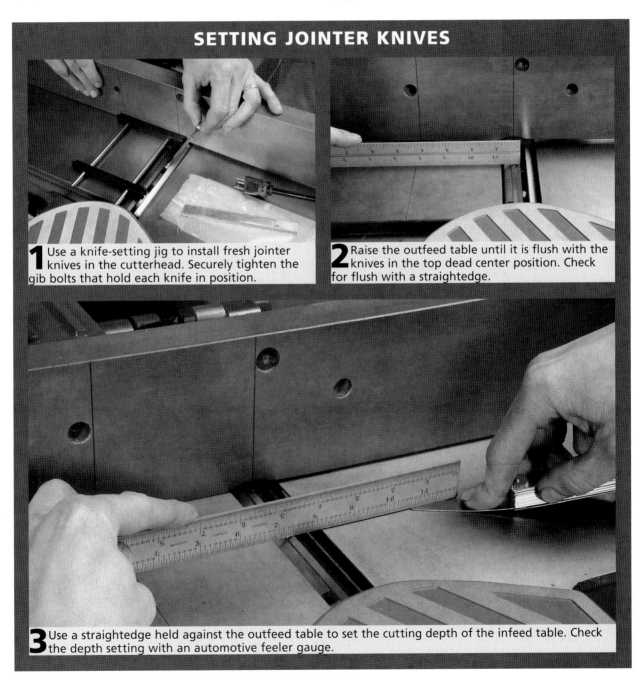

1 Use a knife-setting jig to install fresh jointer knives in the cutterhead. Securely tighten the gib bolts that hold each knife in position.

2 Raise the outfeed table until it is flush with the knives in the top dead center position. Check for flush with a straightedge.

3 Use a straightedge held against the outfeed table to set the cutting depth of the infeed table. Check the depth setting with an automotive feeler gauge.

DRILL PRESS

A well-made drill press kept in a dry shop will work for years without requiring any special care, but eventually you should perform a few maintenance tasks. Open the pulley case on top of your machine and apply a bit of grease to the splined end of the quill shaft that passes through the front pulley cluster. The grease will help the quill move smoothly up and down. Extend the quill all the way down to the bottom of its stroke and spray the outside surface of the column with a dry lubricant to inhibit rust.

Coat the quill column with a light coating of dry lubricant to inhibit rust formation. Wipe off the excess.

Spray dry lubricant behind the outer collar of the chuck so it turns easily.

Spread a dab of grease on the splined end of the quill shaft so it slides easily up and down. Be careful to keep grease off of the drive belts.

The outer collar of your drill press chuck will turn more easily if you apply a little spray lubricant where it meets the inner casting. It's also a good idea to keep the outer surfaces of the chuck jaws lightly lubricated.

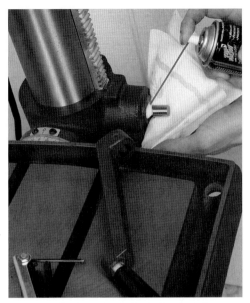

Remove the hand crank and spray dry lubricant into the table's crank gears to keep them meshing fluidly.

Another area that can benefit from occasional lubrication is the shaft where the drill press table handle connects to the table casting. Remove the handle and shoot a bit of spray lube into the opening where the shaft and casting meet. Raise and lower the table a few times to work the lubricant into this seam and around the shaft.

If you've just purchased a new or used drill press, be sure to check the table for squareness to the chuck. To do this, install a long drill bit in the chuck, and raise the table until the bit nearly touches it. Hold a combination square or an engineer's square with the head on the table and the square's rule against the drill bit. The table and bit should form a 90° angle. Move the square around the bit and recheck at several points. Ordinarily, most drill presses have a pin that locks the table at 90°, but this isn't the case for all models. Some lock the table in position by clamp pressure only. These are the styles to check routinely for accuracy.

Check the table for squareness to the chuck by holding a combination square against a long drill bit clamped in place.

EVALUATING DRILL PRESS RUNOUT

In order to drill smooth, clean holes, the chuck and quill shaft on a drill press must spin on a single axis. If your drill press seems to wander as it drills or creates holes with ragged walls, it could be a sign that the machine suffers from excessive runout at the quill. To check for runout, clamp a dial indicator to a magnetic base, and install a long twist bit in the chuck. Set the indicator on the drill press table close to the drill bit, and press the dial's plunger shaft lightly against the drill bit. Turn the dial so the pointer reads zero. Then slowly turn the quill shaft by rotating the drill press's chuck by hand. Check the dial readings as you do this.

A few thousandths inch of runout is fairly typical, but a reading higher than .010 indicates excessive runout. You may be able to reduce your machine's runout by removing and reinstalling the chuck on the quill. A worn chuck may also introduce runout, and replacing it may solve the problem altogether. Otherwise, runout indicates that the quill bearings are worn and need to be replaced—a job best performed by a tool service center or machine shop.

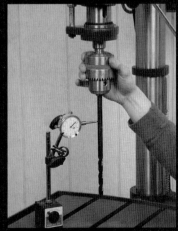

Inspect the chuck and quill spindle for runout using a dial indicator mounted on a magnetic base. Set the dial's plunger against a long drill bit, adjust the pointer to zero and turn the chuck slowly by hand.

RADIAL-ARM SAW

Twenty to thirty years ago, radial-arm saws were as common as table saws in woodworking shops and on the carpenter's jobsite. However, today's portable, highly accurate and inexpensive miter saws have eclipsed the once venerable radial-arm saw. In fact, you won't have many choices these days if you want to buy a new radial-arm saw. A radial-arm saw can still be a versatile and valuable addition to your shop—and inexpensive to buy used. However, maintenance and tuning need to be part of a regular regimen if you want to keep your radial-arm saw in tiptop shape. It has many moving parts that fall out of adjustment more easily than a table saw or miter saw. Be sure to follow the sequence of tune-up operations in the order shown here; one phase of the process will impact another.

Cleaning And Adjusting The Column And Arm

In order to change blade height on a radial-arm saw, you have to raise and lower the arm that holds the motor carriage. In order to accomplish this, the vertical column in back of the saw moves up and down in its base, but the tolerance between these parts is tight. It's important to keep the column clean and the metal protected to ensure that rust or other debris doesn't cause the column to bind in the base casting when it moves. Crank the arm all the way up to expose as much of the column as possible, and wipe it down with mineral spirits from time to time to remove any grime that accumulates here. Coat the column with protective metal spray, or rub on a coat of paste wax and buff it smooth. Avoid using oil or WD-40, which will attract dust.

The column is held in the base casting in two ways: the casting has bolts that squeeze the column like a vise, but there's also a second set of tensioning bolts that press against a softer brass or bronze gib bar. The gib provides an important wear point in the system by taking up any slack between the moving parts.

To check for wear between the base casting and the column, hold the

Protect bare metal on the saw's vertical column with dry spray lubricant to inhibit rust. It will also make the column easier to raise and lower.

front of the saw's arm and wrap your fingers around the column where it meets the base casting. Try to push the arm up and down as well as move it from side to side. If you feel any play between the column and base casting, it's time to tighten the gib tension bolts. The key here is to tighten the gib bolts just enough to take up the play without overtightening them. If the gib bolts are too tight, the column will bind and be difficult to move up and down. You'll also wear out the gib bar more quickly. Tighten the gib bolts a little at a time until the column fits snugly in the base casting but still cranks up and down easily.

Check for play between the base casting and the vertical column by attempting to move the saw's arm up and down while feeling where the casting and column meet.

Eliminate extra play in the column by tightening the gib bolts slightly. Do not overtighten the bolts or you'll restrict column movement.

Use mineral spirits or another mild solvent to clean the roller tracks inside the saw arm. These should be clean, dry and free of rust.

Inspecting And Adjusting The Motor Carriage Bearings

The motor carriage rolls back and forth along the arm on four top-mounted bearings. The bearings follow tracks inside the arm. If these tracks are lubricated with grease or oil, they'll attract dust and wood debris, which will eventually impede smooth movement of the carriage. Use a rag and mineral spirits to wipe away any grime along the tracks as far as you can reach. Roll the carriage out of the way to gain more access to the tracks. Once the tracks are wiped clean,

inspect them closely with a flashlight. If you find any rust along the tracks, remove it with a spray-on rust dissolver. Do not lubricate the tracks. The goal is to keep them clean and dry.

Over many years' use, the motor carriage bearings will begin to wear on the tracks. Two of the four bearings can be adjusted to account for wear. To check for wear, grab the motor carriage with both hands and try to twist it on the arm. If you feel any "give" in the bearings, it's time to take up the slack. Refer to your owner's manual for instructions about accessing the motor carriage bearings. You'll probably need to remove a cap over the end of the arm to reach the adjustment bolts on the bearings. The manual will also indicate which of the two pairs of bearings are adjustable. When you shift the bearings, keep in mind that a miniscule amount of adjustment is all that's probably necessary. The bearings need to fit the tracks without extra play, but they still need to move freely. Check your adjustments by pulling the carriage back and forth. It should roll easily but without any side-to-side "slop" in the action.

The track tends to wear more at the back end since that area is used the most. At a point, adjusting the motor carriage bearings will remove the slack in that area, but then the rest of the track is too tight. When this happens, you'll need to have the track reground by a machine shop.

Check for wear in the motor carriage bearings by grabbing the motor carriage and trying to twist it on the saw arm. There should be no noticeable play.

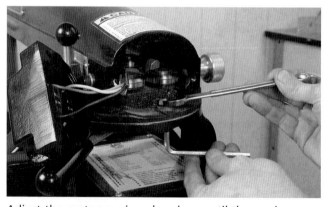
Adjust the motor carriage bearings until the carriage moves back and forth easily without any side-to-side play. Your saw's owner's manual will outline this adjustment process.

Adjusting The Table Parallel To The Arm

A radial-arm saw can be used to make non-through cuts, such as dadoes or rabbets (see pages 119 and 120). In order for these cuts to be of consistent depth, the saw table must be parallel to the motor carriage arm. To align the table and arm, the simplest method is to raise or lower the table using adjuster bolts under the table.

Check the current position of the table by removing the blade and installing a piece of straight scrap onto the arbor. Choose a scrap that's about 14 in. long and a few inches wide. To mount the scrap, drill a hole the same size as the arbor diameter and bolt the scrap in place on the arbor. Turn the scrap so one end faces the table. The bottom end of the scrap will serve as a reference point for checking table height relative to the motor carriage.

Loosen the lever on the saw that allows the arm to swing left and right. Rotate the arm and pull the motor carriage forward over one corner of the table. Lower the arm carefully and insert a thick feeler gauge between the bottom of the reference scrap and the table. Now remove the feeler gauge and slowly swing the arm to the opposite front corner of the table. If the reference edge makes contact with the table as you turn the arm, the table is rising from one corner to the other. You may be able to swivel the arm all the way to the other corner without interference; if so, recheck the table with the same feeler gauge. If the gap matches, the front corners of the table are even with one another from left to right and require no further adjustment. If there's a larger gap at the second corner, the table needs to be raised up to match the first corner. Adjust the front table bolts as needed to level the front corners.

Once the front corners are even, push the motor carriage to the back and check the back two corners of the table with the reference scrap and feeler gauge. Do not raise or lower the arm when moving the carriage from the front corners to the back. Raise or lower the back table adjuster bolts to level the back of the table with the front; doing so will also bring the table into a parallel relationship with the arm.

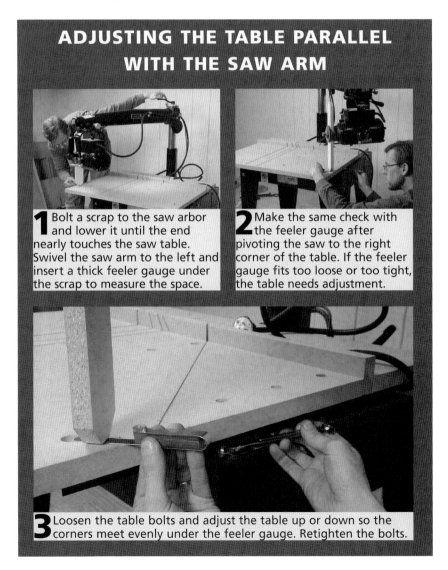

ADJUSTING THE TABLE PARALLEL WITH THE SAW ARM

1 Bolt a scrap to the saw arbor and lower it until the end nearly touches the saw table. Swivel the saw arm to the left and insert a thick feeler gauge under the scrap to measure the space.

2 Make the same check with the feeler gauge after pivoting the saw to the right corner of the table. If the feeler gauge fits too loose or too tight, the table needs adjustment.

3 Loosen the table bolts and adjust the table up or down so the corners meet evenly under the feeler gauge. Retighten the bolts.

Inspect the blade for squareness to the table by resting a combination square against the blade body. There should be no gaps.

Adjust the motor screws that pivot the head up and down to create perpendicularity between the blade and table.

Other Squaring Adjustments

In order to make a truly square cut, the blade must be square to the table and the arm square to the fence. To check for squareness to the table, adjust the blade height for a normal through cut and set a combination square against the blade body and table. Make sure the rule on the square does not touch the blade teeth. Refer to your owner's manual to locate the adjustment bolts for squaring the blade to the table. Often, they will be located behind the bevel tilt scale on the front of the motor carriage. Be sure to unlock the bevel-locking lever before making this adjustment.

A second important test for squareness is the blade's relationship to the fence. To check this, hold a framing square flat against the fence and table with the motor carriage pushed all the way back to the fence. Slide the framing square until it makes light contact with the side of the blade teeth. Now pull the carriage forward slowly to see if the blade teeth remain in contact with the square along the arm travel. If the teeth move closer to or away from the square, you'll need to adjust the arm's settings where it locks to the vertical column. Usually the adjustment bolts will be on or near the lever that allows the arm to pivot left and right.

See your owner's manual for adjusting the saw arm left or right to adjust for square. Adjuster bolts are usually located near the clamp handle on the vertical column.

Check the saw arm for squareness to the fence by pulling the motor carriage along the arm with the blade touching one leg of a framing square. If the blade drifts into or away from the square, it needs to be adjusted.

Correcting for squareness is a finicky process, but it's worth the effort to do carefully. The saw will cut more cleanly, accurately and safely. Check your progress by making test cuts and continuing the adjustment process until the saw makes square crosscuts.

Adjusting The Blade For Heeling

In addition to squaring the saw blade and arm, you also need to be sure the blade is perpendicular to the saw fence and parallel to the arm. If the blade is skewed in relation to the arm, moving the carriage along the arm will cause the blade to cut the wood twice— where the teeth both enter and leave the wood. The condition is called heeling. You'll know your blade is heeling if it leaves burn marks or excessive swirls along the cut edges. Severe heeling increases the chances for binding, which can cause the blade to climb up out of the cut and jerk forward. A skewed blade can also grab cutoff pieces more easily and throw them.

Once the blade is square to the table, you can check

it for heeling. Remove the outer blade collar and reinstall the arbor nut so you can use more of the blade for this test. Hold an accurate framing square against the fence, and tip the perpendicular leg of the square up so it rests flush against the blade diagonally and near the arbor nut. Check for gaps along the blade. If the blade and square don't line up evenly, see your owner's manual to find the trunnion adjuster bolts that shift the motor in this plane. Usually they're located at the rear pivot point where the carriage's yoke holds the motor. Adjust these bolts to shift the motor slightly left or right and eliminate any gaps between the blade and the square.

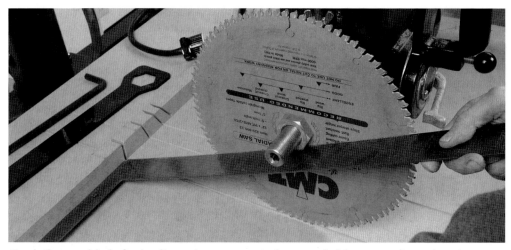

Check the saw blade for heeling using a carpenter's square held at an angle against the blade. There should be no gaps along the blade.

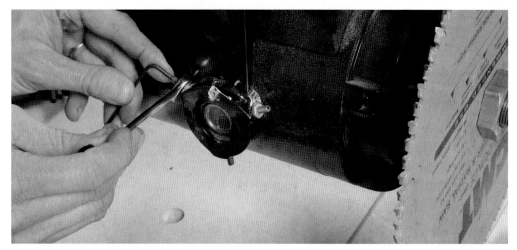

Shift the motor right or left to eliminate heeling by changing the settings of the trunnion adjuster bolts, usually located behind the motor.

TUNING UP A MITER SAW

Compared with a radial-arm saw, tuning a benchtop miter saw is easy. There are far fewer adjustments to make. However, if you transport your saw from the shop to the jobsite, or if you accidentally drop the saw, it's a good idea to check a few important settings before using it again. If your saw has a handle on the motorhead, picking up the saw by this handle can throw the saw out of alignment. Miter saws collect a fair amount of dust and debris, so an occasional cleaning and lubrication will keep the parts moving smoothly.

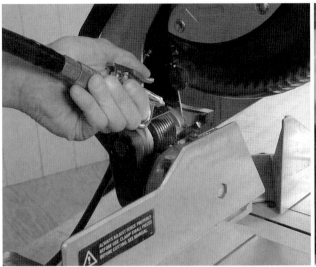

Periodically clean out the elbow joint on a miter saw with compressed air. Then lubricate the moving parts where they slide past one another with dry lubricant spray.

Cleaning And Lubrication

The pivot point where your miter saw's arm connects to the saw base is usually the area that accumulates the most debris. Use compressed air to blow the elbow joint clean, then spray dry lubricant into the seams of the joint. Pivot the saw up and down to work the lubricant into these areas.

Another area to lubricate every now and then is the joint where the saw table swivels on the base. Tip the saw onto its back and clean off any grime around the center table joint. Spray some dry lube into the joint seam and swivel the table a few times to work the lubricant in.

Keep your saw pivoting smoothly by lubricating the joint where the saw table swivels on the base. Access it from underneath the saw.

A short square will tell you whether the saw blade is perpendicular to the table. Look for gaps between the square's rule and the blade body.

Adjust the blade's squareness to the table by turning a pair of setscrews in or out to move the motorhead. Check your owner's manual to find these adjustment screws.

Setting Blade Angles

Your owner's manual will outline how to adjust the blade so it meets the table and fence squarely. Check the settings to see if adjustment is necessary by holding a combination square against the blade body and saw table. Be sure to unplug the saw first. Then hold the square against the fence and blade. Look for gaps next to the blade when you make both checks.

Adjusting the blade for squareness to the table usually involves turning a pair of setscrews located in back of the saw, near the elbow joint. Loosen and back off the blade tilt stops before adjusting the setscrews to allow some room for adjustment, then snug up the tilt stops once the blade aligns with the table.

Saws will vary in terms of how you adjust the blade for squareness to the fence. On the saw shown here, the blade adjusts left and right by

Most miter saws have tilt stops for holding the motorhead at 0° and 45° bevel angles. Once you've adjusted the blade so it's square to the table, snug up the 0° tilt stop.

loosening the screws that hold the table miter scale in place. Refer to your owner's manual to find the proper adjustment screws. Check your adjustments with the square to make sure the settings don't change when you tighten the locking screws.

When the blade is square to the fence and table, remember to adjust the bevel tilt and protractor scale cursors to 0° again.

Set a small square against the saw fence and blade to check for squareness. Lower the motorhead enough so the square does not rest against the blade teeth.

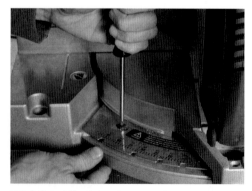

Find the adjustment screws to correct squareness between the fence and blade. Recheck the new setting with a square when you tighten the setscrews.

ROUTER TABLE

A router table may seem like the last tool you'd need to tune up, but in order for the router to cut accurately, it's important that the table is dead flat and the router insert plate is flush with the table. The fence must meet the table squarely, and the fence facings need to be flush with one another. These are simple but important checks to make, especially when you buy a new router table. If you use your router table often, the router will collect grit in the collet, and cleaning out the collet will prevent bits from binding or slipping. If your router table is equipped with a router lift that has a chain, it will get coated with wood dust that will eventually make the lift harder to turn.

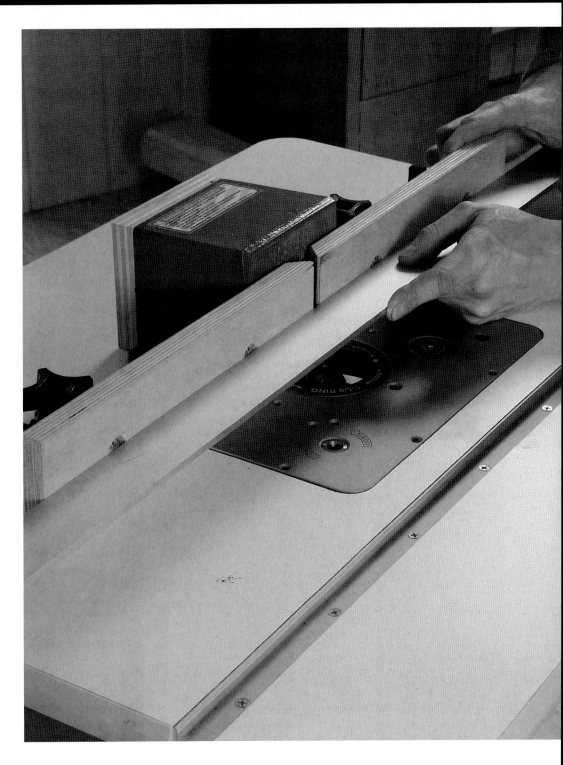

Flattening Reference Surfaces

Use a long reliable straightedge to inspect your router table for flatness. Check across the table's diagonals as well as lengthwise and widthwise. Typically, a router table will sag in the middle under the weight of the router, especially if you use a big router. If there's evidence of low or high spots closer to the edges of the table, insert paper shims under low areas where the tabletop connects to the base. To remedy sagging in the middle of the table, you may have to fasten a pair of cross supports to the bottom face of the tabletop to stiffen it.

Now check the facings on your router table fence. The facings need to be set in parallel planes with one another. For edge profiling, the faces need to be set flush with one another

Check the tabletop of a router table for flatness across its width, length and diagonals. Look closely for gaps under the straightedge, particularly in the insert plate area.

Raise low areas near the edges of the table by inserting shims between the tabletop and the base. Add bottom bracing across the middle of the table if it sags under the weight of the router and insert plate.

For general profiling tasks, fence facings need to be flush with one another to keep workpieces sliding smoothly past the fence. Check them with a long straightedge.

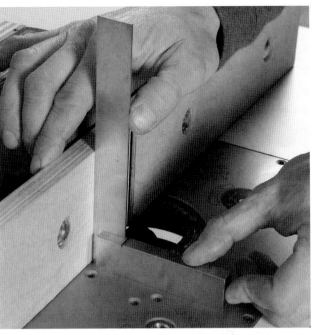

Clamp the router table fence in place and check the facings for squareness to the table. Correct out-of-square facings by adding shims behind them where they make contact with the metal fence body.

to prevent workpieces from catching on the edges as they pass by the bit. You may be able to shim behind a misaligned facing. If it's made of wood, another way to adjust it is by sanding the back surface where the facing meets the fence body. It's also important that the fence meets the table squarely when clamped down for a cut. Check the facings with a square held against the table.

Be sure your router insert plate is flush with the surrounding table sur-faces. Hold the rule of a combination square across the plate and table to check for gaps, and adjust the leveler screws in or out to bring the plate flush with the table. Usually these screws are threaded into the plate, or they may be located beneath the plate on the ledge that supports it. If your insert plate is made of metal, apply a drop of thread locking compound to each leveler screw to prevent it from vibrating out of adjustment.

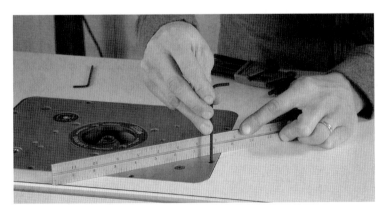

Adjust the leveler screws in the insert plate or around the insert plate opening to bring the plate flush with the table surface. Check your progress using the rule of a combination square.

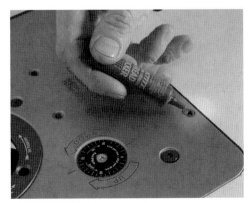

A drop of thread locking compound will help keep setscrews from vibrating out of position on a metal insert plate.

Cleaning The Router Collet And Lift Chain

A router cools itself by drawing air in through the bottom of the motor and out the top. When you invert a router in a router table, much of the fine dust produced during routing gets sucked down through the router motor. Every now and then, blow out the motor with compressed air to remove accumulated dust.

To clean your router's collet, remove the collet nut and use a paper towel wrapped around a pencil to clean out the inner sleeve. Use a rag dampened with mineral spirits to wipe out the tapered boring where the collet sleeve fits into the router.

If your router table has a router lift, use an old toothbrush to brush debris and grease off the router lift chain. Wipe off the sprockets that drive this chain as well. Use a metal protective spray or dry lube to lubricate the chain. Do not use oil or bearing grease on the chain, which will attract wood dust.

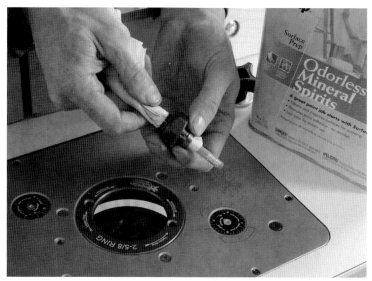

Clean debris out of the collet sleeve with a paper towel wrapped around a pencil. Use mineral spirits to wipe out the tapered bore that holds the collet.

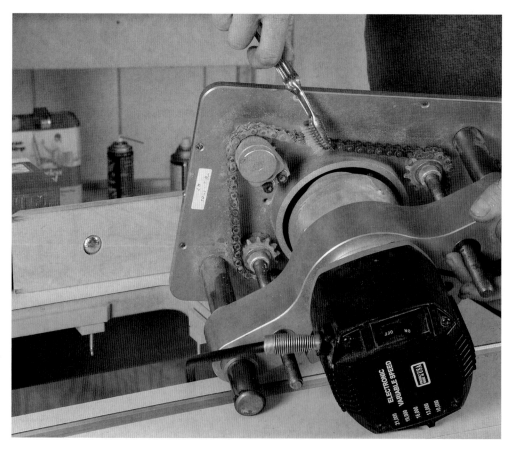

Router lifts with chain drives will accumulate debris on the chain if it is covered with grease. Clean off the grime with a toothbrush, then spray it with a dry lubricant instead of using grease.

CLEANING BLADES AND BITS

Saw blades and router bits get "gummed up" in a hurry. Heat that develops during cutting quickly turns wood pitch into a baked-on coating that reduces the performance of your cutting edges. It also holds heat, which just causes more build-up. The best solvent to use for cleaning bits and blades is a spray or liquid cleaner developed for this purpose. Or soak your blades in mineral spirits or kerosene to soften the debris. Spray-on oven cleaner is another effective solvent, but it's more corrosive than other options; be sure to clean it off thoroughly.

To clean a saw blade, spray or flood the blade with cleaner, allow it to penetrate and soften the grime for a few minutes, then use a soft-bristled brush to scrub the teeth. Clean router bits the same way, but be sure to remove the pilot bearing first for bits that have one. Solvents can dissolve the lubricant inside the bearing and cause it to seize up.

Clean off baked-on residue from your saw blades using blade cleaner and scrubbing with a soft-bristled brush. Wipe the surfaces clean.

Router bits can be cleaned with blade cleaner, but remove pilot bearings first to keep the solvent from dissolving lubricant inside the bearings.

Wipe blades and bits clean with a soft cloth, then spray on some metal protectant to prevent rust, and wipe off the excess. After cleaning a saw blade, inspect all the teeth carefully with a magnifying glass. Check for dull or fractured cutting edges or cracks in the brazing that holds the teeth on the blade body. If you buy economy blades, replace the blade if the teeth are damaged or missing. On an expensive blade, the damaged teeth are worth replacing. It usually costs less than $10 per tooth. You can also have an expensive blade resharpened for much less than replacing it. If the blade has thick teeth, it can often be resharpened several times without replacing the teeth. Return the blade to the manufacturer to have this work done correctly.

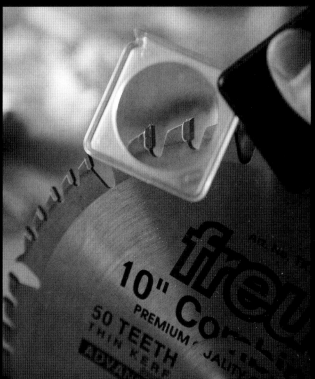

Once the blade teeth are clean, use a magnifying glass to inspect them closely. Look for worn cutting edges, chipped points or other fractures in the carbide and brazing.

SHARPENING CHISELS AND PLANE IRONS

Sharp chisels and hand planes are a joy to use, but the mystery or hassle of sharpening them may keep you from sharpening on a regular basis. Actually, sharpening these edges to serviceable quality isn't really all that difficult or time-consuming once you get the hang of it. If you've never had much luck with conventional sharpening stones, an inexpensive holding jig can make the job much more productive.

There are also a number of wet or dry power sharpening systems that make the job both easy and effective. Dry-grinding sharpeners use adhesive-backed sandpaper on a round platen to provide the sharpening action. The process is similar to holding your chisel against a record player. A tool rest keeps the chisel or plane iron held at the proper angle against the platen, and progressively finer grits take blades from rough grinding through fine honing stages. Wet sharpeners feature round waterstones that spin at slow speeds to provide the cutting action. The stone may be oriented upright, which provides a "hollow ground" edge, or tipped horizontally to form a conventional flat bevel. Both wet and dry power sharpeners have the capacity to provide an edge on par with a hand-sharpened edge. Power sharpeners are expensive, but the convenience and precision they offer may be well worth the investment.

These days, there are several systems for sharpening chisels and plane iron blades. Wet- or dry-grinding power sharpeners work quickly and take much of the guesswork out of the process, or you can use traditional sharpening stones for a lower-cost approach.

Basic Sharpening Process

Whether you use stones or a power sharpener to restore your chisel and plane edges, the sharpening process is basically the same. For severely nicked edges, the first step is to grind the end of the blade smooth and square to remove the nicks. Squaring the end is also important for creating a consistent edge on the blade.

NOTE: *If the edge is already square and without noticeable nicks, there's no need to square up the end further.*

Use an engineer's square held against the blade to mark a square reference line across the back (also called the face) of the blade. Move to the grinder, and set the grinder rest close to the grinding wheel. Hold the blade back against the rest. Gently draw the blade across the stone to remove the edge up to your layout line. Use your fingers to judge heat build-up on the steel as you work. Remove as little metal as possible, and pull the blade

Sharpen your chisels and hand planes as soon as the edges show signs of nicks and wear. The longer you wait, the harder the tools are to use effectively.

away from the wheel at the first sign of heat to prevent the steel from losing its temper. If the edge turns blue, you'll need to start the process over to grind away the blue area. Blue discoloration indicates that the temper is lost; the steel will be too soft to retain an edge. If the wheels on your grinder

SHARPENING WITH STONES

Power sharpening systems speed up the sharpening process, but you can always opt for the more economical and traditional method of sharpening with stones. Sharpening stones are sold in both synthetic and natural forms in various grits. Some stones use water as the principal lubricant, while others use oil. You can also buy ceramic or diamond-impregnated stones that need no lubricant.

The process of sharpening chisel blades or plane irons with stones is similar to power sharpening: flatten and polish the back, grind the bevel, and hone a microbevel. Start with a coarse 800x or 1000x grit for initial grinding, then switch to 4000x grit for final honing. Rub the blade back and forth firmly and evenly against the stone for each stage of sharpening. Be sure to keep the stone lubricated so it develops a slurry of pulverized stone and metal—the slurry contributes to the grinding process. A manual sharpening jig, which holds chisel or plane blades at the correct angle, makes it easier to grind a consistent bevel angle.

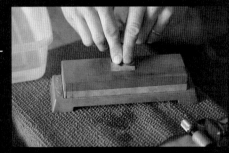

From time to time you'll need to flatten and clean your stones to keep them functioning properly. Lapping kits, which contain powdered silicon carbide and a flat piece of plate glass, are made for this purpose. Or, you can tape a piece of silicon carbide wet/dry sandpaper to a cast-iron tool table and use this setup for flattening stones.

If an edge is severely nicked, draw a line across the steel with a permanent marker so you can grind a fresh square edge and remove the damage.

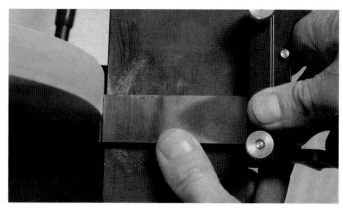

Using a light touch, draw the damaged tool edge past a fine-grit sharpening stone on a grinder. The goal is to grind up to your layout line without discoloring the steel so it loses its temper.

are too coarse to avoid bluing the steel, you may need to replace them with finer grit wheels made for sharpening hand tools. Or, use a metal file instead of the grinder to square the end of the blade.

Once the end of the blade is square, the next step involves flattening the back of the blade. It's important not to bypass this crucial step in the sharpening process. A properly sharpened edge should be beveled on one surface only, with the back remaining absolutely flat. That way, sharpening becomes a process of grinding a fresh bevel surface, with the edge developing from the bevel side, not the back. You only need to flatten the first 1 to 2 in. of the back of the blade—not the entire surface. Some grinding systems allow you to flatten blade backs right on the machine. Otherwise, use a flat

sharpening stone or a piece of fine-grit wet/dry sandpaper fixed to a piece of 1/4-in. plate glass to carry out the flattening process. Then hone the back with finer grit abrasives until it develops a mirror finish.

With the back flattened and polished, check the angle of the blade's bevel with a gauge. (You can purchase a bevel-checking gauge from many woodworking supply catalogs, or it may come with your sharpening system.) Bevel angles ranging from 25° to 30° are common for bench chisels and plane irons.

Grinding the bevel edge on your blades involves pressing the bevel edge against the sharpening surface and holding it at a consistent angle to

If the edge is already flat but dull, flatten and hone the back of the blade to a mirror finish. You only need to do this to a new tool blade. If the back is already flat, proceed to the next step.

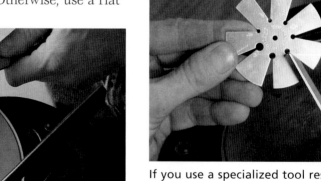

If you use a specialized tool rest for sharpening chisels and plane irons, you'll need to verify the bevel angle in order to set up the rest correctly. This gauge measures a variety of common bevel angles.

On this dry-grinding sharpener, coarse sandpaper abrasives grind the initial bevel to shape. The abrasives spin on a platen similar to a record player. Tools are held in a rest that slides back and forth over the platen.

Adjust the sharpener's tool rest to match the bevel angle on the blade. In this case, the desired bevel angle is 25°.

Grind the bevel until all traces of the old surface are gone and you produce a clean cutting edge that does not reflect light. Be careful not to remove steel too quickly; blue coloration is a sign that the temper is lost.

create a flat surface on the bevel face. On the dry-grinding system shown here, the tool rest can be set to an angle that matches the blade's bevel angle. The chisel or plane iron clamps into a holder that rides on the tool rest to hold the blade at the correct bevel angle, relative to the abrasive platen. Grind the blade until you produce a flat bevel surface. If the blade back is flat and the bevel surface properly ground, you should end up with a knife edge that doesn't reflect light where the blade back and bevel meet.

TIP

A metal tabletop makes a convenient "heat sink" during sharpening to draw heat out of the chisel blade.

If you use a dry-grinding sharpening system, blades will develop an intense amount of heat during grinding and honing. One way to keep blades from overheating is to do your sharpening with the machine on a cast-iron tool table. When the blade heats up, hold it against the cold cast iron, which will act like a "heat sink" and draw the heat quickly out of the steel.

To create a keener edge, some sharpening systems (or sharpening jigs used with sharpening stones) allow for the creation of a microbevel. Making a microbevel simply means creating a slightly steeper bevel near the cutting edge. Microbevels provide an added degree of sharpness, but they also speed up the process of resharpening. If you keep your edges free of nicks, touching up the cutting edge can be as easy as refreshing this microbevel instead of regrinding the whole bevel. Depending on the jig or system you use, the tool rest will adjust easily to hone the microbevel.

Some sharpening systems allow you to hone a steeper razor-sharp microbevel. Provided this cutting edge doesn't get nicked during use, re-sharpening is a simple matter of touching up the microbevel.

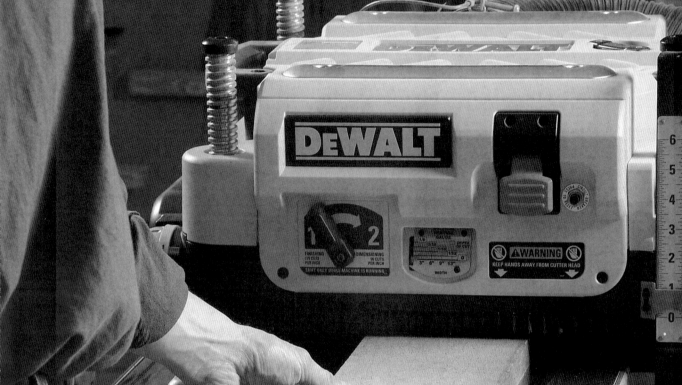

THREE

SURFACING AND STORING LUMBER

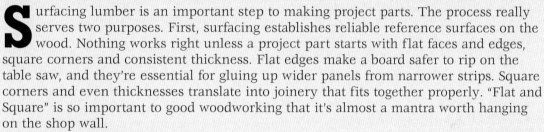

Surfacing lumber is an important step to making project parts. The process really serves two purposes. First, surfacing establishes reliable reference surfaces on the wood. Nothing works right unless a project part starts with flat faces and edges, square corners and consistent thickness. Flat edges make a board safer to rip on the table saw, and they're essential for gluing up wider panels from narrower strips. Square corners and even thicknesses translate into joinery that fits together properly. "Flat and Square" is so important to good woodworking that it's almost a mantra worth hanging on the shop wall.

The second reason for surfacing is that it helps you become familiar with each piece of wood you're planning to use. No two boards are the same, and each piece will have it's own unique strengths and weaknesses you'll have to deal with at the surfacing stage. That includes lumber you buy pre-surfaced at the home center. It might look flat and square on the shelf, but closer inspection will often tell otherwise. If you buy roughsawn lumber, the purpose of surfacing is even more obvious. Prior to surfacing, it's hard to tell what the actual grain and figure of the wood is, and none of the surfaces will be flat or smooth. Some boards will have particularly attractive grain and figure. Other boards may have a tiny knot, split or area of sapwood you'll need to remove. Surfacing gives you the opportunity to make decisions about what boards will work best for each part of your project. It also helps you strategize how best to harvest each piece.

This chapter will walk you through the surfacing process, step by step. Here's where a jointer and thickness planer really earn their place in the home shop, along with a couple good hand planes. You'll learn how to "read" common wood distortions, create reliable reference surfaces on the wood and fix troublesome boards with the correct sequence of jointing and planing. Be sure to surface your wood as close as possible to the time you will use it, otherwise it will eventually change shape and require more surfacing. We'll also review some options for storing lumber and sheet goods properly at the end of this chapter to help keep them tidy, flat and in good condition.

Overview Of The Surfacing Process

There's a time-honored method for surfacing lumber. Many techniques in woodworking can be tackled different ways, but surfacing isn't one of them. Try to follow the same sequence of steps each time you prepare a board to ensure that you'll end up with faces, edges and thicknesses you can count on. Here's the step-by-step process to follow:

1. Take An Initial "Reading" To Evaluate Distortions

The first order of business is to inspect lumber closely to see what irregularities it has. You may have learned that flattening a board face comes first, but that actually comes after knowing which face makes most sense to flatten first. Depending on the condition of the board and the amount of distortion you find, you may need to cut it into narrower or shorter pieces or flatten irregularities

with a hand plane before proceeding to the jointer to flatten that first face. Also, keep in mind what the end result will be for the particular piece of wood you're evaluating. For instance, flattening an 8-ft. board that you plan to use for 2-ft.-long pieces is a mistake; achieving a flat face on the entire board may require removing an excess of wood that then makes the board too thin to be useful.

Start your inspection by holding the board on edge and sighting down the length of the edge. If the edge dips down or rises up from end to end like an archer's bow, the defect is called crook. Particularly long, narrow boards will bend under their own weight, even along the edge—so you may not be witnessing a defect. However, in most cases crooked edges will need to be corrected by machining one edge flat to create a reference surface for the other edge. You'll straighten the edges after flattening the faces.

Next, lay the board on a flat surface and see what happens. Ideally, the entire "down" face will lie flat. If the face is basically flat already, proceed to joint it. Often you won't be so lucky, and the board will indicate some degree of warp. There are three kinds of warp that affect board faces: cup, bow and twist. When only the center of the board or the long edges

Crook and bow will be easy to spot if you sight down the edge of a board.

Lay a board on a flat machine table and see if either face lies flat. Push on the corners; if it rocks, the board is probably twisted.

A "ski jump" shaped distortion is called bowing.

A crooked board arches along its edges.

When just the center or both edges touch, a board is cupping across its faces.

Twisting results in a board rocking on its corners.

touch down, the board is cupping across the grain, similar to the letter "C". If one end of the board rises up like a ski jump, the board is bowing along its length. If only the opposite corners touch down, the board is twisted. On particularly unruly lumber, you may find more than one type of distortion on the same board. Skip to the section on "Surfacing Strategies," page 86, to find out what to do if you need to remedy these kinds of problems.

2. Joint One Face Flat

Here's where the precision surfacing really begins. One flat face becomes a reference surface for making the other face flat as well as flattening the first edge. Orient the flattest face of your board down on the jointer table. Choose the side that touches at the ends rather than the side that rocks in the middle. You'll

also need to figure out how the grain direction runs on this board face. A jointer's cutterhead rotates against the feed direction of the wood, with the knives spinning toward you. Feed

Sometimes the grain direction on the edge of a board will help you figure out how to arrange it on the jointer. The edge grain should point down and with the spin direction of the jointer.

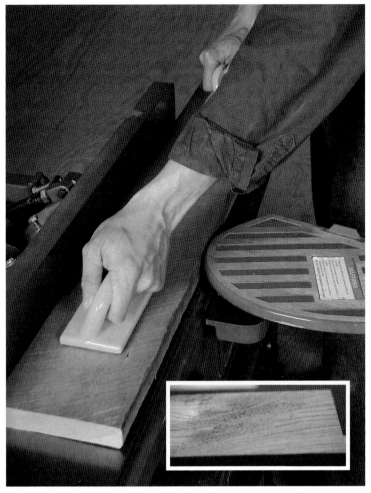

the board into the jointer "with" the grain direction instead of against it to prevent the knives from tearing out bits of wood. (For a basic overview of how to use a jointer, see the photo series on this page.)

It may take several passes to flatten the first face. Each pass will remove more wood until the knives are skimming material off the entire board face. Stop jointing when all traces of the old face are removed and you'll have a fresh, flat board face.

3. Plane The Other Face Flat

With a flat face established, the next step is to flatten the opposite face. A jointer is the wrong tool for this step, because there's no way to be sure the jointed faces will remain parallel. Turn to the planer instead, which maintains parallelism automatically.

Planer knives rotate against the feed direction just like the jointer, so it's a good idea to plane with the grain direction of the wood to prevent tearout. Plane the second face until it's smooth and flat (for more on how to use a planer, see page 91). If tearout seems to occur in some areas regardless of switching the board's direction, it's a sign that the grain direction reverses on this piece

Choose the flattest face of the workpiece to joint first. Take the first pass and look closely at the surface for signs of tearout (see inset photo). If you see it occurring, flip the board end-for-end to joint with the grain instead of against it.

Each pass over the jointer will remove more of the original surface until the knives are removing an even layer of the entire board face. Stop as soon as the jointing produces a smooth, flat face.

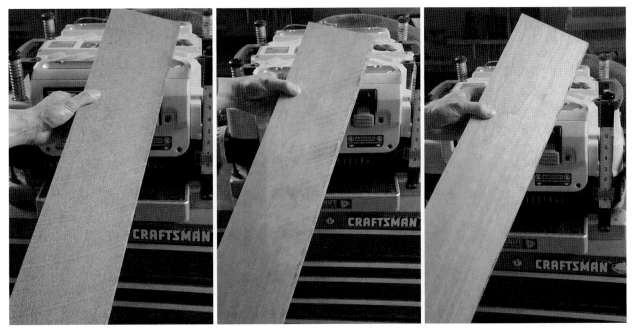

Turn the jointed face down and use your thickness planer to flatten and smooth the other face. Jointing first, then planing will guarantee that both faces will be parallel.

of wood. The best remedy is to plane the face in the direction that offers the most smoothness and least tearout. If the board is within a pass or two of the final thickness you want, set the cutterhead to take the lightest possible passes. Often, this will remove even troublesome areas of tearout. You can also try dampening the surface with water to raise the grain in the tearout areas (see page 92.)

4. Continue Planing To Reach The Desired Thickness

The important thing to remember with this step is to alternate the board faces as you plane it down. This will help maintain the board's original moisture equilibrium so it doesn't warp further. Flipping from face to face also cleans up any jointer knife marks left on the first face. Pay attention to the grain direction as you make each pass. The correct way to maneuver the lumber between passes is to flip the board from one face to the other, and turn it end-for-end. That way, you won't accidentally present the next face to the

machine "against" the grain, which will create tearout. For best results, do not plane off more than $1/32$ to $1/16$ in. of material with each pass. If your planer has two feed speeds, use the faster speed to reduce the board's thickness quickly, then switch to the slower speed for making the final smoothing passes.

5. Joint One Edge Flat And Square

Now that both faces are flat, position one or the other against the jointer fence to flatten an edge and create a square corner. Check your jointer fence first with a combination or engineer's square to be sure the fence and table are square (see page 55). Before you begin, sight down both edges and pick the edge that's most flat. For crooked boards, joint the concave rather than the convex edge, which will remove the tips of the board instead of the hump. The edge will tend to flatten out faster this way, and you'll save more wood. It's also much harder to steady the convex edge.

Make the first pass across the jointer and check the edge for tearout. If

the edge is clean, you've got the grain direction oriented correctly. If tearout is evident, turn the board end-for-end so the opposite face is against the jointer fence. This should remove the tearout. When you make each pass, be sure to keep the face and edge firmly planted against the fence and table. Wider workpieces tend to tip away from the fence if you're not careful. Use push sticks instead of your hands to feed narrow boards across the jointer. Make repeated passes until all traces of the original edge are gone. Then use a square to spot-check the new corner at several places along the board. You want this first corner to be flat and exactly 90° all along its length.

6. Rip The Other Edge Flat And Crosscut To Length

Once you have flat faces and a jointed reference edge, all that's left to do is rip the board to final width on the table saw or bandsaw and crosscut the board to length. It's a good idea to rip about 1/32 in. wider than you need, then joint the sawn edge smooth so you'll end up with two finished edges.

Flatten and square one edge of the workpiece on the jointer. Be sure to keep the board face pressed firmly against the jointer's fence. Check the fresh edge for squareness at several places along its length.

The last step in the squaring process is to rip the other rough edge off your workpiece and crosscut the board to length. For more on ripping and crosscutting, see Chapter Four.

Consider Surfacing Your Lumber Twice

Once you get into the groove of surfacing, it might be tempting to surface all your lumber ahead of when you actually need to use it. Pre-surfacing can be a good idea, because planing makes it easy to read the grain pattern and figure of the wood when you're choosing which boards to use. However, wood is always sensitive to changes in humidity. It will swell during damp summer months and shrink in the winter when the air is heated and dry. Changes in moisture content can lead to distortion, regardless of whether the wood is left in the rough or surfaced to final thickness. If you pre-surface everything, you've got no "wiggle room" to correct any new distortions when the board changes shape.

The better approach is to leave lumber "in the rough" as long as possible until you really need it. Or, skim off just enough of the rough surface of the board so you can evaluate it for grain pattern and figure, but don't take off any more than necessary. This is called "skip" planing. It's also good practice to give new lumber at least two weeks or more to acclimate to your shop before using it. Then, flatten the faces and edges as usual, but don't plane to final thickness. Give the wood a few more days to react to initial surfacing to see if any new distortion happens. A final jointing and planing should take care of any additional warping that happens. Use the wood as soon as possible after the last round of surfacing.

"Skip" planing is a great way to let you see what the figure and color of a board is without planing it to final thickness. Always save final planing until you're ready to use the wood.

Surfacing Strategies To Correct Defects

The tough part about correcting warp is figuring out the best series of steps to fix it. Picking the wrong approach can lead to lots of extra effort or actually make the end result worse than what you started with. You don't want to waste time or waste wood. The goal is to do as little as possible in order to create a reasonably flat surface to take to the jointer. Here are some approaches to try.

Straightening Crooked Edges

Crooked edges are easy to fix. Flatten one face on the jointer, then remove one of the crooked edges to create a flat edge and square corner. For minor crook, just joint the bad edge. If the edge is severely crooked, tack the board to a flat-edged piece of stock and remove the bow at the table saw or bandsaw with a rip cut.

Flattening A Cupped Face

The method for flattening a cupped board will depend on how severe the cupping is as well as how wide and thick the stock is to begin with. If the board cups less than about 1/16 in., flatten the first face as usual. You'll lose a bit of overall thickness by jointing the face flat, but cupping isn't severe enough to merit ripping the board into narrower pieces to flatten it. Orient the board so the concave face is down on the jointer bed to shave off the long edges. To remove cupping on boards wider than your jointer bed, you can flatten the edges with a smoothing plane first, then flatten the opposite face by running the board through the planer. Flip this fully planed face down so it rests on the planer bed, and run the board through to flatten the initial face you treated with a hand plane.

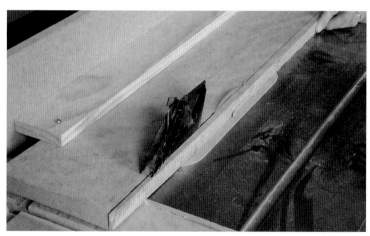

When a board's edges are too uneven or crooked to joint easily, you can flatten one edge by fastening a flat-edged scrap to one edge. Rip the board with the scrap edge against the fence.

Remove the scrap, flip the board end-for-end and rip the other edge flat with the newly flattened edge against the rip fence. Now both edges will be flat and parallel.

If a board is too wide to flatten on your jointer, you can use a smoothing plane instead. Set the plane for a moderately deep cut, and hold it at a skewed angle to the grain so it will cut the wood in a shearing action. Plane with the grain direction.

If the amount of cup is closer to ⅛ in., you can still joint the board face flat but you'll lose more wood. The best way to keep from wasting wood thickness on a severely cupped board is to rip it down the middle using a bandsaw (see page 163) or a table saw (see page 129). Even though you'll end up with two strips of wood instead of one wide board, you can still re-glue the pieces back together after they're individually flattened to form a wider workpiece. **NOTE:** When ripping cupped lumber, position the wood so the convex face is down on the saw table to keep the board from collapsing in on itself and binding the blade.

Remedying Twist And Bow

Boards that twist on both ends are more difficult to salvage than those with a twist on just one end. If the board twists more than about ½ in. overall on lumber less than a couple inches thick it's not worth trying to salvage as a single piece of lumber. Crosscut it into shorter lengths, then use your bandsaw to rip the lengths into narrower strips that are easier to flatten.

On long boards, there may be an area in the middle that's more or less flat already. The easiest way to find out is to use a pair of winding sticks to locate where the distortion starts. Winding sticks are simply a pair of flat, equally sized strips of scrap laid across the grain of a board to use as sighting aids. Make the winding sticks at least as long as the board is wide.

Any pair of flat, equally sized scraps can serve as winding sticks. Paint one white to make it easier to see when using the sticks.

Sometimes you can salvage two narrower boards from one wide cupped board by ripping it down the middle on the bandsaw or table saw. Rip it with the convex face down.

For added visibility, paint them different colors or make one stick white. To use the sticks, lay the piece of lumber on your workbench and place the sticks at opposite ends of the board, then squat down so you can sight just over the top edges of the sticks. On a twisted board, the edges of the sticks will skew rather than appear parallel to one another. Now, move the sticks closer together in stages until the top edges of the sticks appear parallel when you sight across them. Here's where the twist begins. If the sticks never line up, the twist is continuous along the board length.

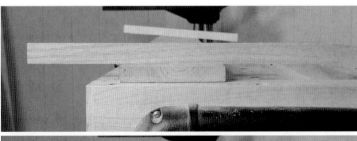

Set a winding stick on each end of the board and look across their top edges to check for twisting. Then move the sticks closer together a little at a time and recheck them. When the edges appear parallel, you've found where the twist begins.

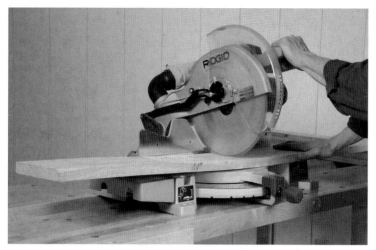

If only part of a bowed board is distorted, cut off the defective area where it begins to deflect.

TIP

USE A PLANER FOR EDGE JOINTING

If you are surfacing multiple narrow strips of wood to the same size, you can use your planer to smooth the last edge of the boards after ripping them to width. The trick is to leave the stock about 1/16 in. wider than the final width. Stack the boards together with the jointed edge down on the planer bed, and run them through the machine "gang style" in a single bundle. This technique works best for stock that's less than about 4 in. wide and at least as long as the planer's length from front to back. You don't want the boards to tip over inside the machine or get stuck between the feed rollers. Make sure there are enough pieces in the bundle to form a stable base. If you're in doubt, clamp them together on the ends with the clamps facing down so they stay clear of the cutters. Orient the grain direction correctly for each board in the gang to help minimize tearout on the planed edge.

If you have a number of same-width workpieces to make, you can send them through the planer on edge and in a group. Grouping the parts helps keep them from tipping over.

To correct twisting on one face, start with a hand plane to plane down the high corners. Plane diagonally to the grain direction in long strokes to knock down the high spots. A jointer or smoothing plane with a long sole is the best choice for this work. Set the plane iron for an aggressive cut to remove material quickly. Then flatten the hand-planed face the rest of the way on the jointer, and proceed with the surfacing process as usual.

If a board bows along its length, you may be able to crosscut it into two shorter flatter pieces. Sometimes a piece of bowed lumber will only distort along part of its length. Cut off the warped section. For severely warped boards, you may have no other choice than to discard the wood or cut it up for the fireplace.

Removing Other Defects

Remove large knots, sap pockets and splits on the ends before you take lumber to the jointer or planer. Check any knots carefully for looseness; a loose knot that falls out can turn into a projectile during machining. Usually, knots will be defects you'll probably remove anyway for appearance's sake. Use a miter saw, radial-arm saw or table saw to crosscut the defective areas off your wood. If the wood doesn't have a flat reference edge, be sure to use a circular saw or jigsaw to cut away the defective areas.

Use a circular saw or jigsaw to remove large end checks before proceeding with further surfacing.

HOW TO USE A JOINTER

Jointing a board involves sliding it over the cutterhead from the infeed side of the machine to the outfeed side. The goal is to maintain even pressure on the wood and move in a fluid motion. To prepare for jointing, set the jointer's infeed table to a light depth of cut (1/32 to 1/16 in.). Stand alongside the infeed table facing the machine, and balance your weight comfortably on both feet. Spread your feed apart so you can rock left and right without losing your balance. If the board you're surfacing is narrower than about 6 in., you'll need two push sticks or rubber-soled push pads to keep your hands safely away from the cutters. Start the machine and press the board down against the infeed table with a push pad in your left hand. Guide the back of the board with your right hand.

A jointer will make the cleanest cuts if you set the infeed table for a light pass. Generally, a cutting depth of 1/32 in. offers a good compromise between cutting efficiency and smoothness.

Start feeding the board into the cutters, keeping even pressure down against the cutterhead as the first end passes over it. Let your left hand guide the front of the board onto the outfeed table, and slowly rock forward on your feet as the cut progresses. Feed pressure transfers from the infeed table to the outfeed table. When your right hand reaches the jointer table, grab another push stick and finish up the first pass.

For long boards, you may have to pivot your body back to the starting position to continue feeding, but try to keep pressure applied to the outfeed side of the table as you reposition yourself. Pausing the cut momentarily won't affect the board surface much, and it will help you maintain your center of balance. Balance is really important when you're working with thick, heavy stock, especially on a small jointer with a short bed length.

To make a jointing pass, stand comfortably beside the machine and guide the front end of the board along the infeed table into the cutterhead. Press down firmly with your left hand holding a push pad or push stick.

When the back end of the board reaches the infeed table, grab a push stick in your right hand and continue feeding the board until it clears the cutterhead. Transfer downward pressure on the board to the outfeed side of the workpiece as the cut progresses. Rock forward on your feet as needed to keep the wood moving smoothly along.

If you find splits in the midsection of a board, be wary of using it. Chances are, the wood contains internal stresses that may cause it to warp again, no matter what you do. The board won't stay flat until all the stresses are relieved. Often, these cracks result from rapid kiln drying where uneven moisture content caused the wood to literally pull itself apart from the inside. This condition is called case hardening or honeycombing. There may be other cracks you won't see until you cut it up or plane it further. Case-hardened wood is best left for kindling.

OTHER COMMON LUMBER DEFECTS

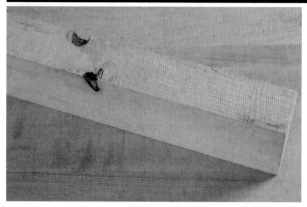

Loose knots are a machining hazard.

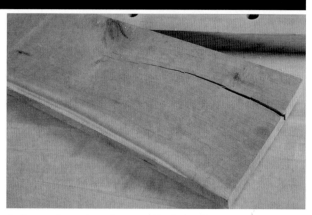

Splits on board ends are called checks.

Splits inside a board may indicate case hardening or wind damaged wood.

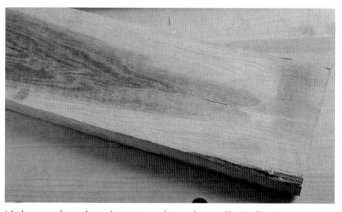

Lighter-colored regions on a board usually indicate sapwood.

Holes and tunnels are a sure sign of insect damage.

Bark along a board edge is called wane.

HOW TO USE A PLANER

Generally, planers are easier to use than jointers. What's most important is that the jointed face of your stock is absolutely flat before you send it through the thickness planer. On ordinary ¾-in.-thick lumber, the feed rollers on a planer apply enough downward force to literally flatten out any residual distortion in the board, but the warp will spring back as soon as the workpiece leaves the planer. You'll be left with a thinner, but equally warped workpiece.

Most benchtop planers have a thickness-setting indicator on the front of the machine so you can set the depth of cut without measuring the board first. If you use the indicator, remember to use the thickest part of the board for setting the initial depth. Otherwise, the board will get stuck in the machine as it planes from thinner to thicker areas, which is hard on the motor. It will also leave gouges and feed roller marks on the wood. With the planer turned off, slip the thickest end of the board under the indicator, and raise or lower the cutterhead until the pointer on the indicator reads your desired depth of cut. For a benchtop planer, don't take off more than about ¹/₃₂ in. of material with each pass, especially on hardwoods.

If you're planing long or heavy lumber, clamp or bolt the planer down on a sturdy work-surface to keep it from tipping over. With everything set and your hearing protection on, turn on the machine and gently feed the wood into the machine. For long boards, lift the back end of the board slightly to prevent the cutterhead from cutting too deeply at the beginning of the pass and creating snipe.

Once the feed rollers are pulling the board through and about half of the board is finished planing, move to the back of the planer to catch the workpiece as it exits. For long workpieces, lift the leading end of the board slightly to keep the planer from sniping the board's trailing end. Flip the board over, turn it end-for-end and lower the cutterhead to prepare for the next pass.

In order to figure out where to set your planer's cutting depth for the first pass, measure the thickness of the workpiece at various places around the board.

Set the thickest end of the board under the planer and lower the cutterhead until the thickness indicator reads about ¹/₃₂ in. This reading tells you how much the machine will remove in the first pass.

Start the planer and push the board into the machine until the feed rollers grab it and start pulling it through.

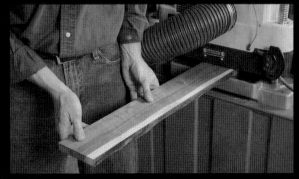

When about half the workpiece has passed through the planer, move around to the outfeed side and catch it as it finishes the pass.

Other Planer Issues To Consider

Planing introduces a number of unique situations you'll probably encounter from time to time as you work with different wood. Here are a few tips to remember:

One way to tame irregular grain direction is to dampen the wood with water and then run it through the planer. Dampness will raise surface fibers so the planer can remove them more easily.

Feeding one workpiece after the next into a planer is a great way to eliminate sniping on the ends of the boards. Keep the boards spaced as closely as possible.

Gang-Planing To Minimize Snipe

Snipe occurs when only one of the planer's two feed rollers are in contact with the wood. Often, the pressure of the roller or the way in which you feed the wood into the machine will tip the front edge of the wood up slightly, and the knives cut it more deeply. You can help equalize the pressure by butting boards end to end as you feed them into the planer. This forms a continuous wood surface for the feed rollers and eliminates snipe on all but the first and last pieces. You'll need a helper to receive the exiting boards if you have many workpieces to plane, but the process is quite efficient. Use scrap pieces as the first and last members of the "train" to prevent snipe from occurring on any of the important workpieces.

Wetting Wood To Reduce Tearout And "Fuzz"

Workpieces with grain patterns that change direction can be difficult to plane smoothly. One way to help tame the irregular grain is to wet it first with water and allow it to soak it in for a few minutes. The water will raise the surface fibers so the planer can shear them off more easily. You don't need to soak the board with wood; a light spritzing is all it takes. Taking lighter passes can also improve surface smoothness in those gnarly areas of a board.

Planing Thin Lumber Safely

Some planers can't be set to plane lumber thinner than 1/4 in. One solution is to make an auxiliary bed for your planer that will offset the cutterhead so it can cut below its minimum depth setting. All it takes is a piece of MDF or melamine the same size as your planer bed with a cleat attached across one end. Set the cleat against the planer bed on the infeed

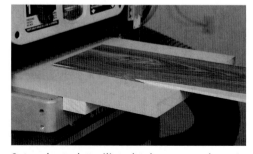

Set a cleated auxiliary bed on your planer's bed to help plane lumber thinner than the machine's minimum depth setting.

side to keep the bed from feeding through the machine. Now, you can effectively lower the cutterhead all the way to the auxiliary bed and plane wood as thin as you wish.

Keep in mind, however, that wood becomes more flexible the thinner it gets. For planing stock that's less than about 1/8 in. thick, mount the strips to a "slave" board with double-sided tape and send the board through the planer along with the strips. This approach will prevent the strips from flexing up and getting trapped in the cutterhead. If that happens, the planer will usually damage the wood.

Planing Short Stock

Every now and then you'll need to plane a short piece of stock that's too short to feed through on its own but too valuable to throw away. Any wood shorter than the distance between the feed rollers is really too short to plane safely without modification. One option is to add a pair of longer runners to the edges of the short board to simulate a longer workpiece. All you need are two strips of scrap around 14 to 16 in. long that are slightly thicker than the wood you want to plane. Fasten the strips to the edges of the workpiece with hot-melt glue, and set the planer's depth of cut to shave off the extra thickness. Send the assembly through the planer as usual.

Use pieces of carpet tape (clear in photo) to secure thin strips of wood to a "slave" board for planing. The slave board will keep thin workpieces from getting caught in the cutterhead.

Dust Collection Reduces Denting

If your planer isn't connected to a dust collector, you already know what a mess it makes. Those chips also blow around inside the machine and get trapped between the feed rollers and the wood, leading to tiny dents in the planed surface. These are really noticeable on softer woods like poplar, pine and cedar, and they can be difficult to sand out later. Keeping your planer's feed rollers clean will help reduce denting, but the best solution is to connect your planer to a dust collector. A collector rated for 500 to 650 cubic feet per minute of suction is all that's really necessary for the home shop, and the machine's cost is actually quite affordable. Best of all, you'll breathe easier and the shop floor will stay much cleaner.

A portable dust collector that draws around 650 cubic feet of air per minute will keep your shop and lungs cleaner. It also helps prevent planers from crushing wood chips into board surfaces and denting them.

Glue a pair of long scrap runners to the edges of a short workpiece before planing it. The runners will simulate a longer board.

Surfacing Wide Lumber

If you are fortunate enough to acquire lumber even wider than the capacity of your jointer or planer, you may wonder how to surface it.

One option is to keep wide lumber in one piece and flatten a face using a hand plane. You'll need to trim the board to a width that will fit your planer, which will sacrifice some wood, but at least the board will stay in one piece.

Another method that sacrifices a bit of wood but allows you to use both your jointer and planer as usual is to essentially rip, joint, plane and reglue the board back together. The photo series shown at left illustrates the process.

Essentially, you'll use the same procedures for jointing and planing sections of the wide board after rip-cutting them to widths that fit the bed width of your jointer. It may feel odd to cut a wide piece of wood into narrow strips, but as you can see in the last photo, the end result still produces a board with grain patterns that blend naturally. This method also provides an effective way to machine-surface a wide piece of stock into a flat, square workpiece quickly. If you do a careful job of jointing and gluing the parts back together, the seams will be almost invisible.

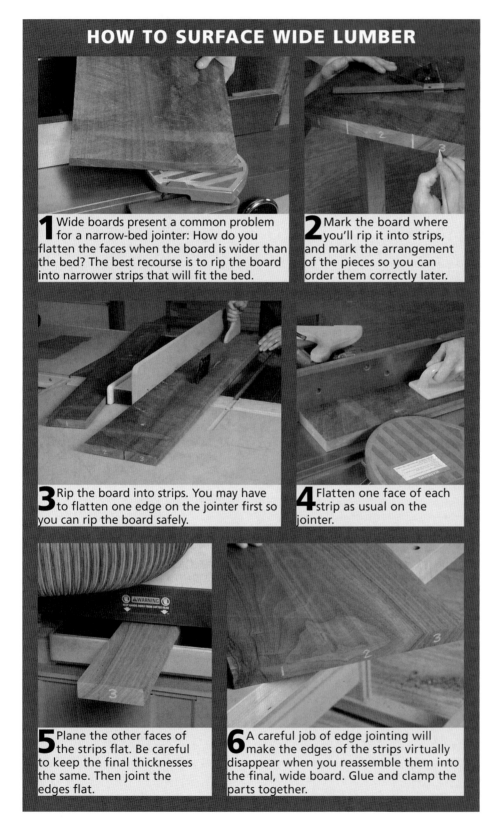

HOW TO SURFACE WIDE LUMBER

1 Wide boards present a common problem for a narrow-bed jointer: How do you flatten the faces when the board is wider than the bed? The best recourse is to rip the board into narrower strips that will fit the bed.

2 Mark the board where you'll rip it into strips, and mark the arrangement of the pieces so you can order them correctly later.

3 Rip the board into strips. You may have to flatten one edge on the jointer first so you can rip the board safely.

4 Flatten one face of each strip as usual on the jointer.

5 Plane the other faces of the strips flat. Be careful to keep the final thicknesses the same. Then joint the edges flat.

6 A careful job of edge jointing will make the edges of the strips virtually disappear when you reassemble them into the final, wide board. Glue and clamp the parts together.

Storing Lumber

Most of us wish we had bigger shops, not only to store more machinery but also to squirrel away more wood. Whether you work in an empty barn or a crowded corner of the basement, sooner or later you'll have to find a reasonable way to store your wood. Obviously, you'll want to keep your lumber as flat and dry as possible, but you also want to be able to find what you need and get it out of the pile fairly easily. There's no perfect way to store wood, and the method that works best for you probably won't work as well for the next woodworker you ask. The location and layout of your shop, the amount of wood you have to store and your own methods of work will impact how you store your board lumber, sheet goods and scraps. Here are a few suggestions to get you started:

Storing Board Lumber

The best way to store dry board lumber is in a horizontal stack. The weight of the stack helps to keep boards flatter, and less of their surface area is exposed to the air to help reduce shrinking and swelling. Sometimes you'll have no choice but to store wood standing on end. The trouble with standing boards vertically is that there's a chance they might bow under their own weight. If the ends of the boards rest on a concrete floor, they can also absorb moisture and swell up. Boards leaning against a wall are also easy to knock over, which is a particular hazard if you have children poking around the shop.

A sturdy shelving system is the best way to store boards horizontally. It can be a free-standing unit, or you can mount shelf standards and brackets to the wall. For safety's sake, try to buy or build a heavy-duty system that's capable of supporting heavy loads. If you attach shelf standards to a stud wall, use thick-shanked lag screws and washers instead or ordi-

Use heavy-duty shelf standards and brackets to build a wall rack for storing stacks of board lumber. Fasten the standards to wall studs with lag screws and large washers.

nary screws. Mount your rack to a load-bearing wall, if possible. Use lead or expanding concrete anchors when fastening to a cement or cinder block wall. If you have to space the shelf standards more than 16 in. apart, lay a stiff shelf board over the brackets to prevent sagging.

Try to keep the shelving system low enough so you can reach the top shelf without needing a ladder. Wrestling the weight of a heavy board while standing on a ladder is a recipe for disaster. Generally, the more shelves you have, the better. Many closely spaced shelves allow you to store smaller stacks of wood on each shelf so they're easier to sort. Smaller piles also weigh less so you can't overload the brackets.

If you are setting up shop for the first time or reorganizing your shop

If you need to stack lumber on a concrete floor, lay a sheet of heavy plastic down first and use scraps for spacers under the wood. If your shop is in the basement, use a dehumidifier to help keep the floor dry.

The proportions of sheet materials may force you to store them on end. Use a strap or piece of rope secured between eyebolts to prevent sheets from accidentally tipping over.

on a major scale, think about conserving energy and preventing back strain. It helps to have your lumber shelving situated close to the door so you don't have to carry lumber very far when it first comes into the shop. Set up your miter or radial-arm saw close to your lumber shelves. That way, you can pull long boards off the shelf and cut them down to rough size, then re-shelve the extras. The less you have to lug a heavy board around the shop, the better.

If you have to stack lumber on a concrete basement or garage floor, be sure to elevate it to keep the bottom boards from absorbing moisture. Concrete acts like a sponge to ground moisture, even in a seemingly dry place.

Storing Sheet Goods

In a perfect world, the best way to store plywood and other sheet goods is flat down on the faces to prevent sagging. But, since most home shops don't have the extra floor space to store sheet goods this way, you'll probably have to stand your sheets on the edges or ends against a wall or in a rack. For safety's sake, wrap a rope or strap around the sheets and fasten it to the wall framing to keep the sheets from tipping over. A pair of heavy screw eyes make good anchors. As you cut down your sheet goods, shuffle smaller pieces to the front of the stack so they're easy to see and get to when you need them. If your shop has a concrete floor, elevate your sheets off the concrete on a piece of scrap or plastic sheeting.

Storing Scrap

The biggest challenge you'll probably have with lumber storage is what to do with all those short scraps. For most of us, it's actually a two-fold problem. The first issue is coming up with a way to store scraps so you can keep them neatly organized and easy to sort through. Most woodworkers store scrap on shelving or in bins of some kind.

Generally, shallower scrap bins and shelves are better than deep ones. A tall garbage container or bin can hold a huge amount of material, but it's hard to keep track of the pieces that end up at the bottom. It also helps to have several smaller bins rather than one big scrap container so you can sort scraps by length or material type.

It helps to store scrap near the saw that creates it. If you own a miter or radial-arm saw, build a scrap storage cabinet that fits underneath with a series of adjustable shelves.

The second issue with storing scrap is deciding what to toss and what to keep. If you're a wood turner, tiny bits of scrap may be useful for turning pens or making custom drawer knobs. On the other hand, if you don't have a lathe, do you really need to hang onto that 4-in. piece of scrap? Only you can decide what's really valuable to save.

Controlling Moisture Levels In The Shop

It's important to monitor and control the amount of moisture in your shop as best you can. Damp air is detrimental to both wood and metal machinery. For a basement shop, buy a hygrometer to help monitor humidity levels from season to season. The ideal humidity level for a woodshop is around 40%. Run a dehumidifier or air-conditioner during the summer to help dry the air and prevent condensation on metal surfaces. Switch to a humidifier in winter months to cut down on static charges and keep your wood from shrinking excessively. The goal is to keep humidity levels relatively constant from season to season. If your shop is in a damp garage, it's tough to control moisture levels most of the time. Weather permitting, open doors and windows and use a fan to create a cross breeze to help keep the concrete floor dry.

As your collection of board lumber and scraps accumulates, you'll need to find sensible ways to store it all. Wall-mounted racks will keep boards flat and easy to reach. A shelf near the miter saw conveniently stores offcuts and other scrap.

A hygrometer is an inexpensive way to help keep track of moisture levels in the shop from season to season.

FOUR

LAYOUT AND PART PREPARATION

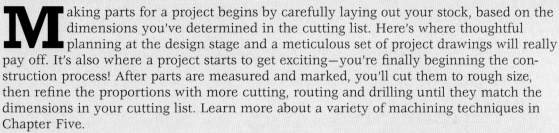

Making parts for a project begins by carefully laying out your stock, based on the dimensions you've determined in the cutting list. Here's where thoughtful planning at the design stage and a meticulous set of project drawings will really pay off. It's also where a project starts to get exciting—you're finally beginning the construction process! After parts are measured and marked, you'll cut them to rough size, then refine the proportions with more cutting, routing and drilling until they match the dimensions in your cutting list. Learn more about a variety of machining techniques in Chapter Five.

This chapter will introduce you to three different strategies for layout and a variety of tips that can make the layout process easier and more efficient. We'll also discuss strategies for measuring and marking, working with sheet goods, making templates and choosing joinery.

Laying out project parts involves more than just drawing a bunch of lines. Since you'll draw each part to full size, careful layout work will show you if you've got enough material to make all the parts on your cutting list. It's also a chance to strategize the best arrangement of parts on each board so you can minimize the amount of wasted wood and cut the parts out easily. This is also your chance to select boards with the best grain pattern and figure for parts you'll want to showcase on your project while leaving less desirable wood for the hidden pieces.

Three Approaches To Part Layout

There are three schools of thought on how to lay out parts. Each option has its merits, and you'll probably use more than one of them based on the project you're building and the amount of time you have to build it. Here's how each strategy works:

Option One: Cut All The Parts

The first approach is to lay out all the parts at once and cut them to final size, one after the next. Project books and magazine articles often advocate this method, because it's a convenient way to move a reader through the layout process with minimal discussion. The main advantage to this method is efficiency. Marking all the parts to size, then cutting them out in one fell swoop tackles part-making in a hurry. The downside is that it leaves you no real margin for error. Once all the workpieces are cut to size, you can't change your mind about the details or proportions of the project. You're committed to the design as is. Mistakes are more costly as well. You'll have to remake some parts from scratch rather than modify other part sizes to account for the mistake. While it's admittedly satisfying to turn all your project lumber into a neat stack of parts, be sure you're really confident with your project designs and part-

making skills if you go this route. Even then, prepare some extra wood from matching stock so you'll be ready when mistakes happen.

Laying out parts doesn't have to be limited to the beginning stages of a project. You may want to size some parts, like drawer fronts, to their face frames after the frames are built. This guarantees a perfect drawer fit.

Option Two: Lay Parts Out As You Go

Layout doesn't have to be an isolated activity that ends before the machining begins. You can approach layout in stages as you work through your project. Layout becomes a task that happens from the beginning of the construction process to nearly the end. For example, if you're building a cabinet with a drawer, you might lay out and cut the sides, bottom and face frame parts, then mill the joinery and assemble the basic box. Once the face frame goes together, you know precisely how big to make the drawer face. The upside to this approach is that you can make little changes to your project, if necessary, as the building process unfolds. It's an especially forgiving method for working through the occasional mistake. If the drawer opening in the face frame looks too small or the doors need to be a bit wider than you planned for in your construction drawings, you can change the proportions without wasting extra time or wood remaking other parts.

Cutting all the parts of a project to final size before building it is a quick way to get the construction process going, but it leaves you little margin for error. Some books and magazines advocate this approach, but use it cautiously.

Sometimes it helps to mark and cut your project parts oversized at the rough-lumber stage if it helps get lumber up off the floor and out of the way. The extra part size is always beneficial, especially if you need to make minor changes to part sizes later.

Option Three: Cut All The Parts, But Leave Them "Loose"

A third option, which is really a combination of the first two approaches, is to lay out and cut all the parts on your cutting list at the beginning, but make them longer and wider than necessary. A half inch or so of extra length and width is probably enough. This approach works well for large projects with long cutting lists that require lots of lumber. Sometimes it helps to reduce a big pile of lumber into smaller pieces right away to get them off the floor and out of your way. This tactic allows you to correct for any minor warpage that may still occur when boards are sized down into smaller pieces. Oversizing your parts also gives you some wiggle room to make minor dimensional changes if something doesn't quite work out as planned. The drawback to this approach is that you'll waste more wood.

Other Layout Tips

Whichever method you choose for laying out and cutting parts, here are some general guidelines to keep in mind:

- **Divide before conquering.** Spread out your boards so that you can see them all at once, and separate them into groupings based on appearance. Start by marking the parts that need to be made from prime material. Usually these parts include drawer faces, panels for doors or tabletops, face frame rails and stiles, and any other pieces that should take advantage of interesting or matching grain pattern and figure. Use the less attractive material where it won't show, such as drawer backs and slides, glue blocks, spacers and cleats.

- **Mix and match to maximize material.** As long as you systemat-

Sort your project lumber carefully by color, grain pattern and defects before you begin to build. Save your best stock for the most visible parts.

ically check parts off your cutting list as you lay them out, you don't have to follow the cutting list in order. Instead, try to keep the overall cutting list in mind, but arrange parts on boards in ways that use the lumber efficiently. This might mean that Part C fits next to Part L on your board layout, which is fine if you're comfortable with the color and grain pattern being what they are on these parts. If, for instance, you have two 13-inch-long parts and a 30-inch-long part to make, look for a board around 5 feet to lay out the three parts. A 6-foot board could work too, of course, but you'll end up with a 1-foot piece of leftover lumber as a cut-off. In the end, the most important thing is that you've accounted for all the parts you need, they're sized accurately and you're happy with the color and grain pattern.

- **Measure at least twice.** It should almost go without saying to the careful woodworker, but be sure to "measure twice," even at the rough layout stage. Get into the habit of double-checking every measurement you make. All it takes is a half second of daydreaming to mark "⅝" when you meant "½".

Try to lay out each board to make the most of it. Arrange the parts to minimize waste areas. If parts need to have matching color and grain pattern, try to make them from the same piece of wood.

- **Label your parts carefully.** The best time to label parts is before you cut a board into pieces. If this isn't practical, label the pieces as soon as you cut them out. Mark each workpiece on a face, an edge and an end. More than likely, you'll machine away at least one of these labels, but one of them will usually stay intact. At some point, parts become unmistakable as you machine them to shape, so the labels are less important. Until that time comes, re-label parts as needed to keep things clear.

- **Mark your waste areas to avoid wasting wood.** It's also important to mark the waste areas clearly when rough-cutting parts during

Label more than one surface of each workpiece so it's still easy to identify when you cut, plane or joint a label or two away. Use a grease pencil or marker so these labels won't rub off easily.

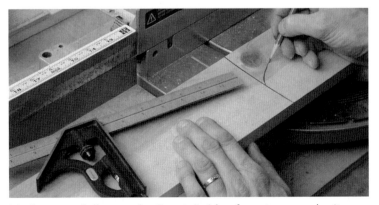

Mark a scratch line on the "waste" side of a cut so you don't accidentally cut on the wrong side of the layout line. Always mark waste areas clearly to minimize mistakes.

the initial layout phase so they're easy to distinguish from the rest of your workpieces. Or, follow a common carpentry practice and make a pencil scratch mark into the waste side of a layout line when you draw the line. The scratch line points you into the waste area. Be sure to set up your saw cuts so the blade cuts along the waste side of a reference line and not into the workpiece. Otherwise, you'll end up with parts a blade-thickness too small.

- **Get the lead out.** Use a permanent marker, brightly colored

If you prefer to label your workpieces with tape, use "self-releasing" painter's tape so the adhesive will peel off easily.

grease pencil or carpenter's pencil with a large lead to label the parts. Part labels should be easy to read and tough to rub off. Masking tape also works for labeling parts, but it can leave adhesive residue on the wood if the tape stays on for too long. Self-releasing painter's tape works best.

- **Drawings don't always tell the whole story.** Just because you can't see hidden parts in your drawings doesn't mean they aren't there. Be careful to include the extra part length required for joinery. This is particularly important for parts with hidden tenons and tongues or for panels that fit into door grooves. Wherever two parts intersect in your drawings, think about that joint before laying out and cutting the two parts. You're in the clear if the parts meet in a butt joint where there's no extra wood connecting the pieces, but other joints may have hidden components that contribute to the overall part length. Your cutting list should have taken this into account already, but check each dimension against your drawings before laying out and cutting the part to size.

When laying out parts, remember to account for the extra length or width that will be necessary to form end joinery.

Layout Tools

There aren't many specialized tools for laying out parts, and you probably own most of what you'll need already. Here are the essential tools:

- No. 2 pencil
- Carpenter's pencil
- Lumber crayon or grease pencil
- White colored pencil (for dark woods)
- Tape measure (10 feet or longer)
- Chalk line
- 3- or 4-foot straightedge
- Combination square with 12-inch or longer blade
- Framing square
- Bevel gauge
- Protractor or angle-setting gauge
- Compass, trammel points
- Marking knife
- Mortising gauge

Marking Tools

For ordinary layout work, a No. 2 pencil will serve you well. The lead is soft enough to leave a bold line without denting the wood, yet it's hard enough to stay sufficiently sharp for many lines. If you make a mistake,

Keep a variety of marking tools on hand for drawing lines. Markers, grease pencils, carpenter's pencils and chalk lines work well for laying out rough stock. A white colored pencil scribes bright lines on dark wood. Use a mechanical pencil for marking your finest layout lines to make joinery or precise cuts.

No. 2 lead is also easy to sand off or wipe away with denatured alcohol. Keep a pencil sharper in the shop so you can touch up your pencil point as soon as it loses the ability to mark a crisp line. Some woodworkers reach for the thicker, square carpenter's pencil or a grease pencil to leave a bolder line. Carpenter's pencils seem to have a harder lead than desk pencils, so they hold up better for marking coarse surfaces. Sharpen them with a utility knife or chisel blade, scooping to the center of the pencil to create a flat, chisel-edged point. A brightly colored grease pencil, chalk or white colored pencil is also handy for marking darker materials like walnut or hardboard.

Some woodworkers prefer to mark knife lines for highly precise cuts. Several tools will tackle this job, including a mortising gauge, marking gauge, utility knife or marking knife.

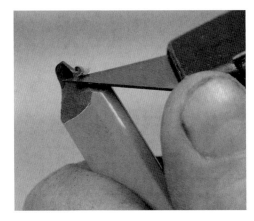

Sharpen a carpenter's pencil with a utility knife. Whittle the wood away all around until you form a knife-like flat edge on the lead.

When scribing lines with a marking knife, pull it along a straightedge or square with the blade's bevels facing outward. Watch your progress closely to keep the blade from drifting off course.

For marking fine lines or laying out joinery, a mechanical drafting pencil with replaceable leads provides more precision. Or, use a sharp marking knife, mortising gauge or sharp utility knife to cut your layout lines into the wood. A knife blade cuts a fine line that's still fairly easy to see, especially when it crosses the grain, and it severs the wood fibers to help reduce splintering when you saw along the layout line. If you need to change a knife blade layout line, it's fairly easy to "erase" with a little sanding.

Measuring Basics

Measuring line lengths with a steel tape measure is nothing new. Tape measures are as dependable in the woodshop as they are on the job site. For the rough layout stage, it's fine to use the metal clip at the end of the tape to set the starting length of the line. However, once you cut your workpieces to rough size, it's a good idea to modify how you use the tape. Instead of indexing line lengths off of the moveable clip, which can introduce errors on exacting measurements, use the 1-in. mark as the start-

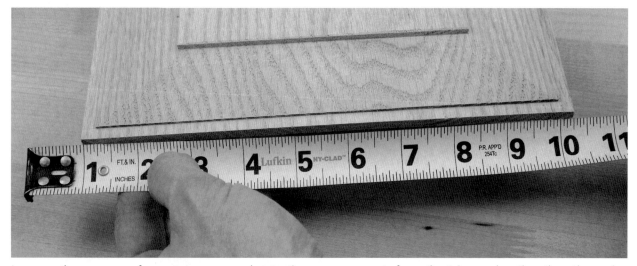

Improve the accuracy of your tape measure by starting measurements from the 1-in. mark rather than the end clip, then subtract 1 in. from the final measurement. In this photo, the panel is 9¼ in. wide.

ing point. Then be sure to subtract 1 in. from the final measurement.

Tape measures work well for measuring parts that are longer or wider than the length of your combination square or steel rule, but switch to a rule as part sizes become smaller. It's easier to set a flat rule against a short workpiece than trying to hold the body of the tape measure, flex the tape flat and mark a cutoff line. The rule on a high-quality combination square will also have scales subdivided into 16th, 32nd and even 64th inch increments. The added precision isn't essential for rough-cutting, but it will make all the difference when centering a dowel hole or laying out a mortise.

Another approach that makes sense from time to time is to set aside your rulers and tapes altogether. If, for instance, you're fitting a drawer face to a face frame opening and the face frame is already completed, use the actual opening to size the drawer face. Make tick marks on the workpiece to mark off the width and length of the opening, then add or subtract from these "real world" measurements to fit the drawer face

Use a precise measuring tool for laying out or checking joinery. A high-quality combination square will provide accurate readings down to 1/64 in.

inside the opening or to create a lip around the edges. If you need to cut dadoes across a cabinet side panel to fit a plywood shelf, use the shelf to mark the dado. Hold the shelf in position and trace the dado's position and width. This way, there's no need to fuss with measuring and drawing a pair of lines $23/32$ in. apart.

Another approach to layout is to use the actual parts instead of a rule to mark locations, widths or thicknesses. Here, a shelf works like a template for marking the precise width of the dadoes required to house it.

Drawing Layout Lines

Laying out parts involves drawing accurate lines. You'll need to mark long and short straight lines, perpendicular and parallel lines, angled lines, curves and circles. Whether you are drawing a rough-cutting line to split a sheet of plywood in two or marking the exact location for a rabbet shoulder, try to approach each marking task with the same degree of care and precision. Reliable lines are the building blocks that produce accurate parts and true reference edges.

Drawing Straight Lines

A long steel rule or the rule of your combination square makes it easy to draw short straight lines. The task gets a bit trickier when drawing longer lines, especially on full-size sheet goods. One option is to snap a chalk line between a pair of tick marks on the ends of the sheet. Just pull the chalk line taut, lift it a few inches off the sheet and release it to snap a relatively clean cutting line. Chalk lines aren't accurate enough to make a final layout line, but they'll give you a quick reference for lining up a circular saw or jigsaw to make that first long cut. For greater accuracy, you can also use the edge of another sheet of plywood as a straightedge. Factory edges on plywood, melamine or MDF are generally straight enough for layout work, provided the edge is clean and undamaged. A third option is to simply mark a series of ticks off the edge or end of the sheet where you want the line to be, then connect the marks with a steel rule to create the line. Make sure the reference edge on the sheet is straight if you use this method.

A quick way to "draw" a reference line on a long sheet of plywood is to snap a chalk line rather than using a pencil and straightedge. Pull the line taut, lift it off the surface and let it snap down to create a straight line.

It's easy to draw a line parallel to a part edge using a combination square. Lock the rule and hold a pencil against the end of the rule, then pull the square and pencil along the edge.

Drawing Parallel Lines

If you are drawing a line parallel to the edge or end of a board, a handy carpenter's trick is to use the end of your combination square to draw the line. Simply extend the rule of the square off the head the distance you want the line to be from the board's reference edge or end. Then, hold the head of the square against the reference surface and your pencil against the end of the rule. Slide the square's head along the board to mark a parallel line.

For extreme accuracy, especially when laying out joinery, some woodworkers use a mortising or marking gauge to scribe parallel lines (see the box on page 110). A mortising gauge has a pair of sharp pins that establish a pair of parallel scratches to set the long sides of a mortise or to mark the thickness of a tenon. Mortising gauges work well for incising lines on face, edge and end grain. Dragging the head of the tool along the reference surface indexes the scratch lines.

A marking gauge has just one sharp point or cutting wheel to mark a line. Marking gauges are helpful for indexing the pins and tails of dovetails or the shoulders of rabbets and tongues, where one knife line is all you need.

A marking gauge with a sharpened cutting wheel scores clean shoulder lines for laying out a tenon. It also neatly severs the wood fibers to prevent tearout when cutting the tenon to shape.

109

USING A MORTISING GAUGE

Let's say you want to mark the dimensions of a centered mortise on the edge of a face frame rail. A mortising gauge can help you scribe the width of the mortise as well as center it on the workpiece. Here's how: To set the width of the mortise, place the router bit, mortising chisel or drill bit you'll use to cut the mortise between the pins on the gauge and adjust them until the pins touch the cutting edges of the bit. Next, set the adjustable fence of the mortising gauge against the face of the workpiece and slide the fence one way or the other until the pins are roughly centered on the thickness of the stock. Lock the fence and press the pins lightly into the wood to create reference dimples. Flip the gauge to the opposite face of the workpiece to see if the pins still line up with the dimples. If they do, the pins are centered on the workpiece. If they don't, move the fence slightly to adjust the pin positions. Flip the gauge back and forth a few times and make fine adjustments to the fence until the pins are perfectly centered. Then drag the gauge along the wood to cut lines for the mortise sides. It may take a few passes to scratch lines deep enough to see. Use a square and marking knife or pencil to draw the ends of the mortise. For off-centered mortises, skip the flipping step and index the fence off of the workpiece using one of the pins to measure the offset.

HOW-TO USE A MORTISING GAUGE

1 Adjust the sharpened pins on a mortising gauge to match the width of the mortising chisel, drill bit or router bit you'll use to cut the mortise.

2 Slide the adjustable fence on the gauge to set the mortise's location on the workpiece. If the mortise should be centered, press the points lightly into the stock, then flip the gauge to the other face to see if the points still line up with the dimples.

3 Pull the gauge along the workpiece with the fence pressed firmly against the wood to scribe lines for the mortise walls.

4 Mark layout lines for the ends of the mortise with a knife and combination square. You're now ready to cut it to shape.

Drawing Perpendicular Lines

A combination square, try square or engineer's square are the right tools to reach for when you need to draw a perpendicular line. A trusty square is as important to good measuring and marking as a tape measure or graduated steel rule. Hold the head of the square firmly against a board's reference surface to mark a square line. When you need to draw a series of square lines around a board to create the shoulders of a tenon or a tongue, mark one square line, then use it as a reference for setting the square to draw adjacent lines around the board faces and edges.

A combination square is the most versatile square to own. The head of the square has fences for checking or marking both 45° and 90° angles, and the rule can be extended and locked at any length to set parallel lines or to gauge mortise depths. It's helpful to have two sizes of combination squares in your collection: a 12- to 16-in. combination square and a shorter 6-in. size for marking smaller parts.

A carpenter's framing square or even a drywall square will also work for laying out perpendicular lines,

Squares are indispensable shop tools. You'll appreciate having both large and small combination squares for general layout work. A try square or all-metal engineer's square will be helpful for tool and fence setups.

but these squares aren't always as accurate as smaller squares designed for greater precision.

Squares ensure perpendicularity when laying out parts. A square will transfer lines around a workpiece quickly without measuring.

You'll need an accurate way to measure and draw angled lines. A protractor or other angle-setting gauge will establish the angle, and a bevel gauge transfers the angle onto the workpiece.

Measuring And Marking Angled Lines

A combination square will allow you to mark 45° or 135° angles, but you'll need a different set of measuring and marking tools to create other angled lines. If you need to duplicate an existing angle from a workpiece or a drawing, a bevel gauge is the proper tool for the task. Essentially, a bevel gauge is a square with a moveable blade that can be locked to any angle. Bevel gauges are also handy for recording a tool blade angle if you need to reset the saw and then find that original angle again. To use a bevel gauge, set the stock of the square against one reference surface or line, and pivot the blade until it lines up with the other reference surface or line. Lock the blade to hold the angle.

When you need to create a new angle on a workpiece, use a protractor or another angle-setting gauge to set the bevel gauge accurately. Hold the bevel gauge stock against the reference surface of the angle-setting device or protractor, and line the blade up with the angle reference line.

Drawing Circles And Curves

Curves can add grace and elegance to a project filled with rectilinear shapes. Face frame rails, long bench stretchers, chair backrests and table-tops can often be improved with a gentle curve. It helps to have a few strategies for laying out curves when occasions call for them. Curves can be easy to duplicate by simply tracing them off an original shape, such as the scalloped bottom rail of a dresser. When you need to create a new curve or copy an existing curve that can't be traced easily, woodworking and art supply stores sell flexible strips for shaping into curves. Often these devices have a lead core so the curve will conform to the shape you need while still being stiff enough to trace against. A piece of heavy-gauge electrical wire also works well for this purpose. If you need to create a uniform, gentle arc, an easy tech-

The large reference lines and proportions of an angle-setting gauge provide greater accuracy than a small protractor when setting angles.

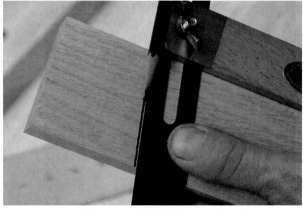

Once you've adjusted and locked your bevel gauge to an accurate angle, use it like an ordinary square to transfer the angle to the workpiece.

A narrow strip of thin plywood flexed between two nails makes a uniform, smooth arch shape.

A compass, trammel points, a flexible strip or even stiff electrical wire are all good options for shaping and drawing curved lines.

nique is to flex a strip of thin plywood, hardboard or wood against a few nails driven into the workpiece. Use a nail to hold each end of the strip and another nail to set the apex of the arc.

Circles are easiest to draw with an ordinary compass. The 8-in. size will suffice for most small layout work. Make sure your compass can be locked securely so it holds its setting when used on rough-surfaced wood. Buy a pair of trammel points for marking larger circles. Trammel points clamp to a dowel or strip of wood and function like an oversized compass. One trammel has a com-

pass point to set the center of the circle, and the other trammel holds a pencil for scribing the shape. Depending on the length of dowel or wood strip you use, you can draw a limitless range of circle sizes.

Trammel points work like an oversized compass for drawing circles of any size. Your only limitation is the length of the rod or bar that holds the points in position.

A piece of heavy-gauge electrical wire creates a quick template to transfer a part shape to another workpiece. Of course, it isn't as accurate as a dedicated template with a fixed shape.

Working With Sheet Goods

Plywood, melamine board and medium-density fiberboard (MDF) certainly play an important role in woodworking. Large sheets enable you to create broad panels without gluing up individual pieces of wood. Plywood with an attractive face veneer is ideal for making cabinet carcass parts and back panels. Melamine provides smooth, pre-finished surfaces that are easy to clean, and MDF is handy for building jigs or hard, flat worksurfaces.

One thing to keep in mind as you lay out parts on plywood is to orient the face grain correctly. Generally, grain direction should follow the longest dimension of a workpiece and run vertically on vertical parts. This is an aesthetic consideration and not a functional one, in an attempt to mimic solid wood. Running the grain the other direction will accentuate the fact that the wood is veneer.

In terms of preparing parts from sheet material, the biggest issue you'll face is how to manage the weight and bulky proportions of full sheets. Try to organize the layout lines so one or two long cuts will divide the sheet into more manageable pieces. The easiest and most efficient cuts are straight passes that split one piece into two. Avoid arranging the parts on your sheets so cutting lines intersect and dead-end in the middle of the sheet. Sometimes these situations are unavoidable, but the cuts are more fussy to make, and it's easy to accidentally cut too far and damage an adjacent workpiece.

If you're working alone or with particularly heavy sheets like MDF, it's safer to cut them down to size on the floor with a power saw instead of on the table saw. Trying to work against gravity and wrestle a 100-pound sheet of MDF over a table saw is a recipe for trouble, and cutting accuracy will probably suffer as well. Instead, lay strips of scrap or short 2x4s on the floor to form spacers, and use a circular saw and straightedge to cut the sheet into pieces. Place enough spacers under the sheet to keep it from sagging, and arrange the spacers close to the cutting lines. Set your blade depth about a quarter inch deeper than the thickness of the sheet material. Don't worry about keeping the spacers clear of the saw path; just lean on the sheet as you cut it so your weight keeps the spacers from shifting, and saw right across the spacers.

Arrange scrap spacers underneath sheet goods to keep them from sagging and the blade clear of the floor when cutting with a circular saw or jigsaw.

TIP

A sheet of 1- to 2-in.-thick dense-foam insulation board makes an excellent floor spacer for cutting sheet goods. It provides full support beneath the sheet, won't damage your saw blade and even helps reduce tearout along the sawn edges.

Foam Board

Foam insulation board makes an inexpensive and supportive spacer underneath sheet goods for cutting them down to size.

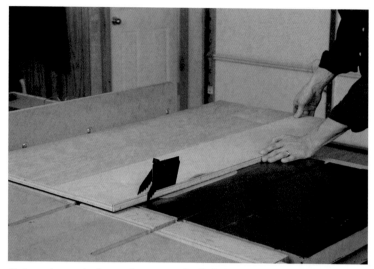

Cut parts made from sheet goods slightly oversized when you first break up the sheet, then use a table saw to trim them to final size.

outfeed support behind the saw to keep panels from tipping off the machine or worse, to prevent a small saw from tipping over. Sometimes you may have no choice but to cut a full sheet on the table saw. In these situations, have a helper catch the pieces as they leave the saw. A helper should not pull or try to guide the cuts but simply support the weight of the material to keep it from tipping.

It's a good idea to cut your sheet goods parts a little larger than necessary, then trim the parts to final size on the table saw or with a router and straightedge guide. Here's a helpful cutting order to follow: When roughing pieces out of plywood sheet stock, it's best to make the oversize rip cut first, than an oversize crosscut, followed by a finish crosscut to your layout line and then the finish rip cut. Make your initial "rough" cuts about $1/16$ to $1/8$ in. outside your final trim cuts.

When you use a table saw for final trimming, be sure to set up adequate

A router, equipped with a straight bit and guided against a clamped straightedge, is another good option for trimming sheet materials cleanly and to final size.

Making Templates

Templates are simply patterns for making parts, and they serve several important purposes for woodworking. When you need to draw an intricate part shape, it's easier to sketch on a piece of tagboard or paper than it is directly on the wood. Once you're happy with the shape, cut it out to create a basic pattern for tracing the shape onto the workpiece. If you mount your paper pattern to a stiff backer such as hardboard and cut it out, the template is even easier to trace against, and you can use it again and again.

Aside from its value as a tracing aid, a stiff template makes it easy to duplicate parts accurately with a router. Use the template to trace the shape onto your workpiece, and cut the part out slightly oversized with a bandsaw or jigsaw. Then, attach the template to the rough-cut workpiece with double-sided carpet tape or dabs of hot-melt glue. A piloted straight bit in your router will follow the edge of the template and trim the workpiece exactly to final size (see page 214).

If you have a bunch of identical parts to cut out, stack the workpieces together and secure them with strips of double-sided tape. Trace the template shape on the top workpiece. Cut all the parts at once with your bandsaw, and sand them to final shape and size before pulling the pieces apart. It's a quick way to duplicate parts "gang style."

You can also use templates as router guides when you need to cut out an inside shape or make an inlay. It's easy to rout precise hinge mortises or even use your router to drill shelf pin holes if you create a template to guide the bit.

Making A Template

An accurate template starts with an accurate drawing. Sketch your part carefully to shape on paper, tagboard or graph paper. When you're making templates from published plans, use a photocopier to enlarge the part to full size so you don't have to draw it. Then attach the paper pattern to whatever backer material you prefer with spray adhesive. Hardboard, MDF, void-free plywood or sheet plastic all make good material for templates. Cut out the template with a jigsaw or bandsaw, sawing just outside your layout lines. Refine the shape by filing and sanding.

Mount a template to hardboard or other stiff backer material with spray adhesive.

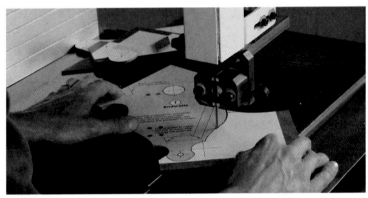
Cut the template to shape. One way to prevent miscuts that can ruin a template is to cut just outside the layout lines.

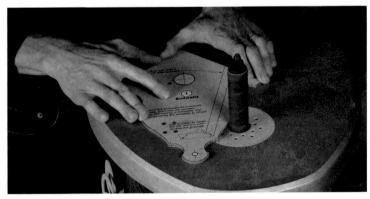
Carefully sand or file the template up to the layout lines to refine its shape. A benchtop drum sander is ideal for this job.

CHOOSING JOINERY

Modern woodworking glues and fasteners form reasonably strong connections between two workpieces, but usually a bead of glue or a few screws won't hold up over the long term. When furniture or cabinet parts have to bear loads or withstand twisting, shearing and pulling forces, they need to physically lock together. Here's where joints are important. By machining two parts so they interlock, friction helps hold the pieces together so the joint doesn't rely entirely on the glue bond or the strength of the screw threads. Intertwined parts benefit from the grain strength of one another.

Another important feature of joints is their pleasing shape. The classic dovetail or box joint has an eye-catching geometry that captures your attention and serves as a hallmark of fine craftsmanship. More importantly, all those intricate pins and tails add up to huge surface areas for glue, which improves its adhesive strength. A thin layer of glue spread over a broad area is substantially stronger than a thick layer confined to a small place.

There are literally dozens of joint styles to choose from, and entire books are devoted to the subject of joinery alone. Most joints can be made in different ways with a variety of power and hand tools. You don't have to master every style to be a competent woodworker. Knowing how to make a half dozen or so different joints really well will probably suffice for most projects you need to build. As your skills grow or your interests change, you can always experiment with more complex joinery, and those styles are explained in other books.

The following twelve joint styles in this chapter are a good core group for general woodworking. Use the brief descriptions of each joint to help you decide which joints best suit your needs. Then refer to Chapter Five to learn more about how to make these joints with various tools and setups.

Butt Joints

Butt joints are the simplest joint style to build, made by combining the end of one part with the end, face or edge of another part. Both parts of the joint are cut square and joined with glue, nails, screws or a combination of glue and fasteners.

Butt joint.

Rabbet joint.

You can also connect the parts with biscuits and dowels. Simplicity and speed are the biggest advantages to using butt joints, but since the joint parts don't interlock, they tend to be the weakest option. End grain does not accept glue well, and the joint has very little surface area. Other types of joinery are designed to increase the surface area.

Applications

Box corners; light-duty cabinet, shelving or drawer construction; edge-glued panels or face-glued blanks

Tooling Options

Use your table saw, miter saw or radial-arm saw to rip and crosscut the joint parts to shape. Drive nails or countersunk screws across the joint whenever possible, and use glue to help improve strength.

Rabbet Joints

Rabbets are two-sided cutouts that form an offset tongue on the edge or end of a workpiece. They add a little more surface area for glue than a butt joint, and the parts are semi-interlocking which improves overall joint strength. You can combine rabbets together to make flat or right-angle joints or fit a rabbet into a dado for an even stronger interlocking connection. Reinforce rabbet joints with glue and nails or screws driven across the joint.

Applications

Box corners; fitting back panels or shelving into cabinet carcases; edge-glued panels

Tooling Options

Rabbets can be cut with a standard blade on a table saw or radial-arm saw, but the process is faster with a dado blade. You can also make rabbets with a router or router table using a straight bit or piloted rabbeting bit.

Dado & Groove Joints

Dadoes and grooves are three-sided cuts that do not pass all the way through a workpiece. Dadoes run across the grain, and grooves follow the grain. You can use a dado or groove on one workpiece to house the edge or end of another workpiece form reasonably strong joinery, especially when the joint needs to support a great deal of weight. Dado and groove joints are superior to butt joints but not as strong as fully interlocking styles such as mortise and tenon, dovetail or box joints.

Applications

Fitting shelving into casework; installing dividers in cabinetry or drawers

Tooling Options

Use your table saw or radial-arm saw equipped with a dado blade to cut dadoes and grooves. A router and straightedge guide or router table and fence are excellent options as well. Use a straight bit to make the cuts.

Tongue & Groove Joints

Tongue and groove joints feature a centered tongue that fits into a matching groove on the ends or edges of the mating joint part. Since the tongue portion of the joint has twice the number of stepped surfaces as a rabbet, it contributes more surface area for a stronger glue bond. It typically isn't necessary to reinforce the joint with nails or screws.

Applications

Fitting thick panels into door frames; making edge-glued panels; joining face frame rails and stiles; light-duty door frame joints

Housed dado joint.

Tooling Options

A table saw and dado blade will cut both the tongues and grooves of this joint. A router or router table equipped with straight, slot-cutting or rabbeting bits will also mill this joint effectively.

Tongue and groove joint.

Lap Joints

A lap is simply a wide rabbet cut into the end of a workpiece. You can combine two lapped workpieces to form a semi-interlocking right angle joint, or fit a lap into a wide dado to make a "T"-shaped joint. Lap joints form cross-grain connections that hold up fairly well with glue alone. However, strength improves considerably if you drive a couple dowels or screws across the joint to create a mechanical connection.

Applications

Light-duty door joints; face frame construction; joining stretchers to table legs; joinery for outdoor furniture

Tooling Options

A radial-arm saw and dado set are ideal for cutting lap joints, especially

Lap joint.

Mortise and tenon joint.

on long or heavy workpieces. A table saw and dado blade or router and wide straight bit are other good options. A bandsaw will also cut lap joints, but the parts should be short enough to maneuver safely on the saw table.

Mortise & Tenon Joints

Mortise and tenon joints are among the strongest woodworking joints you can make. The mortise is usually a stopped groove in one workpiece, with square or rounded ends. It is sized to fit a four-sided tongue, called a tenon, on the mating workpiece. The interlocking nature of the parts, combined with huge surface areas for glue, make this joint an excellent choice for both load-bearing and high-stress applications. Glue is usually sufficient for holding the parts together, but you can lock the parts permanently with cross dowels, wedges or pegs.

Mortise and tenon joints also work well for knockdown applications by simply omitting the glue. Generally, a removable wedged-shape tusk holds the parts together in these situations so the joints are easy to take apart. Mortise and tenons are relatively easy to make, and the clever connection of the parts makes them equally enjoyable to build.

Applications

Frame and chair construction; joinery for outdoor furniture

Tooling Options

Mortises can be cut by hand with chisels, but typically they're milled with a drill press, mortising machine or router and straight bit. The usual convention is to cut the mortise first, then make the tenon fit the mortise. A table saw or radial-arm saw are both good choices for cutting tenons, using either a standard blade or dado blade. You can also make tenons with a straight bit on the router table.

Biscuit Joints

Biscuit joints are made with a simple and safe tool called a biscuit joiner. Essentially, a biscuit joint is really just a modified mortise and tenon joint. The biscuit joiner cuts a curve-shaped slot into each face of the joint to fit a football-shaped biscuit of compressed wood. The biscuit acts like a loose tenon to bridge the joint parts. It contributes surface area for glue and also creates a mechanical connection. Biscuits can be used for all butt joint variations as well as to reinforce miter and bevel joints.

Applications

Edge-glued panels; face frame and picture frame joints; box and cabinet carcase construction; attaching light-to medium-duty shelving in bookcases

Tooling

Biscuit joiner; router and biscuit-joining bit

Pocket Screw Joints

Pocket screw joints are another excellent way to reinforce the basic butt or miter joint. You'll need a specialized drilling jig to create the deep, pocket-style holes that characterize this joint. The holes are bored at

Biscuit joint.

steep angles into one workpiece, and panhead screws are driven into the deep holes to draw the joint together. Pocket screw joints are easy to make and form surprisingly strong connections. If you place them on the back side of a frame or inside a box, they're also easy to hide.

Applications

Face frame and picture frame joints; box and cabinet carcase construction; attaching aprons to table legs

Tooling

Power drill, pocket hole jig and stepped drill bit; pocket hole screws

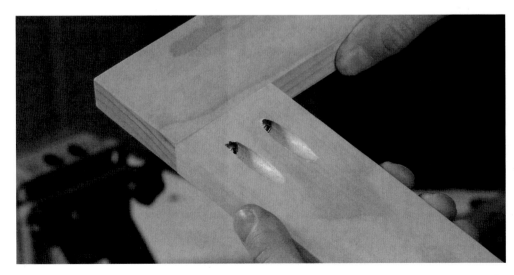

Pocket screw joint.

Dowel joint.

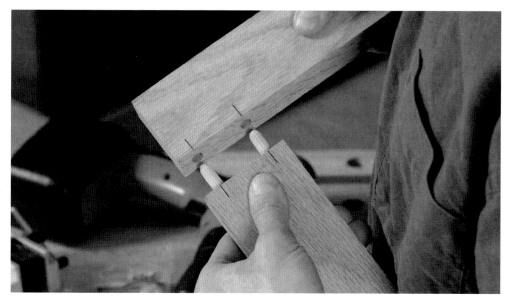

Dowel Joints

Dowels can be added to a variety of joints to create mechanical connections. They are simple to make if you use a drilling jig or a pair of dowel points to mark the dowel locations carefully. Without an accurate method for registering the dowel holes, these joints are much more difficult to build. Dowel joints aren't as strong as mortise and tenon joints, but they are significantly stronger than a butt joint reinforced with glue and nails.

Applications

Face frame construction; door joints; box and cabinet carcase construction; installing light- to medium-duty shelving in cabinets

Tooling Options

A portable drill and doweling jig or dowel points are the usual tools for making dowel joints, but a drill press and fence will also work.

Cope And Stick Joints

You've probably seen manufactured cabinet doors are constructed with cope and stick joints. Another name for cope and stick is "rail and stile" joint. You'll need a specialized pair of bits and a router table to build cope and stick joints: one bit for making the sticking cuts and another bit for the cope cuts.

Cope and stick bits are designed to make mirror image cuts. The sticking bit produces a decorative profile around the inside edges of the door frame as well as a slot for holding a wood or glass panel. The cope cut is made only on the ends of the rails to fit into the sticking cut on the stiles.

Applications

Door frame construction

Tooling

Router table, cope and stick bit set

Cope and stick joint.

Box Joints

Box joints consist of square-ended pins and slots that fit together to form strong, mechanical corner joints. Usually, the pattern of pins and slots is uniform across the joint, but you can also vary the spacing to create unique patterns. In the same way that the pins and tails of a dovetail joint increase surface area for glue, box joints also use glue to its best advantage. Box joints are fairly exacting to build and require a jig to set the pin and slot spacing. Once the jig is set correctly, these joints are easy to cut.

Box joint.

Applications

Box, drawer and small cabinet construction

Tooling Options

Table saw and dado blade or router table and straight bit; box joint jig

Dovetail Joints

Anyone who appreciates fine furniture knows what a dovetail joint looks like. That familiar wedge pattern of interlocking pins and tails is probably the most universal and desirable joint style of them all. Dovetails are the perfect combination of pleasing geometry, clever engineering and practical strength. There are two typical styles of this joint: half-blind dovetails, where the ends of the tails are hidden, and through dovetails that expose the ends of the pins and tails. Dovetails can be spaced in a regular or variable pattern across the joint. Some woodworkers prefer to cut dovetails by hand, but a dovetailing jig and a router makes the joint more approachable if you're just getting started.

Applications

Drawer and box construction

Tooling Options

Handsaws and chisels or a dovetailing jig, dovetail bit and handheld router

Dovetail joint.

FIVE

POWER TOOL TECHNIQUES

Once you've got your stock properly surfaced and flattened, it's time to turn that pristine lumber into projects parts. If you are like most home woodworkers, you probably use power tools for cutting parts and milling joinery. These days, power tools are the logical choice for most woodworkers. They're highly accurate, easy to obtain and outfitted with more and better features than ever before. Some hand tool purists will argue that today's sophisticated woodworking machines have taken a measure of skill out of woodworking, but I disagree. It still takes a combination of correct technique and years of experience to use your power tools to their full advantage. We may not be using as many dovetail saws and spokeshaves as our forebears did, but power tool woodworking is nevertheless a challenging, efficient and enjoyable way to work with wood.

This chapter will take a somewhat unique, tool-by-tool approach to teaching power tool techniques. Unlike many books, which are structured so the techniques drive the tool choice, we'll take a different path. If, for instance, you need to make a rip cut with a table saw, turn to the table saw section to find the proper ripping technique. In the same way, if you need to make a miter cut but don't have a miter saw, you can learn how to cut miters with a bandsaw, table saw or radial-arm saw by turning to those tool sections. If you are a relatively new woodworker, this approach will help you learn a variety of different techniques for the specific tools you own. Use the sections like an enhanced owner's manual. Maybe you are a more seasoned woodworker already; this chapter will also teach you about those advanced techniques you've always been curious to learn. Ever tried raising a panel, resawing or cutting cope and stick joints? How about routing through dovetail joints with a jig? You'll find those answers here, along with many more.

Overview Of Common Cuts

Before we begin the tool technique sections, here is a brief overview of some common cutting and joint-making operations you'll see repeated in this chapter. Familiarize yourself with these terms so you can apply them to whatever tool is being discussed.

Rip Cuts

Making rip cuts, or *ripping* as it's sometimes called, involves cutting a board along its length, following the wood grain. For sheet goods such as plywood or MDF, there is no continuous wood grain through the material. Here, rips cuts serve more as a way to reduce a part to correct width. Rip cuts made close to the edge of a workpiece also help form a flat reference edge or remove damaged or defective material. The process for making a rip cut on most woodworking machines involves feeding the wood through the blade with one flat edge pressed against the tool's fence.

Crosscuts

Crosscuts are cuts made across the width of a workpiece. On solid wood, a crosscut runs across the wood grain to establish the length of a workpiece. On a table saw or bandsaw, you'll usually use the tool's miter gauge to support the workpiece from behind when making a crosscut. Crosscutting with a miter saw or radial-arm saw involves holding the wood against the saw fence and plunging or pulling the blade through the workpiece.

Angled Cuts

There are three primary types of angle cuts in woodworking—miter cuts, bevel cuts and tapers. The terms "miter" and "bevel" are sometimes used interchangeably, which makes the nomenclature a bit confusing. A miter cut refers to a cut made across the grain on the end of the workpiece. Essentially, it's an angled crosscut; think of an ordinary picture frame joint as the classic example of a 45° miter cut. A bevel cut is normally an angled cut made along the edge of a workpiece with the blade tipped to an angle other than 90°. Box parts are sometimes cut with 45° bevels and reinforced with thin splines to create attractive joints.

Compound miter cuts are made by combining both miter and bevel cuts. Typically, the cut crosses the grain at an angle like a miter, but with the added difference that the blade is also tipped off of 90°.

Taper cuts are rip cuts made at an angle to the edge or face of a workpiece to reduce its proportion from one end to the other. Shaker-style table legs are often tapered on one or two faces. Tapering reduces the overall bulk of a workpiece and can help a project appear "lighter" and more elegant. Cutting tapers usually involves holding a workpiece in a jig at an angle to the tool's fence and sliding the jig and leg along the fence. The fence remains parallel to the blade; only the orientation of the workpiece changes. Tapers can also be cut without a jig on the bandsaw.

Rabbet, Dado And Groove Cuts

Rabbets, dadoes and grooves are all examples of "non-through" machine cuts. Whether you make these cuts with a saw or router, only part of the workpiece will be removed and the wood is never cut in two. All three cuts are used primarily for joinery, although you'll sometimes see small rabbets or narrow grooves used as stylistic details called "reveals" or "shadow lines". Refer to the joint overview on pages 118 and 119 to learn more about rabbet, dado and groove joint options.

Curve Cuts

Curve cuts are self-explanatory. They can be made with or across the grain as well as through the thickness of a workpiece. Handheld jigsaws, bandsaws and scroll saws are the usual choices for cutting curves.

Mortise Cuts

Mortises are made exclusively for joinery, usually to house a square- or round-edged tongue called a tenon. Cutting a mortise is actually more of a drilling than a sawing operation. A drill bit, mortising chisel or router bit are plunged into a workpiece to excavate the waste. Mortises are usually closed on all sides except for the opening where the tenon fits in, although sometimes a mortise passes all the way through the workpiece so the end of the tenon shows.

Other Joinery Cuts

Box joints, dovetails, lap joints and a variety of other specialized joints can also be made with many woodworking machines. See pages 117 to 123 in Chapter Four for an overview of a dozen different joints you can make and various tool options for making them.

Quick Guide To Machine Options

As you'll see in the tool technique sections to follow, some woodworking machines like the table saw are suitable for a variety of different cutting operations. Other machines have more specialized applications. The following chart provides a quick overview of each cutting tool that will be covered in this chapter with a guide to the various cuts it makes. If you're unclear about what your tool options are for making a particular cut, this chart should help.

TOOL	RIP CUTS	CROSSCUTS	TAPER CUTS	MITER/ BEVEL CUTS	CURVE CUTS
Table Saw	•	•	•	•	
Bandsaw	•	•	•	•	•
Radial-Arm Saw	•	•		•	
Miter Saw		•		•	
Handheld Router					•
Router Table					
Mortising Machine					
Biscuit Joiner					

TOOL	DADO/GROOVE CUTS	PANEL RAISING	COVE CUTS	OTHER JOINERY CUTS
Table Saw	•	•	•	•
Bandsaw				
Radial-Arm Saw	•			
Miter Saw				
Handheld Router	•		•	•
Router Table	•	•	•	•
Mortising Machine				•
Biscuit Joiner				•

TABLE SAW TECHNIQUES

Table saws are wonderfully versatile machines. With an accurate fence, adequate power and enough workpiece support around the saw, most types of woodworking cuts are possible on this tool alone. The biggest safety concern with table saws is a condition called kickback. Kickback usually occurs during rip cuts when workpieces bind between the fence and blade on the "exit" side of the blade. Sometimes kickback is caused by a misaligned fence, but often the problem is actually the wood. Rip cuts can release long-grain tension from the wood that occurs naturally in some boards. Released tension can cause the kerf opening behind the blade to close up as the cut progresses. When the kerf closes, the wood can pinch the blade enough to allow the blade to lift it off the table and throw it back powerfully in the direction of the operator.

There are a number of precautions you can take to avoid kickback: Be sure to use the guard and splitter that come with your saw whenever you are making rip and crosscuts. Table saw splitters are safety devices designed specifically to prevent this condition from happening. Adjust your saw fence and miter slots so they are parallel to the blade and to one another (see the tune-up procedure in Chapter Two). Use a sharp clean blade, and avoid rip-cutting wet lumber or boards without a flat reference edge.

Basic Rip-Cutting Procedure

The basic technique for making rip cuts on a table saw is simple: set and lock the rip fence a distance away from the blade that matches the width of the workpiece you want to make, then slide the board along the fence and through the blade from one end to the other. You'll need to modify your rip-cutting procedure depending on the proportions of the wood you are cutting, and those situations are covered in detail later in this section. Here is the basic rip-cutting process to follow for cutting lumber with ordinary dimensions.

1. Verify The Blade-To-Fence Settings On The Scale Cursor

Your saw's rip fence has a cursor and scale along the front fence rail that are designed to help you set up the width of rip cuts accurately. It's important to occasionally check the accuracy of your rip fence settings off of the blade. Fences eventually fall out of alignment with use and wear. If you switch from one blade to another, differences in blade thickness will also affect the scale's relationship to the blade.

To check the blade-to-fence relationship, slide and lock the fence a few inches from the blade and so the cursor lines up exactly with one of the inch marks on the fence scale. Use the rule of your combination square to measure the distance between the fence and the closest edge of the blade teeth to the fence. Measure carefully here; this distance should exactly match the cursor's scale setting. If it doesn't, loosen the screws that hold the cursor plate in place and adjust it as needed.

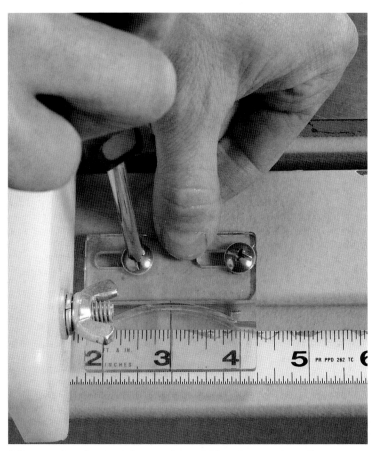

To set the width of a rip cut, measure from the fence to the closest edge of the blade teeth. In this photo, the saw is set for a 3-in.-wide rip cut.

After you've checked the cutting width using a rule, adjust your rip fence's cursor so the scale reading matches the ruler measurement. You should now be able to use the fence scale instead of a ruler to set up cuts.

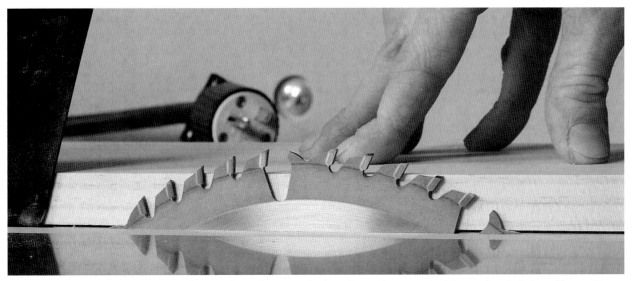

Raise the saw blade until the teeth rise about ¼ in. to ½ in. above the wood. This cutting height will provide a good compromise between blade efficiency and safety.

2. Set The Blade Height For The Stock You Are Cutting

Opinions vary as to how high to set the blade teeth above a workpiece. Setting the blade low, so just the tips of the teeth pass through the wood, reduces your danger of being seriously cut if an accident happens. On the flip side, the low blade setting increases blade heat and friction in the cut because more teeth are contacting the wood. A high blade setting, of course, places your body in greater danger of getting cut, but it can provide a cleaner, smoother cut than a blade set low. Low-powered saws can benefit by setting the blade high. A reasonable compromise is to set the blade so the teeth rise about ¼ to ½ in. above the wood. If your saw struggles to make a cut with the blade set at this height, try a slightly higher setting or slow down your feed rate when pushing wood through the cut.

3. Set And Lock The Rip Fence To Establish The Width Of Cut

If you trust the accuracy of your saw's rip fence and have checked the blade-to-fence index as discussed in Step One, use the fence scale and cursor to lock the width setting. Or,

make a mark on your workpiece instead, and slide the fence accordingly until the layout mark lines up with the edges of the blade teeth closest to the rip fence.

If you are cutting a long board or heavy workpiece, be sure to set up a support table or roller stand behind the saw to keep workpieces from tipping off the saw as you complete the cut (see the sidebar on page 136).

You can also set the width of cut by adjusting the rip fence off of a layout mark on your workpiece. Cut on the waste side of the layout line.

4. Making The Cut

When making a rip cut, it's important to always keep your body out of the line of fire in case of kickback. On a table saw, this means that you should never stand directly in line with the blade or the back end of the wood. A good practice is to stand to the left of the workpiece and so your left foot touches the left corner of your saw base. If it feels more comfortable, lean your left hip against the front fence rail to give yourself even more stability during cutting. Adjust your stance so you feel well balanced and with your weight evenly distributed on both feet.

Inspect the stock you plan to rip and make sure the edge that will follow the rip fence is sufficiently flat. For more on flattening board edges, see Chapter Three.

During a rip cut, you'll use your left hand to apply pressure to the left edge of the board, which will keep the wood pressed against the rip fence. Boards should never drift away from the fence during ripping, or a kickback is likely to happen—and at the very least you'll end up with a sloppy cut. Your left hand is not a feed hand for making the cut; it only applies pressure against the fence. Never let your left hand drift toward the blade as the cut progresses. Keep your hand pressed firmly down on the saw table and in one place throughout the cut; a good spot is near the front edge of the saw table and at least 6 to 8 inches from the blade. If you are uncomfortable using your left hand near the blade, clamp a featherboard to the saw table and use it instead of your hand to apply pressure against the left edge of the wood.

Your right hand serves as the primary feed hand for ripping. It's okay to wrap your fingers around the back edge of the board when starting the cut. As soon as the back edge of the board reaches the saw table, grab a push stick or push pad in your right hand to feed the board the rest of the way through. Never let your right hand come within 6 in. of the blade unless you are holding a push stick or push pad to protect yourself. Place a push stick on the saw table on the side opposite the fence so you can reach it easily when you need it.

With your body properly positioned in back of the saw and outfeed support and push sticks at the ready, start the saw and set the workpiece on the saw table. Press the workpiece against the fence with your left hand as you slide it slowly into the blade with your right. Once the teeth engage the wood, feed the workpiece smoothly and fairly quickly. You can feed the wood as fast

Stand comfortably behind the saw and to the left of the workpiece when making rip cuts. For added stability, touch your left foot to the saw base. You may even want to lean your left hip against the saw near the end of the cut to help keep your balance.

To start a rip cut, stand to the left of the workpiece—never in line with it. Have a push stick close by, and keep the workpiece pressed firmly against the fence with your left hand or a featherboard. Feed the wood into the blade with a gentle, smooth motion.

as the saw's motor will accept it, but don't feed so quickly that you lose control of the wood. Rapid feed rates will help reduce burning and saw marks on the cut edge. Slow down your feed rate if the saw begins to labor in the cut; you'll know that by a change in the way the motor sounds.

Switch to a push stick in your right hand when the board end

reaches the table, and continue feeding the wood past the blade to complete the cut. The "offcut" piece will stop next to the blade as soon as the blade cuts the workpiece in two. Leave the offcut where it is, but slide the piece in your right hand all the way clear of the blade. Shut off the saw, then clear the offcut away when the blade stops spinning.

If a situation develops during ripping where the blade slows down and the saw seems unable to complete the cut, slow your feed rate down as much as necessary to prevent stalling the blade completely. The most important goal is to finish the cut and prevent the blade from stopping—a dangerous situation that invites kickback. If you have no option but to stop the cut midway, press the wood down tightly against the saw table with your right hand and quickly reach down to turn off the saw with your left hand. Keep the wood pinned down on the saw until the motor stops, then pull the wood back and out of the cut. Before making another rip cut, figure out why the cut stalled. Check your fence alignment and board carefully for problems.

When the end of the board reaches the front of the saw, pause the cut and grab a push stick in your right hand. Keep your left hand near the front of the saw throughout the cut. Continue feeding with the push stick.

Finish the cut using just the push stick in your right hand. Feed the wood completely past the blade, but leave the cutoff piece where it is until you turn off the saw and the blade stops spinning.

Ripping Narrow Workpieces

From time to time you'll need to rip strips narrower than the thickness of your push stick or push pad will allow. Narrow rip cuts may also compromise the space between the saw's guard/splitter assembly and the rip fence. There are several options for making narrow rip cuts safely. One option is to set up the cut so the narrow portion becomes the "offcut" on the side of the blade opposite the fence. If you need to make several rip cuts so the thin workpieces match, a thin push stick may allow you to make the cuts conventionally and still allow enough clearance past the guard and splitter. Or, try the low fence or notched jig shown in the photos here for making repetitious, narrow rip cuts.

OPTIONS FOR RIPPING NARROW WORKPIECES

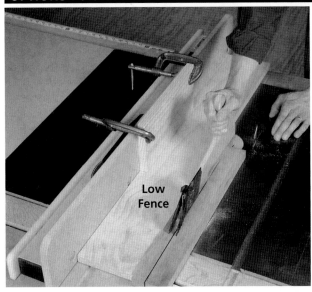

A low fence clamped to the rip fence provides more clearance for your right hand when ripping a series of narrow workpieces with one fence setting.

Another safe alternative for ripping narrow stock is to set up the cut so the narrow piece becomes the offcut. Guide the workpiece on the wide side.

A wide piece of notched scrap makes a handy jig for ripping narrow workpieces safely. It's a good solution for repetitious narrow rip-cutting.

Make a narrow push stick from hardboard or thin plywood to guide narrow strips between the fence and blade when that need occurs. A featherboard keeps narrow workpieces from drifting away from the fence.

ZERO-CLEARANCE THROATPLATES

Most throatplates that come standard on table saws have blade openings that are too wide to cut thin or small workpieces safely. Sliver-sized offcuts tend to fall down in the blade opening, and narrow strips can catch in the blade slot and interrupt the cut. The solution is to buy or make your own zero-clearance throatplate to replace the one that comes with your saw, then raise the blade through it to cut a blade slot that tightly hugs the blade body. The thin blade opening will provide better support and closure. A zero-clearance throatplate is an excellent, low-cost enhancement to your table saw. Use it for all general cutting except for when you need to tip the blade to make bevel cuts. In those situations, switch back to the throatplate that came with your saw.

Any flat, smooth scrap plywood, MDF or stable hardwood stock will work for making zero-clearance throatplates. The stock thickness should match the depth of the throatplate opening on your saw. Follow the photos shown here to make the plates. It's a good idea to make several plates at once and keep a few on hand for making zero-clearance dado throatplates as well.

MAKE A ZERO-CLEARANCE THROATPLATE

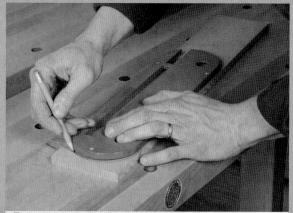

1 Use your saw's metal throatplate as a template for drawing a zero-clearance throatplate to shape.

2 Cut the throatplate to shape just outside the layout lines.

3 Sand up to your layout lines, checking the fit of the throatplate in the saw periodically. It should slip easily into the throatplate opening.

4 Cut the kerf in the new throatplate by holding it down with the saw's rip fence locked in place. Raise the blade slowly through the plate. Be sure the fence is positioned clear of the blade.

Ripping Long Workpieces

Rip-cutting stock longer than ordinary is still safe to do on a table saw, provided you have adequate outfeed support behind the saw. You don't want long or heavy workpieces tipping off the saw. Cutting workpieces on a table saw should never be a "see-sawing" exercise.

Another issue to take into account with long workpieces is that you may have to stand a distance away from the front of the saw to start the cut. When possible, try to keep your body as close to the saw as you can so you don't have to walk the wood into the saw to make the cut.

If the length of the workpiece or its weight mandates that you have to stand away from machine at first, clamp a pair of featherboards to the rip fence and saw table to keep the wood pressed down and against the rip fence. Use the workpiece as a gauge for setting up the featherboards; their positions should provide a fair amount of pressure against the wood but not so tightly that you can't slide it through without binding. A good rule of thumb is to set the finger tension on the featherboards so they flex slightly when the workpiece engages them.

The rip-cutting procedure for long workpieces is similar to making an ordinary rip cut, but with a few alterations. When you must stand away from the saw to start the cut, elevate the back end of the workpiece slightly to ensure that the front end is flat against the saw table. Walk the wood slowly into the blade to begin and advance the cut. Be careful to keep the wood tracking along the fence as usual; walking the wood will make this more difficult to do than standing next to the saw. As soon as it's reasonable, resume your normal stance next to the saw, and complete the cut as you would for a typical rip cut.

Use a pair of clamped featherboards alongside and above the wood to keep workpieces tracking properly when ripping long boards. Install them ahead of the blade.

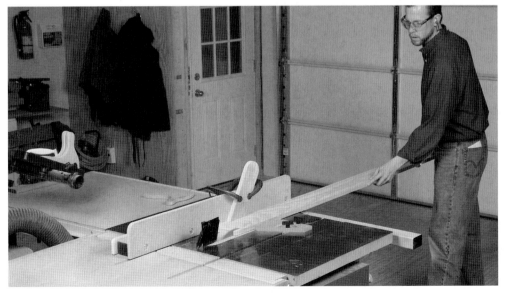

Raise the back end of a long workpiece slightly to keep the front end pressed down against the saw table when ripping it. Then slowly walk the board into the cut until you reach the saw table. Finish the cut as usual.

OUTFEED SUPPORT OPTIONS

Ripping long, wide or heavy workpieces will be much easier and safer to do if you set up a sturdy form of outfeed support behind the saw. There are lots of options for providing adequate outfeed support. You can buy many types of roller stands from woodworking suppliers that come with adjustable stands. A tall sawhorse or worktable can work just as well or even better than a roller stand. What's important is that your outfeed device is large enough to provide adequate support and sufficiently sturdy so it doesn't tip or shift when a workpiece slides over it. Weight it down if necessary to make sure it stays put. Set the height of the support slightly lower than the height of your saw table to prevent workpieces from catching on the edge as they leave the saw. Another good option for larger saws is to fasten a fixed or folding table directly to the saw to create a permanent source of outfeed support whenever you need it. The one shown here folds up and down to conserve floor space.

Set up a temporary means of outfeed support for smaller saws. A roller stand, short worktable or even a tall saw horse will all work well.

On a larger saw, you may wish to retrofit a permanent outfeed support table to it. This one folds up and down for storage.

Ripping Waney Or Crooked Edges

Bark-covered, rough or crooked-edged boards may be too defective to flatten easily on a jointer. Still, you can't rip them safely without a flat edge to reference against the saw fence. A simple way to create a flat edge on a defective-edged board is to screw it to a flat-edged piece of scrap as shown in the photos here. Position the screws near the edge of the workpiece so you can cut away the screw holes later. The flat-edged scrap will provide a reference edge for the defective workpiece. Set up the rip fence so the blade will trim off one rough edge of the workpiece to create the flat edge you need. Then unscrew the boards, flip the workpiece so the cut edge is against the fence and rip the second edge as usual.

On boards with two waney edges, screw the edge of the board to a straight-edged piece of scrap so you can rip the other edge straight and true. Once one edge is flat, rip the other edge without the scrap attached.

Ripping Thick Stock

It's possible to rip lumber thicker than the maximum blade height of your table saw, but the procedure will require you to remove the splitter and guard. If you are uncomfortable doing this, a much safer method is to rip thick stock on a bandsaw (see below).

The process for cutting thick stock on a table saw is straightforward: Set the blade height to cut at least halfway through the thickness of the workpiece. Make the first rip cut carefully and slowly to keep from stalling the blade—it will require lots of power from your saw. Once the first cut is made, turn the workpiece over and make a second rip cut to slice the workpiece in two. Before making the second cut, check to be sure the blade lines up with the first cut.

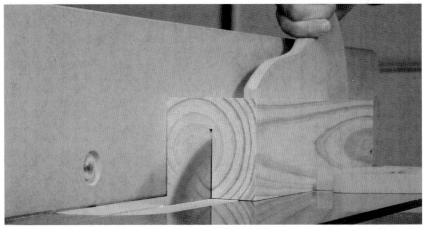

You can rip workpieces almost twice as thick as the maximum blade height. Set the blade so it will cut more than halfway through the workpiece.

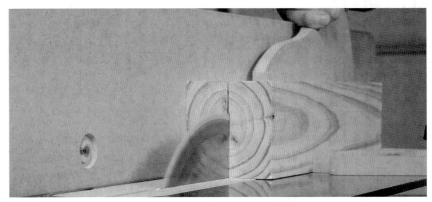

Flip the workpiece over and make a second rip cut to cut the workpiece in two. A featherboard will help maintain side pressure against the fence for both cuts.

If you have a bandsaw, it's a safer alternative than a table saw for ripping thick stock. The bandsaw won't create a kickback hazard like a table saw.

Ripping Short Or Thin Stock

Ripping workpieces shorter than a foot or so in length can still be a safe operation, provided you use a push stick or push pad to guide the cut. Set the blade height low for an added measure of safety. An even safer way to rip short stock is to use a crosscut sled. For more on crosscut sleds, see page 147.

Before cutting thin materials such as plastic laminate, check the fit of your rip fence against the saw table when it's clamped in place. Even a thin gap between the fence and table can allow the laminate to slip through during cutting and ruin the cut. If there's a gap, clamp a piece of flat-edged scrap to the fence to close the gap, then cut the laminate as you would any other sheet material. Use a low blade setting and push pad to keep the laminate from fluttering near the blade.

Always use a pushing device such as a foam-bottom push pad or a push stick to guide short workpieces when you rip them to width. Never push with your fingers.

Use a piece of scrap clamped to the saw fence to close up any gap when ripping plastic laminate or thin veneer.

Set up a beveled rip cut so the offcut will fall away from the blade. Otherwise, it could get trapped between the blade and fence and kick back.

Making Angled Rip Cuts

There are two types of angled rip cuts you can make on a table saw: bevel rips and tapers. A beveled rip cut is simply a conventional rip cut made with the blade tipped to an angle other than 90°. When setting up a beveled rip cut, position the fence on the side of the table opposite the direction the blade tips. In other words, if your table saw blade tips left, set the fence to the right of the blade. Doing this will prevent the blade from creating a tunnel over the portion of the workpiece next to the fence, which could trap the wood and create a kickback situation. Make the rip cut as usual, with the saw's splitter and guard in place.

Cutting tapers on a table saw will require that you support the workpiece in a tapering jig that slides along the saw fence during cutting. Strore-bought tapering jigs work like

TAPERING JIGS

Fabricated tapering jigs are fairly inexpensive to buy, but they're also easy to make yourself. The shop-made jig shown here isn't adjustable, however it has the added advantage of a clamp that holds workpieces securely against the jig's base during cutting.

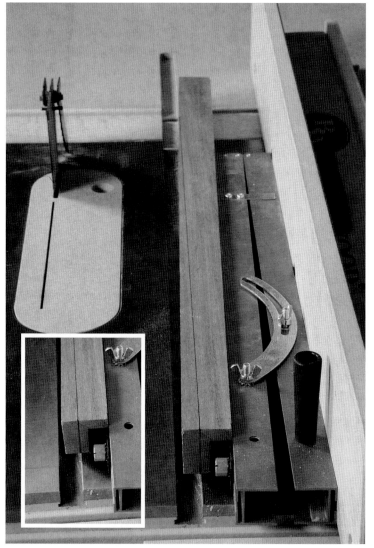

Adjust the tapering jig and the rip fence until the taper cut line aligns with one of the miter slots. Lock the tapering jig.

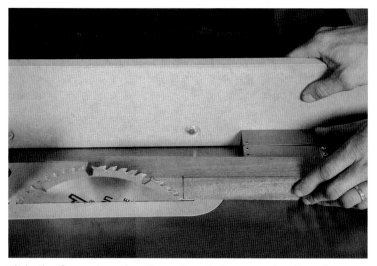

Slide the fence, tapering jig and workpiece over to align the layout line with the blade. Lock the rip fence.

an adjustable bevel square. The workpiece rests against a moveable leg on the jig, and the other leg rides along the rip fence. Set up the cut by lining up the cutting line on your workpiece with one of the miter slots on the saw table. Set the jig against the workpiece and slide the rip fence over until the other leg of the tapering jig rests fully against the fence. Lock the jig setting. Now move the fence and jig together to line up the cutting line on your workpiece with the blade. Lock down the fence. Make the cut by sliding the jig and workpiece along the fence. Depending on the proportions of your workpiece, you can use strips of carpet tape or a push stick to hold the wood against the jig during the cut.

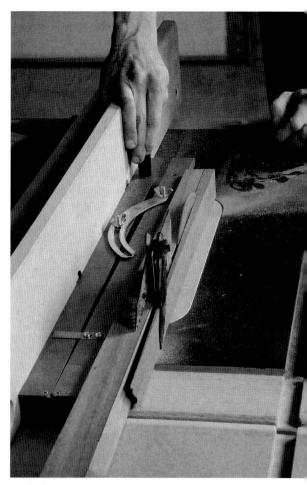

Push the tapering jig and workpiece along the fence to make the cut. For added support, use double-sided tape or a push stick to hold the workpiece against the tapering jig.

Ripping Large Sheet Good Panels

The safest approach for ripping full-sized sheets of plywood, MDF or melamine is to cut them into smaller pieces with a jigsaw or circular saw first, then trim them to final size on the table saw. However, if your table saw has a stable base and plenty of side and outfeed support, you can also rip large panels to size fairly easily at the table saw. Make sure the panel's weight isn't more than you can lift or maneuver easily; you'll need to guide it accurately over the saw just as you would any other rip cut, so it's important that you can maintain control of the panel.

Once you've set up sturdy outfeed and side support next to the saw, start the cut by lifting the sheet onto the saw table and pressing the reference edge against the rip fence. Stand at the left rear corner of the sheet with your left hand acting as a pressure point to keep the panel pressed firmly against the fence. Your right hand feeds the sheet through. Feed the panel into the blade, walking it slowly into the cut. Keep your eyes on the fence to make sure the edge of the panel follows the fence through the entire cut. If the panel begins to drift, shift your body position slightly to get the edge back on track. A little change in feed pressure is usually all it takes to correct a wandering cut.

As the cut progresses, you can move from the left rear corner of the sheet to standing directly behind the sheet. Again, move slowly and carefully when you change positions. When the saw cuts the sheet in two, push the portion of the sheet guided by your right hand completely past the blade before turning off the saw.

Before cutting large sheet materials, set up a sturdy outfeed support device to keep workpieces from tipping off the saw. Start the cut with your body near the corner of the sheet.

As the cut progresses, move around behind the sheet so you can support it on both sides of the blade.

Feed the sheet until it's cut in two, pushing the portion in your right hand completely past the blade. Turn off the saw before clearing off the two workpieces.

Cutting Raised Panels

It's easy to raise panels for cabinet doors on a table saw, and there's no special blade to buy. The process involves making a series of shallow cuts to define the center square area, then four taller bevel rip cuts to slice the facets of the panel to shape. The following photo series will take you through the entire process, step by step. There are a number of safety issues to keep in mind when making the tall bevel-rip cuts for these panels. First, make sure your saw's rip fence is properly adjusted and parallel with the blade. You'll need to remove the saw's guard and splitter to allow room for the panel to slide past the blade in the vertical position, so it's imperative that the blade not bind the workpiece during cutting. Second, attach a tall auxiliary fence to the rip fence to provide extra support behind the panel

HOW TO CUT RAISED PANELS

1 Mark the "field" area of the panel with four layout lines.

2 Make rip cuts approximately ⅛ in. deep along the four layout lines to create the panel's "shadow" lines.

3 Lay out the bevel angles on the panel, and set a bevel gauge to this angle.

4 Tilt the saw blade using the bevel gauge to set the correct blade angle. Raising the blade to full height will help establish this angle accurately.

workpiece—you'll be cutting the panel by standing it on its narrow edges and ends. Adding a tall, broad surface to the fence will prevent the panel from rocking or tipping during cutting. Third, make sure your panel material is surfaced absolutely flat. Finally, cut the short ends of the panel first, then the long edges. This will help to reduce tearout where the long grain meets the short grain.

When making the tall bevel cuts, try to push the panel past the blade as smoothly and rapidly as the saw's motor will allow. A rapid cut will help prevent the blade from scorching the wood—it's never fun to have to plane or sand out burn marks! Raising panels on a table saw will inevitably leave some blade marks or small burns on the cut edges. The quickest way to remove these is to use a sharp block plane to shave off the damage. A small cabinet scraper or hand-sanding will also remove the marks quickly and easily.

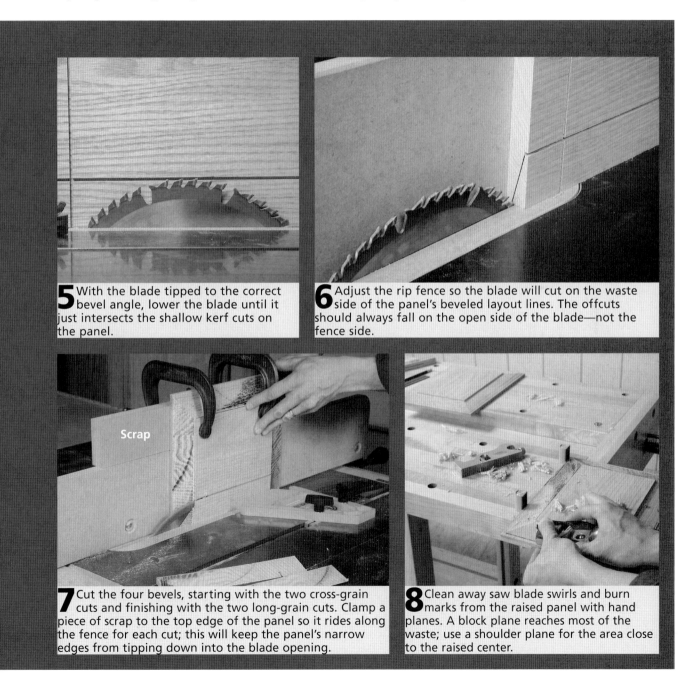

5 With the blade tipped to the correct bevel angle, lower the blade until it just intersects the shallow kerf cuts on the panel.

6 Adjust the rip fence so the blade will cut on the waste side of the panel's beveled layout lines. The offcuts should always fall on the open side of the blade—not the fence side.

7 Cut the four bevels, starting with the two cross-grain cuts and finishing with the two long-grain cuts. Clamp a piece of scrap to the top edge of the panel so it rides along the fence for each cut; this will keep the panel's narrow edges from tipping down into the blade opening.

8 Clean away saw blade swirls and burn marks from the raised panel with hand planes. A block plane reaches most of the waste; use a shoulder plane for the area close to the raised center.

To line up a crosscut, set the workpiece against the miter gauge and line up the blade with a layout mark on the wood. Adjust the workpiece so the blade will cut on the waste side of the line.

Holding the workpiece securely against the miter gauge, slide the gauge past the blade to make the crosscut. Keep your hands and shirtsleeves clear of the blade.

Crosscutting With A Table Saw

Crosscutting on the table saw is a simple operation done with your saw's miter gauge. To make the cut, set the miter gauge to 0° and hold the workpiece against the miter gauge fence. With the saw turned off, slide the gauge and workpiece up to the blade to line up the blade with a reference mark or line you've drawn on your workpiece. Then back up the gauge and workpiece, start the saw and slide the gauge completely past the blade to make the cut. Make sure your rip fence does not touch the workpiece or its offcut during crosscutting; the rip fence can trap a cutoff piece against the blade and lead to kickback.

To make a miter cut, unlock the miter gauge knob and swivel the head of the gauge to whatever angle you need to cut. Tighten the knob down firmly to lock the angle setting. Hold your workpiece securely against the gauge when making the crosscut—angling the fence reduces the miter gauge's fence support, especially when it's set to a steep angle. Workpieces will tend to creep along the fence as you slide the gauge past the blade if you're not careful.

Options For Making Repetitive Crosscuts

Sometimes a project may require you to crosscut a number of parts to exactly the same size. Cutting drawer components or parts for face frames are two typical examples. You can line up each cut by eye, but odds are you won't end up with part lengths that match. Instead, try the following two approaches to create easy ways to index your crosscuts for perfect results.

Use A Stop Block Clamped To An Extension Fence

See the tip box below to mount an extension fence to your miter gauge. Make the fence longer than the workpieces you need to cut to the same size. To index the crosscuts, set a workpiece against the miter gauge

Clamping a stop block to your miter gauge's extension fence is a helpful way to keep workpieces from creeping when making miter cuts.

and align the cutoff line on the workpiece with the blade. Clamp a stop block to the extension fence on the opposite end of the workpiece. Now, each crosscut you make will create workpieces with matching lengths.

TIP

MITER GAUGE EXTENSION FENCES

Miter gauges that come with most table saws have fences that are too short to provide enough support for many crosscutting applications. An easy way to improve the performance and accuracy of your miter gauge is to fasten a length of scrap wood to the fence. Your gauge probably has two holes drilled through the fence for this purpose. The scrap fence can really be any length you choose—12 to 16 in. is a good general length to use. Make the scrap 3 to 4 in. wide so it's easy to grip with your hands without losing control of the workpiece in front of it. Position and fasten the fence to the miter gauge so the blade will cut a slot through it when using it the first time. The blade slot will give you a convenient reference for lining up your cuts—it shows the exact path of the blade and it will greatly reduce tearout. Positioning the extension fence so it crosses the blade also allows the fence to help sweep cutoff pieces clear after making a crosscut.

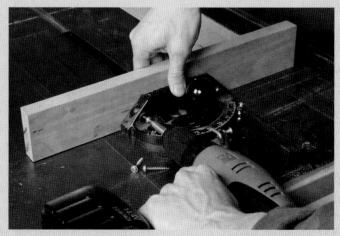

Adding a scrap extension fence to your miter gauge will improve workpiece support for cutting long or tall workpieces.

Index Crosscuts Using The Rip Fence

A second method for making repetitive crosscuts is to use the rip fence and a stop block to create matching part lengths. In this scenario, clamp the stop block to the rip fence near the front of the saw. Set a workpiece against the miter gauge and slide the wood over to meet the rip fence stop block. Move the rip fence one direction or the other until the cutoff line on the workpiece lines up with the blade, and lock down the fence. Make sure the stop block and workpiece will not make contact with one another during the cut; this could lead to a kickback. The stop block serves only as a reference for lining up the workpiece before beginning the cut. Make each crosscut by sliding the workpiece over to the stop block, holding it firmly against the miter gauge and pushing the gauge past the blade as usual. Each cutoff you make will be exactly the same length.

INDEX CROSSCUTS USING THE RIP FENCE

Stop Block

Clamp a stop block to the rip fence far enough in front of the blade so the workpiece will not touch it when it contacts the blade. Adjust the rip fence so the stop block will align the cutting line on the workpiece with the blade.

Using the stop block to register the workpiece, each crosscut will produce same-length cutoffs without the need for more layout lines.

A crosscut sled acts like an oversized miter gauge to support long boards for crosscutting. A bar or two underneath the sled follows one or both miter slots and controls the sled's path past the blade.

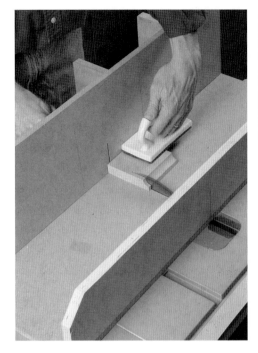

A crosscut sled also provides a safe, controlled means to crosscut short stock. Always use a holddown of some sort to keep your hand clear of the blade when cutting small workpieces.

Crosscut Sleds

For some crosscutting operations, a miter gauge is an inadequate or even unsafe fixture to use. Particularly long or wide workpieces are hard to control when crosscutting with a small miter gauge. Tiny workpieces are also difficult to hold when you have to slide them over the saw table against the miter gauge, and they can put your fingers dangerously close to the saw blade. In these sorts of situations, a crosscut sled can really help. Crosscut sleds take many forms, but the basic design is fairly similar. Essentially, a crosscut sled is a panel with one or two runners underneath that fit in the saw's miter gauge slots. The runners help the panel slide in a controlled path over the saw blade. One or two fences on the panel hold it together and provide a backup surface for workpieces when crosscutting. Use the sled just as you would your miter gauge: set the workpiece against the rear fence and slide the sled past the blade to make a crosscut. The sled allows you to keep the workpiece immobilized and adequately supported.

Crosscut sled designs will vary. Some have a single runner that fits the miter slot, but most designs use two runners and a tall fence on both the front and back.

Cutting Rabbets

Rabbets are two-sided cutouts in the end or edge of a workpiece that create an offset tongue (see page 118 for more on rabbet joints). They can be cut on a table saw with either a standard blade or a dado blade. When a rabbet follows the length of a workpiece, use the rip fence to guide the necessary cuts. To cut rabbets into the end of a workpiece, you can use the miter gauge alone or a combination of the miter gauge and rip fence.

The following two photo sequences will show you the technique for cutting rabbets with either a dado blade or a standard blade.

Cutting Rabbets With A Dado Blade

Install a dado blade in the saw and stack the cutters to form a cutting width wider than the rabbet you wish to make. Clamp a sacrificial fence facing to your saw's rip fence with a recess that allows the blade to fit inside. You'll use the amount of projection of the blade from the rip fence to help set the rabbet's proportions.

Draw reference lines on your workpiece to mark the proportions of the rabbet. With the workpiece lying flat on the saw table, raise the dado blade until the teeth reach the "cheek" line of the rabbet (the horizontal reference line on your workpiece). Now set the workpiece against the miter gauge and so the end touches the rip fence. Move the fence and workpiece until the edge of the dado blade intersects the "shoulder" line of the rabbet (the vertical reference line on your workpiece). Lock the rip fence here.

Raise the dado blade until the teeth reach the rabbet's cheek line.

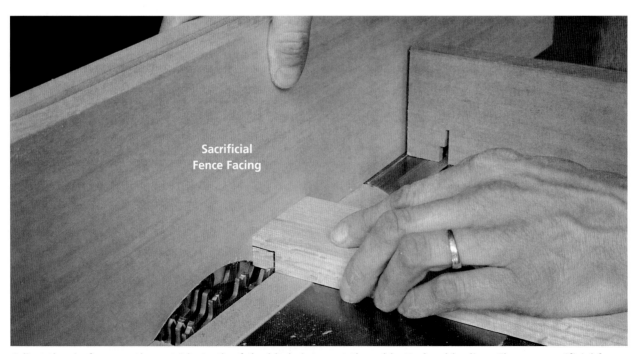

Sacrificial Fence Facing

Adjust the rip fence so the outside teeth of the blade intersect the rabbet's shoulder line. Clamp a sacrificial fence facing to the rip fence to partially cover the exposed blade.

Cut the rabbet in one pass using the miter gauge to back up the workpiece, just as you would make a typical crosscut. The saw's settings should cut the rabbet to exact size. A scrap extension fence on your miter gauge will help reduce tearout on the back edge of the cut.

Cutting Rabbets With A Standard Blade

Rabbets are also easy to cut in two passes with a standard saw blade instead of a dado set. You'll make the shoulder cut with the workpiece flat on the saw table and backed up against the miter gauge. Raise the blade until the tips of the teeth intersect the rabbet's cheek line. Line up the blade with the rabbet's shoulder, and slide the rip fence over until it touches the end of the workpiece. The fence will prevent the workpiece from shifting during the cut. Or, you can simply hold the wood tightly against the miter gauge and make the cut without the aid of the rip fence.

To cut the cheek surface, one option is to make a series of repeated passes over the blade, shifting the workpiece a little each time to "nibble" away the rest of the waste. Or, you can stand the workpiece on end against the rip fence and cut the cheek in one pass instead (see the right photo shown here). If you cut the cheek this way, install a zero-clearance throatplate in your saw (see page 134). Back up the cut with

Back up the workpiece with the miter gauge, and make the rabbet cut just as you would a normal crosscut. Feed slowly and smoothly past the dado blade.

a piece of scrap wood behind the workpiece to keep it from rocking or tipping during the cut. Set the rip fence so the blade intersects the cheek line and cuts on the waste side of the layout line.

To cut a rabbet with a standard blade, make the shoulder cut with the workpiece backed up against the miter gauge.

Scrap

Cut the rabbet cheek with the workpiece standing on end against the rip fence. Back the workpiece up with a wide piece of scrap stock to help stabilize it vertically.

Cutting Dadoes And Grooves

Dadoes are non-through cuts made across the grain of a workpiece (for more about dado joints, see page 119). When cutting a dado across a narrow workpiece, use the miter gauge to back up the workpiece. Set up your dado blade so its width matches the dado you want to cut. Raise the blade until the teeth reach to the dado's depth. Make the cut by sliding the miter gauge past the blade, just as you would make an ordinary crosscut. Use a scrap fence attached to your miter gauge to keep the dado blade from splintering the wood as it exits the cut.

When you need to cut a dado across a wide panel, you can guide the workpiece along the rip fence instead of using the miter gauge.

Grooves are long-grain, non-through cuts made into the face or the edge of a workpiece. Use the rip fence to guide groove cuts, whether you are cutting them into the face or the edge of a workpiece. Set the width of your dado blade to match the groove width, and raise the blade so it will cut the groove to full depth. Use featherboards to help keep workpieces from veering away from the rip fence when making groove cuts.

Tongue and groove joints are easy to make with a dado blade and sacrificial fence attached to the rip fence.

Dadoes are cross-grain cuts that do not cut a workpiece in two. When cutting a dado across a narrow workpiece, back the cut up with your miter gauge.

Dadoes provide a sturdy means of capturing another workpiece, because the resulting joint makes an interlocking connection. The joint shown here is called a housed dado.

Grooves are long-grain cuts that do not pass all the way through the workpiece. You can make them on faces or edges with a dado blade. Featherboards help keep the workpiece snug to the table and rip fence.

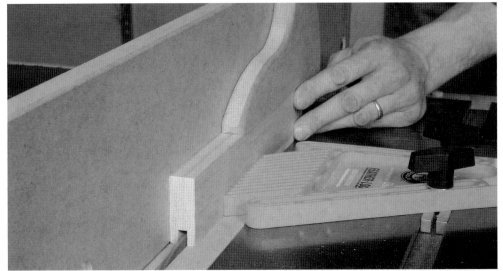

The first step in making a tongue and groove joint is to cut the groove along the edge of one workpiece. Flip the workpiece end-for-end and make a second pass with the same fence setting to center the groove.

Cut the groove portion of the joint first. **NOTE:** *Be sure to start with workpieces that are the same thickness.* A handy trick for centering the groove precisely along the edge of the workpiece is to make the groove in two passes, flipping the workpiece end-for-end for the second pass. Two passes will automatically center the cut on the workpiece.

Once the groove is made, reset the rip fence for cutting the tongue side of the joint. The tongue is really nothing more than a pair of rabbet cuts that leave a centered portion of the wood intact. Use the wall of the grooved piece as an index for setting up the blade to make the tongue cuts: make the dado blade project out from the fence the same distance as the thickness of the groove wall. Lower the blade slightly from the height you used to cut the groove to allow the tongue to seat fully in the groove. Two passes along the rip fence will mill the tongue to shape. It should slip into the groove with slight friction but not tightly. If the tongue is too tight, unlock the fence and tap the fence so the dado blade projects slightly further than before. The slightest shift in the fence is probably all that's required here. Make two more passes to shave the tongue for a better fit.

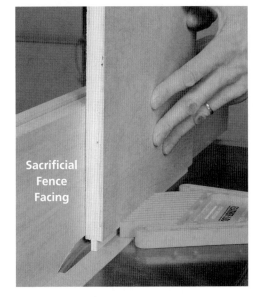

Install a sacrificial fence facing and reset the rip fence for making the tongue. It's really just a pair of rabbet cuts. Make two passes to cut the tongue. Test your setup on scrap first to make sure the tongue will fit the groove.

The tongue should slip into the groove with a bit of friction, but you shouldn't need to apply force. A slightly short tongue will leave some clear space in the bottom of the joint for excess glue.

151

Cutting Tenons

Tenons are elongated tongues cut on the ends of workpieces. Generally, only one tenon is cut on the end, although a particularly large joint may require two tenons. Usually the tenon is centered on the end of the workpiece, but off-centered tenons are also sometimes used. Tenons are made to fit into matching-shaped, square-ended holes called mortises (for more on mortise and tenon joints, see page 120). The easiest way to fit a mortise and tenon joint together is to cut the mortise first, then make the tenon fit the mortise. (For more on cutting mortises, see pages 187, 195 and 216). To save yourself frustration as well as wasted wood, make the following tenon cuts on scrap stock first to fine-tune your saw settings before cutting the actual workpieces.

Cutting Tenons With A Standard Blade

Cutting tenons with a standard saw blade is similar to cutting rabbets. The first step is to make the shallow shoulder cuts that determine the overall length of the tenon. Follow the photo sequence shown below, using the mortised workpiece as a gauge for setting blade height and positioning the rip fence. When the shoulder cuts are set up correctly, use the miter gauge to back up the tenon workpiece, and make a pair of cuts into both faces of the workpiece to create the first two broad tenon shoulders. The end of the workpiece should slide along the rip fence to help index these two cuts.

Once the shoulder cuts are made, raise the saw blade until it just intersects the shoulder cuts. This taller blade setting will create the broad cheek cuts. The safest way to make the cheek cuts is to clamp the workpiece on end in a tenoning jig (see next page). Adjust the jig laterally until the blade intersects the bottoms

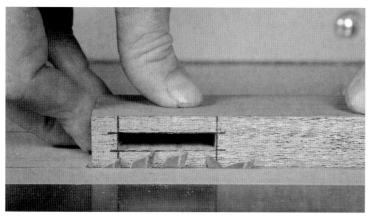

Use your mortised workpiece to help set the blade for cutting the tenon shoulders. The tips of the blade teeth should line up with the mortise walls.

Measure the depth of the mortise to determine where to set the rip fence to cut the correct tenon length. Extend and lock the rule of a combination square to gauge the depth.

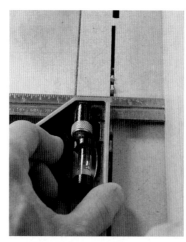

Set the rip fence using the locked combination square as a reference. The head of the square should rest against the outside face of the blade.

Two passes across each face of the workpiece will create the two tenon shoulder cuts. Try this setup on scrap first. Back up the cuts with a miter gauge.

With the shoulder cuts completed, raise the blade until the teeth just intersect the shoulder cuts. Check the blade with a square to make sure it is perpendicular to the table.

You can use a tenoning jig to trim the tenon cheeks in two passes. Set this cut up carefully; the blade should meet the shoulder cuts precisely and form a clean corner.

of the shoulder cuts. Cut the tenon cheeks in two passes, flipping the workpiece from one face to the other and reclamping in the jig to make each cheek cut. If you don't have a tenoning jig, you can also make these cheek cuts vertically by backing up the workpiece with a large, square edged piece of scrap and sliding both along the rip fence. Position the fence so the wastepieces fall onto the open saw table when the blade cuts them free. Do not set up the cut so the wastepieces are trapped between the fence and blade; they will bind in the cut and shoot back at you.

Tenons typically have two types of surfaces—the broad cheeks and shoulders you've now made and another pair of short shoulders and cheeks made along the edges of the workpiece. The combination of both sets of shoulders and cheeks creates a four-sided, centered tongue. Make the short shoulders and cheeks next. Use the mortised workpiece again to set the blade height accordingly for trimming the short shoulders. Line up the rip fence carefully with the end of the workpiece so the blade cuts the short shoulders in exactly the same place as the long shoulders. Set the workpiece

OPTIONS FOR TENONING JIGS

As with most popular woodworking jigs, you can buy manufactured tenoning jigs or build your own from scrap. Jigs you buy will have a bar that fits in the miter slot for locating the jig, and most styles have micro-adjust features for fine-tuning setups. The clamp offers excellent support for holding long workpieces on end. Another option is to make your own tenoning jig from scrap. There are numerous styles of shop-made tenoning jigs. The one shown here fits over the rip fence beam to slide across the saw table. It has a clamp for holding workpieces securely against the jig's baseplate.

If the tenon has a pair of short shoulders and cheeks, use the mortised workpiece again to set the blade height. This setting will establish the width of the short shoulders.

on edge against the miter gauge to make the first shoulder cut, then nibble away the rest of the waste in a series of repeated passes, shifting the workpiece away from the blade a little more each time until you reach the end of the tenon. This process will create the short cheek. Flip the workpiece to the other edge and repeat the nibble cuts to make the second short shoulder and cheek.

Once your tenon is cut, try to fit it into the mortise. It should slide in with a bit of friction, but you shouldn't have to force or pound the parts together. If

Use the rip fence to line the blade up with the broad shoulder cuts you've already made on the tenon workpiece. Two more passes cuts the short shoulders. Back up these cuts with the miter gauge.

Nibble away the rest of the waste out to the ends of the tenon to create the short cheeks. Flip the workpiece over and repeat to make the second short shoulder and cheek.

TIP

TENON RULE OF THIRDS

A general rule of thumb for sizing tenons is to make the tenon about 1/3 the thickness of the workpiece. So, on a 3/4-in.-thick workpiece, the tenon is 1/4 in. thick, and each of the broad shoulders is 1/4 in. These proportions make the tenon thick enough to offer plenty of strength, and the deep shoulders help the joint resist racking. This sizing isn't set in stone; you may need to vary the proportions of the tenons you make for some joints, depending on the size of the workpieces and the strength requirements of the final joint. However, err on the side of making the tenon at least 1/3 as thick as the workpiece; a thinner tenon compromises its strength.

The general guideline for designing tenons is to make them 1/3 the thickness of the workpiece (right in photo). Thinner tenons lose strength, and thicker tenons compromise the strength of the mortise walls.

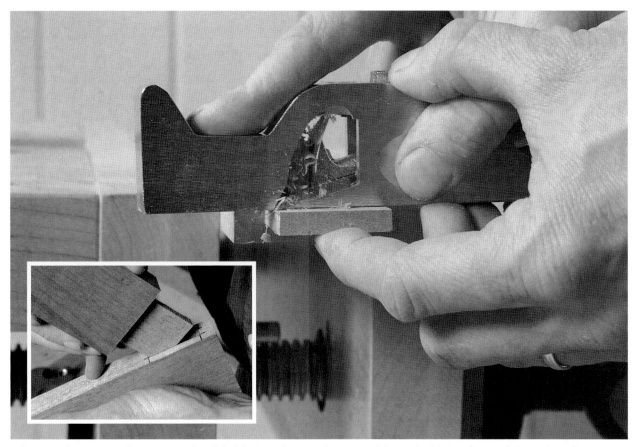

When made accurately, a tenon should slide into its mortise smoothly and without force. If the tenon fits tightly, plane a few shavings off the cheeks to improve the fit.

the tenon fits too tightly, use a shoulder plane or sharp chisel to pare down the cheeks until the tenon slips into place. On the other hand, if the tenon is too loose to begin with, the best recourse is usually to start over and make another tenon on a fresh workpiece. Here's where it really pays to make each stage of the tenon cuts on a piece of matching scrap stock to avoid mistakes.

Cutting Tenons With A Dado Blade

Tenons are quick and easy to cut with a wide dado blade—the blade will remove more waste with each pass than a standard blade, and it allows you to cut both the shoulder and the cheek simultaneously. Use the rip fence as a guide for setting the length of the tenon, just as you would when using a standard blade. Back up the cuts with the miter gauge. The height

of the blade establishes the cheeks. Make the broad shoulder cuts with the workpiece held against the miter gauge. Several side-by-side passes will

A wide dado blade makes tenons efficiently, because the shoulder cuts also form a substantial portion of the cheeks. Back up these cuts with the miter gauge. Use the rip fence as a stop block to index the shoulder cuts.

A few side-by-side passes with the dado blade finishes the broad shoulders and cheeks.

Reset the dado blade height, if necessary, but keep the fence position the same to cut the short shoulders and cheeks. Nibble away the waste.

cut away the waste. Once the broad cheeks and shoulders are formed, change the blade height if necessary to set up the short shoulder and cheek cuts, but leave the rip fence locked where it is. Tip the workpiece on edge to make the remaining shoulder/cheek cuts.

INSTALLING A STACKED DADO BLADE

Dado blades are made in two styles: wobble dadoes and stackable dadoes. A wobble dado will have one or two blades mounted on an adjustable hub. Turning a dial on the hub skews the blade or blades on the hub to cut different dado widths. On stacked sets, the dado consists of a pair of outer blades, called scoring blades, that look similar to ordinary saw blades and a set of four to six tooth "chipper" blades. The outer blades have teeth that bevel either left or right—one for each side of the cut—to create the walls of the dado. The chipper blades remove the rest of the waste in between. When you install a stacked set, arrange the blades so the teeth do not touch and the chippers fan out evenly around the arbor. This will distribute the blade weight uniformly to help reduce vibration during cutting.

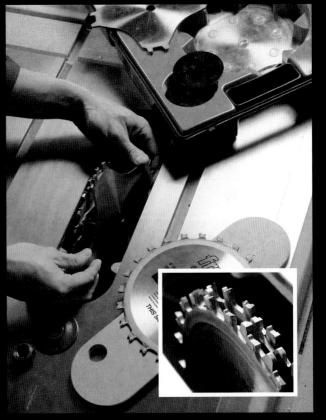

When you mount a stacked dado blade on the saw's arbor, install the chipper blades so they fan out evenly and the teeth do not touch.

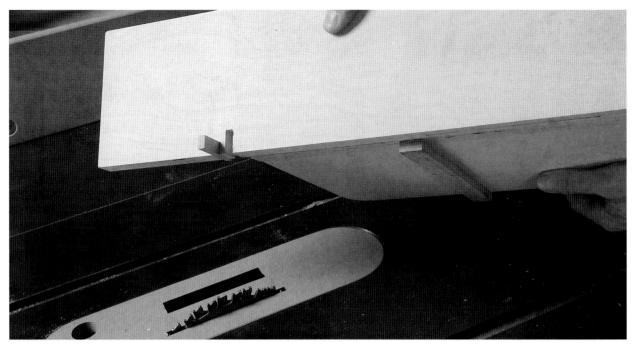

Most box joint jigs consist of a sled with a runner that slides in the saw's miter slot. A facing with a pin indexes the workpieces automatically to form the pin and slot box joint pattern.

Cutting Box Joints

Box joints provide a beautiful symmetry of straight pins and slots that interlock. These are great joints to use for box-building of all sorts, including bookshelves, chests and drawers. They were often used for joining crates and boxes before the advent of cardboard. All the surface area formed between the pins and slots provides a broad area for glue, which makes these joints both sturdy and attractive. The photo sequence on the next few pages illustrates how to cut this joint with a table saw and a dado blade, but you can use the same approach and jig for making box joints with a straight bit in a router table.

Box Joint Jigs

The secret to cutting a repetitive series of equal-width pins and slots is to use a simple indexing jig. Styles of box joint jigs vary, to some degree. The type you see here is most typical: it consists of a sled with a runner attached that slides in the saw's miter slot. The sled holds workpieces on end and keeps them square in relation to

the blade. A second facing with a small protruding pin clamps to the sled. The pin is used to index one pin or slot from the next as you cut them. Make your jig about 12 to 14 inches wide and about 6 in. tall to provide ample vertical backup support for workpieces. Use a strip of dimensionally stable hardwood, such as hard maple, to make the jig runner and the indexing pin. Size the runner carefully so it slips into the miter slot with just the slightest amount of play; it should slide but not move from side to side in the slot. A sloppy fit of the runner in the slot will create poorly fitting joints.

Setting Up The Jig

To prepare the jig for use, install the outer blades and chippers of your dado set until the combined blade thickness matches the width of the jig pin precisely. Use paper spaces between the blade parts if necessary to make fine blade width adjustments. Raise the blade and use it to adjust the facing on the jig so the blade fits squarely in the jig slot. The fixed pin on the jig should be located exactly one pin's width away from the blade.

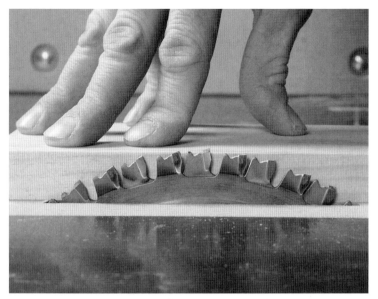

Set the dado blade height to match the stock thickness of the joint, then raise the blade about 1/32 in. higher.

Cutting The Pins And Slots

With the jig adjusted for your dado blade, the first step in milling the parts is to lay out the joint and set an accurate bit height. Ideally, your workpieces should be cut to a width that's evenly divisible by the pin thickness of the jig. It's also a good idea to design the joint parts so the outer edges of one workpiece have pins on them. A joint that begins with a pin on one end and ends with a slot looks out of balance, so plan accordingly on your project.

If both workpieces are the same thickness, raise the blade to match this thickness. Sometimes, however, you may want to make box joints on parts with two different thicknesses, such as drawers with 3/4-in. faces and 1/2-in. sides. In this case, set the blade height to match the workpiece that will have pins on both outside edges. Cut these first.

Begin the slot-cutting process by butting a pin-ended workpiece against the jig's pin and holding or clamping it in place against the jig fence. Cut the first slot, which also creates the first pin. Feed the workpiece and jig slowly across the table and through the blade.

Once the first slot is cut, slip the slot over the jig's pin to index the next pin and slot cut. Cut this slot, then proceed across the rest of the workpiece in the same fashion to cut all the slots and pins to shape. If the opposite end of the workpiece will receive the same configuration of pins and slots, make these now by flipping the board end-for-end.

Hold the workpiece against the jig with one edge resting against the jig's pin. Slide the jig through the blade to cut the first joint slot, which also forms the first pin.

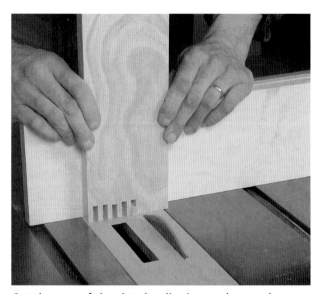

Cut the rest of the slots by slipping each new slot over the jig pin to index and cut the next slot and pin. Cut all across the first board, flip it end-for-end and repeat on the other end, if necessary.

Once the pin-ended board is milled, use it to index the first cut on the slot-ended board. Be sure to change the blade height now, if the joint parts aren't the same thickness. To cut the first slot, slip the outermost slot of the pin-ended board (the workpiece you've already cut) over the jig's pin, and butt the mating board against the first. Cut the first slot along the edge of this board with both workpieces held firmly against the jig fence.

Continue cutting slots across the face of this board until you've cut the other end slot. If your workpieces are accurately sized to width, the outermost slots should end up being the same width.

Test-fit the joint. The parts should slide together with a bit of friction, but you shouldn't have to force them. If the fit is too tight or loose, you'll need to unclamp and shift the pin facing on the jig slightly and cut new parts. Just the slightest shift of the facing will change how the parts go together, so be careful when making any changes. Another common problem is that the endmost slots or pins don't end up equally sized. The solution here is to recalculate your part widths and make sure they're evenly divisible by the pin thickness. Box joints are definitely worth trying on test material first to dial in an exact fit. Don't get discour-

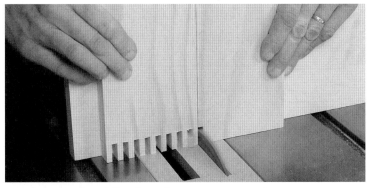

Use the completed first board to set up a complementary pattern of pins and slots on the mating workpiece. Fitting the first slot of the first board onto the jig, you can cut the second board with a slot on its edge rather than a pin.

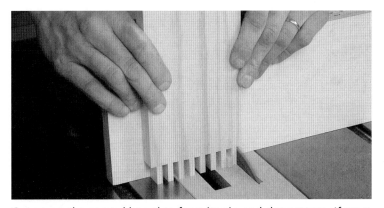

Cut across the second board to form its pin-and-slot pattern. If your jig is cutting accurately and the workpieces are sized correctly for the jig, the outermost cuts should form equally sized slots.

aged if you have to try test joints several times before arriving at the proper fit—it's worth the extra effort.

Test-fit the joint to see how the parts mesh together. A proper fit should not bind or show any gaps. Adjusting the jig's facing slightly will usually improve the fit.

Cutting Coves On A Table Saw

One of the more unusual, yet surprisingly effective, techniques you can accomplish on a table saw is cutting wide coves. Cove-cutting will enable you to make custom crown and furniture moldings in any species of wood you choose, and there's no special blade to buy. A standard saw blade will make reasonably smooth cove cuts, but be sure the blade you use is sharp and clean. Even the table saw size is inconse-

quential: a larger cabinet or contractor's saw with more power certainly helps, but you can still cut cove molding without difficulty on a smaller benchtop saw.

To make cove molding, you'll use the side curvature of the blade to shave the workpiece to shape. In a sense, the table saw becomes a makeshift shaper. By clamping a fence at an angle to the blade, you'll feed the wood at an angle to the blade. If you change the angle of the fence and the height of the blade, you'll change the curvature of the cove. This way, it's possible to cut a

MAKING COVES ON A TABLE SAW

1 Draw the cove profile on the end of a test workpiece and use it for setting up and trying the procedure. Cut two scrap blocks that match the width of the cove as well.

2 You can use a standard or fine-toothed saw blade to cut coves. Raise the blade to match the highest point of the cove's arc.

3 Hold the scrap blocks in between another pair of long, straight pieces of scrap stock. Turn the parts on the saw table until the edges of the long scraps just touch the front and back edges of the blade. This establishes the angle of approach for the clamped fence.

6 Clamp the angled fence securely to the saw. Install a featherboard to keep the workpiece pressed firmly against the angled fence during cutting. OPTION: You can replace the featherboard with a second long clamped fence, if you prefer, to form a "tunnel" for the cove workpiece to slide through. Either method works well.

7 Lower the blade to a cutting height of about 1/16 in. to make the first pass. Cutting the cove to shape will be a "shaving" process made with many shallow passes. Use a push pad and featherboard to guide the test piece along the angled fence.

wide range of cove sizes and profiles. What's important to remember about cutting coves is that the process involves making many repeated passes, raising the blade only slightly with each pass. The harder the wood, the shallower each cut should be.

The photo sequence on these pages will show you how to set up and perform a typical cove cut. You'll need a long, straight strip of scrap for the angled saw fence, several large clamps to hold it in place and two spacer blocks that match the width of the cove shape you want to make. It's a good idea to try this technique out first on scrap stock of the same species and proportion as your actual workpieces. It'll provide a good testing grounds for making fine adjustments to the fence settings as well as determining how deep to set the blade for each pass. Plan on making several test pieces to arrive at the final setup you'll want for the molding you're making. If you can connect your table saw to a shop vacuum or dust collector, that's also advisable for this operation—cove-cutting creates lots of fine dust.

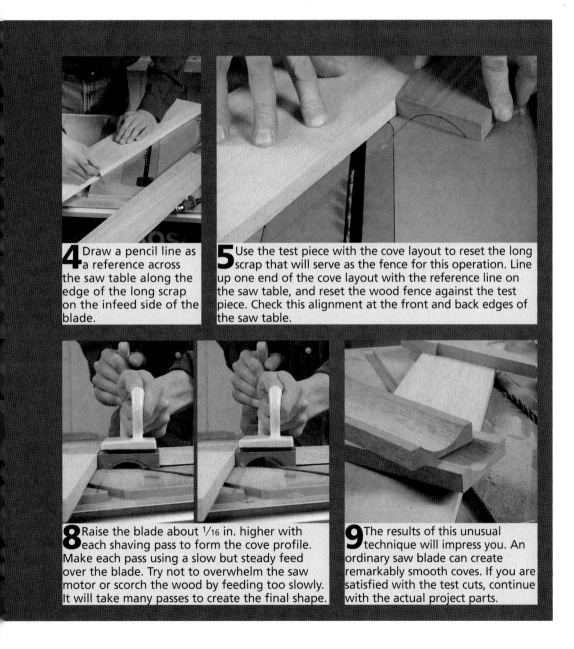

4 Draw a pencil line as a reference across the saw table along the edge of the long scrap on the infeed side of the blade.

5 Use the test piece with the cove layout to reset the long scrap that will serve as the fence for this operation. Line up one end of the cove layout with the reference line on the saw table, and reset the wood fence against the test piece. Check this alignment at the front and back edges of the saw table.

8 Raise the blade about 1/16 in. higher with each shaving pass to form the cove profile. Make each pass using a slow but steady feed over the blade. Try not to overwhelm the saw motor or scorch the wood by feeding too slowly. It will take many passes to create the final shape.

9 The results of this unusual technique will impress you. An ordinary saw blade can create remarkably smooth coves. If you are satisfied with the test cuts, continue with the actual project parts.

BANDSAW TECHNIQUES

If excessive dust, noise and potential kickback hazards leave something to be desired about table saws, you'll love a bandsaw. It can rip and crosscut as accurately as a table saw, with the added advantage of also being able to cut curves. However, the cut is generally not as smooth as you'll get with a well-tuned table saw. A bandsaw's continuous blade is much thinner than a standard table saw blade, so it wastes less wood in the cut. The blade also moves in a linear rather than circular fashion; it presses workpieces down against the table instead of forward and opposite the feed direction—a major contribution to kickback. The blade's narrow profile is relatively unaffected when wood pinches the kerf closed behind the cut. This sort of pinching is the other factor that produces typical kickback.

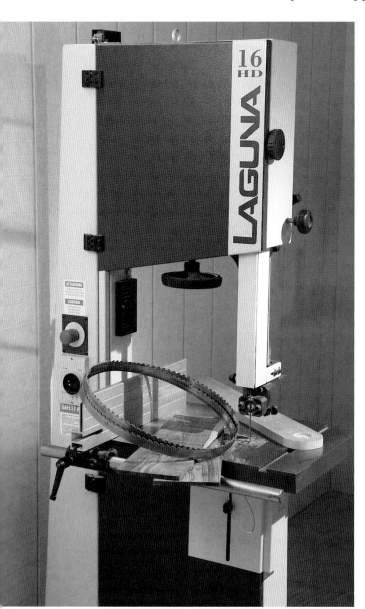

There are numerous other good attributes to bandsaws. Bandsaws are helpful for making freehand rip cuts when you don't have the advantage of a flat edge to ride against the fence. The thin blade profile is better suited for resawing than a table saw blade, and the process is safer because the guard stays in place. A band-style blade cuts with less vibration than a circular blade so it cuts more quietly, and the moveable upper guard is fully adjustable for optimal safety.

No cutting tool is perfect or capable of all possible operations. A bandsaw can't make non-through cuts like a table saw or router. Its table is typically smaller than that of a table or radial-arm saw, which can compromise workpiece support to some degree. However, a bandsaw's strengths definitely outweigh its limitations, and it is a useful addition to any home shop. If you are in the market to buy a bandsaw, a 14- to 16-in. size will cover most project needs. Blades for a 14-in. saw will be easy to find and reasonably priced.

If you are a new bandsaw user, here are a few tips to keep in mind: Be sure to apply adequate tension to the blade before making any type of cut; you'll need to raise the amount of tension as blade widths increase. (See your saw owner's manual for recommendations on tensioning the blade.) It's also a good practice to check the position of the blade guides regularly and release the tension on the blade if you don't plan on using your bandsaw within a few days. Constant blade tension can prematurely wear the saw's tension spring and flywheel tires as well as the blade.

The following section overviews a range of cutting techniques to try with your bandsaw.

Rip-Cutting With A Bandsaw

Although bandsaw blades have measurable width, the blade body doesn't function like a wide, flat plane as circular blades do. The band-style blade eliminates the kickback hazards associated with table and radial-arm saws, so you can make rip cuts without using a fence. Freehand rip-cutting is a simple matter of pushing the wood through the blade and guiding the cut along your layout line. Gently steer the wood left or right as necessary to keep the blade following the line. You'll appreciate the advan-tage of freehand ripping whenever you need to cut off waney or crooked edges. There's also no problem of the blade "double cutting" the wood and leaving burn marks like a table saw can, because a bandsaw makes long cuts along the front edge of the blade.

For greater accuracy, you can also make rip cuts similar to the table saw method using the saw's rip fence or even a board clamped to the saw table. See the photo sequence shown here to learn the proper setup and procedure for making a fence-guided rip cut. Make sure to set up plenty of outfeed and side support next to the saw when ripping wide or long workpieces. Use a push stick to keep your hands out of

Rip-cutting rough, or waney-edged boards is a safe procedure on a bandsaw, thanks to its narrow blade and linear cutting action. Unlike a table saw, one edge does not have to follow the rip fence.

MAKING RIP CUTS ON A BANDSAW

1 When ripping long boards on a bandsaw, set up a sturdy form of outfeed support behind the saw to keep workpieces from tipping off as you cut them.

2 Raise the upper blade guides to allow about 1/4 in. of clearance above the wood for normal cutting. The blade guides serve as a protective guard.

3 If you prefer, you can use a rip fence clamped to the saw table to make a rip cut, similar to a table saw. A rip fence will provide greater accuracy than guiding the cut by eye. Set the fence so the blade aligns with a reference mark on the workpiece.

4 Start the cut by feeding the wood along the fence. Stand to one side of the workpiece. Use one hand near the front of the saw table to guide the wood into the blade and your other hand to feed it forward.

5 When your feed hand reaches the saw table, grab a push stick to complete the cut so you can keep your fingers a safe distance from the blade. Push the wood completely past the blade, and turn off the saw before removing the pieces.

harm's way whenever you are ripping workpieces that place your fingers within about 6 in. of the blade. Lower the guard so it's positioned about 1/4 in. above the workpiece, and lock it in position. If workpieces tend to veer off the fence during ripping, you may need to adjust your saw's fence for blade drift. Or, switch to a fresh, sharp blade and see if that improves cutting quality. Dull blades can also cause wandering.

Bevel rip cuts are easy to make on a bandsaw. Most saws have tables that can be tipped off of 90° for this purpose. Set the table angle to match the bevel angle you want to cut, and feed the workpiece through the blade like a normal rip cut. If the bevel angle is severe, position the rip fence below the workpiece instead of above it so you don't have to work against gravity when making the cut.

Cutting Tapers

Since freehand rip cuts are safe to make on a bandsaw, you can also make taper cuts freehand, if you prefer. To keep the cut on course, feed the workpiece into the blade slowly and steadily. Keep your eyes focused on the cutting line a few inches in front of the blade, and make left or right adjustments to the wood gradually to correct the cut if it begins to drift off the cutting line. Use a push stick to guide particularly narrow workpieces such as table legs, when your hands approach the blade.

For greater accuracy, an adjustable tapering jig instead of cutting it freehand. In this case, the rip fence will guide one leg of the jig as you slide it and the workpiece through the cut. Set up the taper cut by adjusting the rip fence and jig until the "entry" point of the cut on your workpiece lines up with the blade. Then open or close the jig so the "exit" point of the layout line aligns with the blade. These steps will provide the coarse adjustment to the jig and fence, but you'll probably have to check the entry and exit points of the cut a few more times and fine-tune the fence and jig settings until the layout line is perfectly lined up for the cut. Make the cut by sliding the jig and workpiece along the fence. For narrow workpieces, use a push stick to hold the wood against the jig to prevent it from creeping out of place.

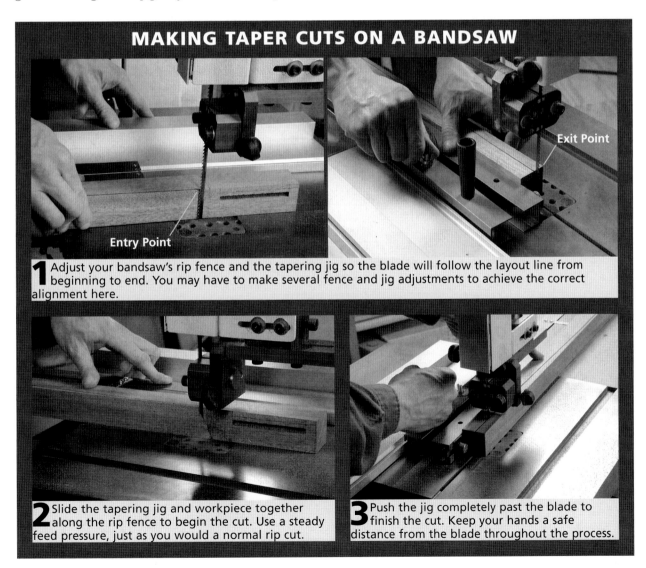

MAKING TAPER CUTS ON A BANDSAW

Exit Point

Entry Point

1 Adjust your bandsaw's rip fence and the tapering jig so the blade will follow the layout line from beginning to end. You may have to make several fence and jig adjustments to achieve the correct alignment here.

2 Slide the tapering jig and workpiece together along the rip fence to begin the cut. Use a steady feed pressure, just as you would a normal rip cut.

3 Push the jig completely past the blade to finish the cut. Keep your hands a safe distance from the blade throughout the process.

Crosscutting And Cutting Angles

The process for making crosscuts or angle cuts is the same on a bandsaw as a table saw. If your saw comes with a miter gauge, hold the workpiece against it to guide the crosscut. Pivot the miter gauge off of 90° to cut miters. Some bandsaws don't include a miter gauge, but the one on your table saw probably fits the slot in the bandsaw table as well. Or, you can simply make your crosscuts freehand if you're comfortable guiding the cut by eye.

Crosscutting with a bandsaw is similar to a table saw. For best accuracy, use a miter gauge in the saw's miter slot to back up the workpiece. Or, you can guide these cuts freehand.

Sometimes you may need to cut several workpieces to the same length. Make these sorts of repetitive crosscuts using a stop block clamped to the rip fence, just like a table saw. Adjust the rip fence so the distance between the stop block and the blade matches the length of workpiece you want to make. Back up each cut with the miter gauge.

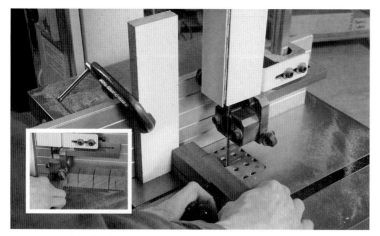

Use a stop block clamped to the rip fence if you want to make several identical-length parts. The fence automatically indexes the part length.

Cutting Curves

A bandsaw can perform numerous types of cuts, but you'll really appreciate its curve-cutting capability. If a jigsaw is all you've ever used for cutting curves, a bandsaw will seem like a dream tool. It offers excellent control and leaves smooth, clean cuts. Any narrow bandsaw blade can negotiate a broad curve cut if it's sharp and tensioned adequately. However, the tighter the curve, the narrower the blade must be. A 1/4-in.-wide blade is a good general-purpose size for cutting curves down to a radius of about 3/4 in. Narrower 1/8-in. blades will allow you to navigate even tighter curves. The downside to narrower blades is stiffness: cutting thick, hard material with a narrow blade can cause the blade to deflect and produce a bowed cut. Raising the blade tension will help, but thin blades just aren't as stiff as wider blades.

A 1/4-in.-wide blade with 6 teeth per inch is a good all-around curve-cutting blade. Blades with higher tooth counts will cut more smoothly but also more slowly.

Bandsaw blades are manufactured in standard, hook-tooth and skip-tooth patterns. Standard-tooth blades have the finest teeth and produce the smoothest cuts, but the blade cuts slowly. Hook- and skip-tooth blade styles have large, coarse teeth made for cutting soft- to average-hardness lumbers quickly. These tooth styles are excellent for ripping and resawing, and they'll also cut curves, but the tradeoff is rougher cut edges. Try the different tooth patterns to see which configuration you like best for the work you do. If you sand your sawn edges anyway, the difference in cutting quality may not be a significant issue.

Curve-cutting is generally a free-hand operation where you guide the cut by eye. For a gentle, continuous curve, simply feed the wood slowly into the blade and make gradual adjustments to feed direction as soon as the blade drifts off your reference line. When cutting more complex curve shapes, or combinations of curve and straight cuts, plan how you'll make the cut before you begin. Where a curve cut dead-ends in a straight cut, try not to back the blade out of a long kerf in order to make the adjacent cut. Backing out a blade can pull it out of the guides or even off the saw's flywheels if you aren't careful, especially if the saw is still running. The better approach is to make short, connecting cuts to the long curve first, then make the long cut to remove the waste piece. Keep cuts moving forward across the saw table whenever possible.

Be careful when negotiating extremely tight curve cuts; it's possible to bind the blade in its kerf and twist or even break it. The easy way to avoid this problem is by making a series of short relief cuts in the waste material adjacent to the curved cutting line. Relief cuts enable you to slice off portions of a tight radius and give the blade room to navigate the curve. When the layout of the workpiece won't allow for relief cuts, switch to a narrower blade so you can make the turn you need without binding the blade.

One last issue with curve cuts concerns the size of your saw table and the maximum distance from the blade to the vertical column of the saw. There's a limit to how long a workpiece you can pivot on your saw table before it contacts the column. Rehearse your cut, turning the wood around on the saw table to see if the column will cause problems. You may need to slice off extra waste from the corners of the

Cutting tight curves can twist and even break a bandsaw blade. The solution is to make several short relief cuts first. They'll give the blade room to follow the curve without binding.

workpiece or cut the curve from both ends in order to accommodate the capacity of your machine.

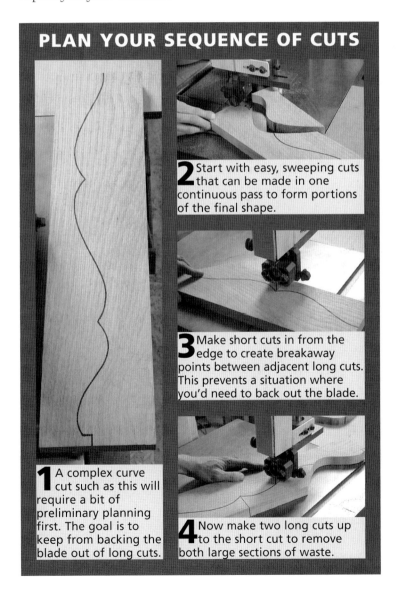

PLAN YOUR SEQUENCE OF CUTS

1 A complex curve cut such as this will require a bit of preliminary planning first. The goal is to keep from backing the blade out of long cuts.

2 Start with easy, sweeping cuts that can be made in one continuous pass to form portions of the final shape.

3 Make short cuts in from the edge to create breakaway points between adjacent long cuts. This prevents a situation where you'd need to back out the blade.

4 Now make two long cuts up to the short cut to remove both large sections of waste.

Cutting Circles

It's easy to cut perfect circles for small tabletops, wheels and so forth on your bandsaw by using a simple pivoting jig. The styles of these jigs vary widely, but most amount to a long jig base that clamps to the saw table with a pivot pin for turning the workpiece through the cut. The one shown here uses a removable dowel for the pivot pin. The distance from the center of the dowel pin to the blade establishes the radius of the circle.

To cut a circle, first draw it on your workpiece to find the center.

Make the edge of the circle intersect the edge of the workpiece to provide a convenient starting point for the blade. Drill a shallow hole partway through the workpiece so it fits over the pivot dowel, and locate the dowel on the jig at the correct radius length. To cut the circle, install the workpiece on the jig and turn it clockwise through the cut. If the jig is clamped firmly and the blade is properly tensioned, the saw will cut an exact circle around the pivot pin. It's a simple process, but you'll marvel at the accuracy.

A shop-made circle-cutting jig will cut perfect circles without guiding the cut by eye. The workpiece simply revolves around a fixed dowel pin to guide the cut.

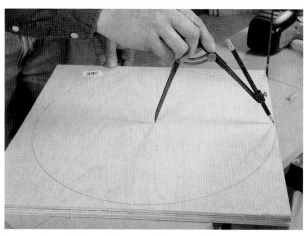

Draw the circle to shape with one edge touching the edge of the workpiece. This is where the blade will begin the cut.

Drill a stopped hole at the center of the circle for the dowel. Then install the dowel and workpiece on the jig.

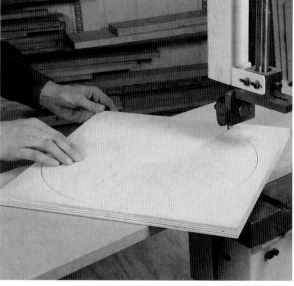

Feed the wood into the blade and slowly rotate the workpiece around its center point to cut the circle out.

Resawing

Resawing is a handy technique for making the most of your thick, figured or expensive lumber. The process involves standing the workpiece on edge and ripping it into thinner slabs by cutting across the face. Resawing allows you to create sheets of book-matched veneer or to reduce lumber to thinner dimensions without planing it all away. Choose a wide hook- or skip-tooth blade for resawing. You'll get the best results if you use the widest blade your saw will accept: blades in the ½- to 1-in.-wide range will provide the stiffness you'll need to keep these tall cuts from bowing. Plus, an aggressive tooth pattern will cut quickly and clear the sawdust efficiently.

Aside from using the proper blade, the other factor that affects resawing is your choice of fence. A standard rip fence will work for resawing, but it's important to carefully adjust it for blade drift. A wide saw blade will only increase the tendency of the wood to veer off course if the blade drifts. A better option is to make a simple "point" fence, as shown here, and clamp it to your rip fence or directly to the saw table. A point fence provides a line of bearing support for the wood—which is all the cut really requires—but it also allows you to steer the workpiece left or right to keep the cut tracking properly. Make the point fence at least 6 in. tall; wider is even better. Create a thin, flat contact surface on the edge of the fence or gently round it over so the wood glides against it easily.

Make sure your initial stock has a flat edge and face to hold against the saw table and fence. The wood needs to remain square to the table throughout the cut, otherwise you'll end up slicing off wedges instead of

Resawing is a process of ripping a workpiece into thinner pieces by sawing parallel to its faces. The bandsaw is well suited for this job.

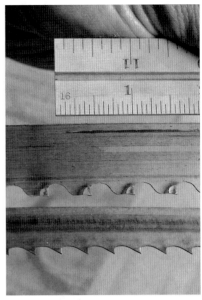

Use a wide skip- or hook-tooth blade with 2 to 3 teeth per inch for resawing. Blade widths in the ½- to 1-in. range are ideal.

slabs or thin sheets with consistent thickness. Feed the wood slowly through the cut, allowing the blade the time it needs to clear the sawdust and not bog down. Make your left and right adjustments gradually if the blade starts to drift off course. Once you've sliced off a piece, plane the

A shop-made "point" fence clamped to the table or rip fence allows you to steer workpieces left or right to keep the cut on course.

sawn face of the starter workpiece again so that each cutoff has one planed face. When you're finished resawing, run your slabs through the planer with the smooth faces down to clean up the sawn faces. For smoothing thin sheets of veneer, be sure to install a "slave board" in the planer.

HOW TO RESAW ON A BANDSAW

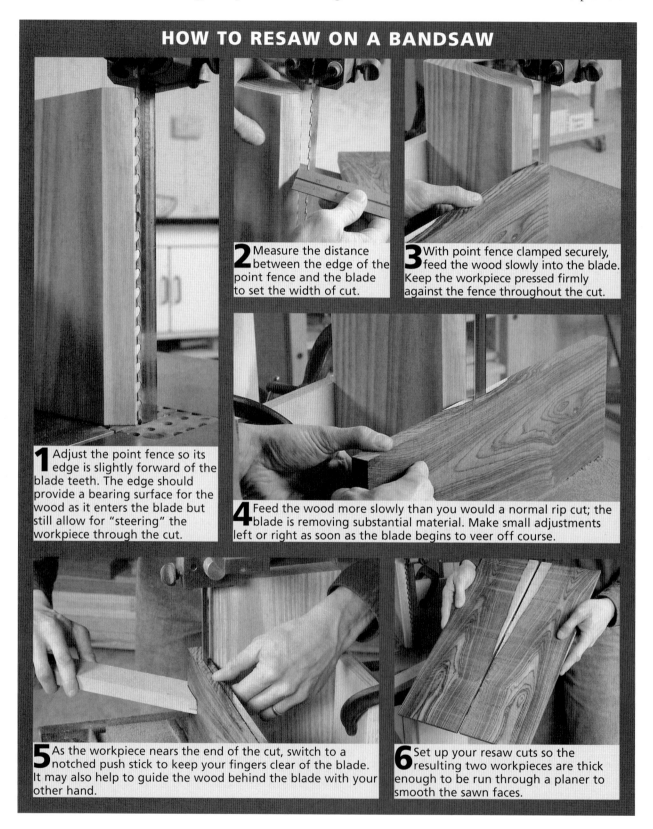

2 Measure the distance between the edge of the point fence and the blade to set the width of cut.

3 With point fence clamped securely, feed the wood slowly into the blade. Keep the workpiece pressed firmly against the fence throughout the cut.

1 Adjust the point fence so its edge is slightly forward of the blade teeth. The edge should provide a bearing surface for the wood as it enters the blade but still allow for "steering" the workpiece through the cut.

4 Feed the wood more slowly than you would a normal rip cut; the blade is removing substantial material. Make small adjustments left or right as soon as the blade begins to veer off course.

5 As the workpiece nears the end of the cut, switch to a notched push stick to keep your fingers clear of the blade. It may also help to guide the wood behind the blade with your other hand.

6 Set up your resaw cuts so the resulting two workpieces are thick enough to be run through a planer to smooth the sawn faces.

RADIAL-ARM SAW TECHNIQUES

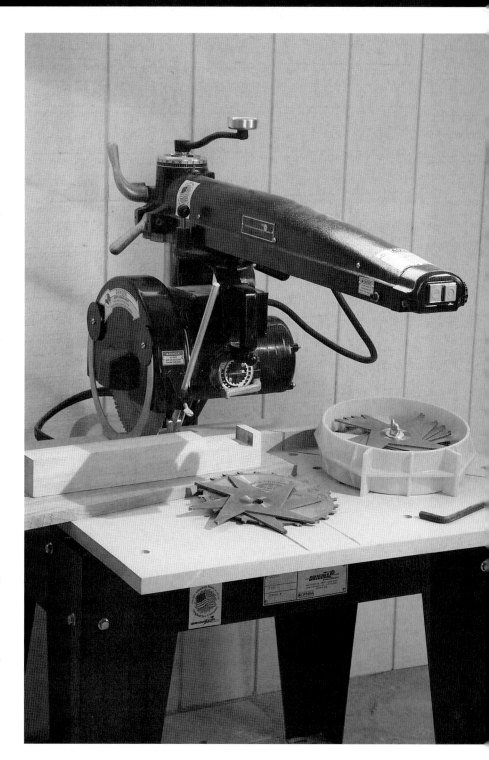

Until the mid 1980s, radial-arm saws were common in home woodshops and on the contractor's job site. However, they've been eclipsed in popularity by today's highly accurate and more affordable miter saws. You can still buy radial-arm saws from some manufacturers, and they're a common sight at auctions and garage sales. Once you own one, you'll see how versatile and handy these old standby saws really are. In a sense, a radial-arm saw functions like a table saw with the motor hanging above the table instead of beneath it. A radial-arm saw is capable of making crosscuts, angle cuts and rip cuts. You can also outfit it with a dado blade for cutting joinery. It's becoming harder to find technique books for radial-arm saws, but we'll show you how to use one here.

This section will also teach you the various cuts you can make with a miter saw. Miter saws make fewer types of cuts than radial-arm saws, but they are easier to use and safe for even novice woodworkers. Once you learn a few techniques and tips, you'll find that a miter saw will cut with hairsplitting accuracy. It's definitely the tool to choose when you are crosscutting moldings and trim, making picture frames or even building that deck or fence.

Crosscutting With A Radial-Arm Saw

Making crosscuts with a radial-arm saw involves pulling the motor from the back of the saw to the front, through the workpiece. The blade

Line up the edge of a blade tooth with your layout mark to set up a crosscut, just as you would on other saws.

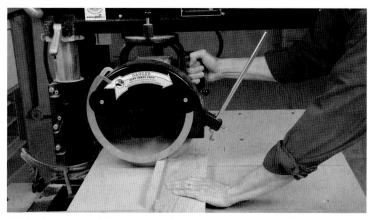

With the motor fully retracted, start the saw and pull the motor forward and into the workpiece. Hold the wood firmly against the fence with your left elbow locked.

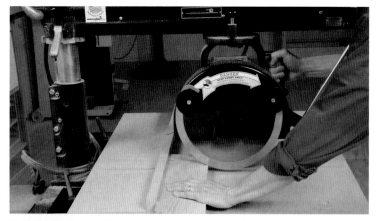

Pull the motor with a slow and steady motion all the way through the workpiece. Once the wood is cut in two, slowly retract the motor back to the starting position. Turn off the saw before clearing away the workpieces.

spins clockwise, in the same direction as the pull stroke. During crosscutting, you must be careful not to pull the motor too quickly through the cut; it's possible to overfeed the blade and stall the motor. In extreme instances, the blade can even climb up and out of the cut and come toward you. A gentle, controlled pulling motion is all it takes to make the cut. Always let the motor and blade do the work. Your hand is simply a guide to move the blade through the wood.

When using a radial-arm saw, your stance in front of the saw will also help you counteract its tendency to self-feed. Stand a comfortable distance in front of the saw so you can reach the fence on the table with your left hand and pull the saw motor through the cut with your right. The goal is to lock your left elbow to anchor the wood securely against the fence and rotate your upper body to pull the saw motor through the wood. If you can lock your right elbow when pulling the motor through, you can use your upper body strength to overpower the saw if it begins to self-feed.

To make a crosscut, first lower the saw's arm on the column until the tips of the blade teeth are slightly below the surface of the table in the table kerf slot. Make sure the blade rotates freely in the kerf before proceeding with the cut. Set the workpiece against the fence, and pull the motor forward slightly to line up the blade reference mark on the workpiece. Position the workpiece so the blade will cut on the waste side of the line, then hold it firmly against the fence with your left arm locked. Make sure your left hand is clear of the blade's path by at least 10 to 12 in. Push the motor fully to the back of the saw, start the saw and pull the blade slowly through the wood with your right hand. As soon as the blade cuts the wood in two, slowly retract it to the starting position and turn off the motor. There's no need to pull the blade any farther through the wood than what's necessary to complete the cut. When the blade stops spinning, remove the workpiece and cutoff from the saw table.

It's easy to make repetitive crosscuts on a radial-arm saw if you clamp a long stop block to the fence board. Use a sample workpiece of the length you want as an index for positioning the stop block on the fence. You'll need a stop block that's long enough to allow the clamp to clear the motor or the blade guard, depending on which side of the blade you set up the block. After making the first cut, shut off the saw and wait for the blade to stop before retracting it to the starting position. Then remove the cutoff piece, slide the workpiece against the stop block again and cut the next piece.

A long, narrow piece of scrap clamped to the fence can serve as a stop block for making repetitive crosscuts. Make sure the clamp is clear of the saw motor.

Cutting Miters And Bevels

To cut miters on a radial-arm saw, refer to your owner's manual for instructions on how to unlock the saw's arm on the column so it can swivel radially left or right. Usually, there will be a clamp lever at the top of the column for this purpose. First raise the blade up out of the table kerf slot, then unlock the radial clamp. Slowly swing the arm left or right to set the miter angle you wish to make. A scale on top of the arm will help you find the correct angle. If you are making a 45° miter cut, most saws will have a preset detent for locking the radial clamp accurately.

If the saw has been used to cut miters before, there may be a blade kerf slot already cut into the table surface for the angle you're

making. In that case, lower the blade until the tips of the teeth are just below the table surface. Set the workpiece against the fence and line up the blade with your cutting line, just as you would a normal crosscut. Start the saw and pull the blade through the workpiece to make the cut. For greater accuracy, clamp a stop block to the fence so it touches the far end of the workpiece. This will help keep the workpiece from shifting along the fence during the cut. It's also a handy way to set up repetitive miter cuts.

On most radial-arm saws, making miter cuts involves swiveling and locking the saw arm on the vertical column.

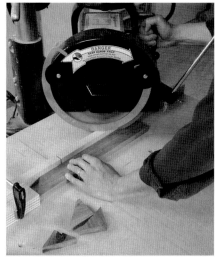

A stop block clamped to the saw fence will ensure that mitered workpieces are exactly the same length.

An angled jig, clamped to the fence, allows you to cut miters without changing the angle of the blade. A short fence along the angled edge of the jig makes it easier to hold the workpiece tightly in place.

In situations where there's no blade kerf slot for the angle you are cutting, you'll need to cut a new kerf slot. Start the saw with the blade fully retracted and with no workpiece against the fence. Lower the blade until the teeth graze the table, then pull the blade across the table and through the fence to cut the slot.

Another option for cutting miter angles is to keep the saw arm locked at 90° and use a jig like the one shown above to hold the workpiece at an angle to the blade. Make the jig so it clamps securely to the fence board.

Be careful to keep any metal fasteners you use to make the jig clear of the blade. Hold the workpiece firmly against the jig and pull the blade through to make the crosscut, just as you do for a typical square crosscut.

Making Beveled Crosscuts

The motor on your radial-arm saw can be tipped on its yoke for making beveled crosscuts. See your owner's manual to locate the bevel locking lever. Raise the saw arm so the blade is about 4 to 6 in. above the table. Unlock the bevel clamp and gently pivot the motor to set the bevel angle. A bevel scale on the front of the saw's yoke will help you find the correct angle. Lock the clamp again. Lower the arm so the blade recesses in a crosscut kerf made in the saw table. Cut a fresh kerf if you need to so the blade has a clear channel to follow when making the cut. Make the bevel cut by pulling the blade through the workpiece.

Compound Angle Cuts

You can also combine miter and bevel settings on your saw to make compound cuts. Follow the instructions for setting up miter and bevel cuts (above) to prepare the saw. Pull the blade through the workpiece to make these compound angle cuts.

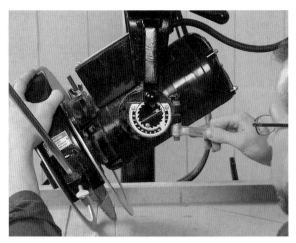

To set up bevel cuts, raise the saw motor high enough above the table so you can pivot the motor to the angle you want. Cut a relief kerf through the fence and into the table if one doesn't exist for this bevel angle already.

Make beveled crosscuts just as you would an ordinary crosscut. Start with the motor fully retracted to the vertical column, and pull it slowly through the wood. Set up the cut so short sections of waste rest on the table and do not lie on the blade as they are cut free.

Making Rip Cuts

Radial-arm saws are capable of making rip cuts, similar to a table saw, however this technique requires extreme caution. It's imperative to set up and make these cuts carefully to ensure your safety. The best material to rip on a radial-arm saw is plywood, MDF or other sheet goods that do not have natural grain direction. On a table saw, the splitter will help keep solid lumber from pinching the blade behind the cut, which can lead to kickback. Your radial-arm saw may or may not have a splitter component on the antikickback rod that you'll use for ripping. Therefore, there's no physical divider to prevent the wood from closing up during a cut. If you have to rip solid lumber, be sure to flatten one face and edge carefully to create reliable reference surfaces to slide along the table and fence. (For more on surfacing lumber, see Chapter Three.)

Aside from choosing and preparing stock carefully, it's important to set up your saw properly for ripping. Refer to your owner's manual for the correct procedure. The basic setup involves pivoting the saw's yoke so the blade is parallel to the fence board. Most saws will have a lock that engages when the yoke pivots to the ripping position. You can rip with the blade facing you or facing the fence, whichever you prefer.

When the blade faces you, the saw is set up for wider ripping capacity. You'll stand on the left side of the saw in this configuration and feed the workpiece from left to right. If you orient the blade to face the fence, you'll stand on the right side of the saw and feed from right to left across the saw table. Always feed workpieces into the blade so the teeth are rising up from underneath the workpiece. Never feed the wood into the blade with the teeth cutting downward. The blade will have a tendency to self-feed, pulling the wood out of your hands. At best, you'll lose control of the cut and possibly damage your saw. At worst, the blade will pull your hands through as well.

Follow the photo sequence shown here to set up and carry out a rip cut with the blade facing the front of the saw. To set up the width of cut, pull the motor along the arm until the distance from the blade to the fence matches the workpiece width you want to make. Lock the motor carriage on the arm (most saws will have a clamp knob on the carriage for this purpose). Lower the blade to create a shallow kerf cut in the saw table.

To set up a radial-arm saw for ripping, pivot the motor so the blade is parallel to the front of the saw table.

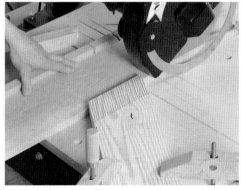

When ripping narrow workpieces or solid wood, install a featherboard ahead of the blade to keep workpieces pressed securely against the fence. Never install a featherboard behind the blade, where it could close up the cut and create a dangerous kickback situation.

Move the motor carriage along the saw arm until the blade lines up with a reference mark on your workpiece. Lock the motor carriage securely.

175

Rotate the blade guard down until it almost touches the workpiece. It will serve as both a shield and a holddown during ripping.

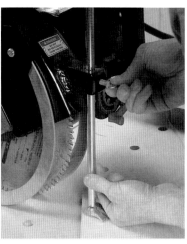

Lower and lock the antikickback rod so the fingers drag lightly on the wood. In the event of kickback, the fingers will dig in and keep the blade from pulling the wood backward.

With the width of cut established, set up the blade guard for ripping. On a radial-arm saw, the blade guard pivots forward and down to shield as much of the leading edge of the blade as possible during ripping. The front edge of the guard also serves as a holddown in the event the blade lifts the workpiece off the table. Use your workpiece as a spacer for positioning

the guard; set the guard about 1/8 in. above the workpiece. Once the guard is set and tightened on the motor housing, lower and lock the antikickback rod on the back side of the guard. Set the rod height so it just clears the top of the workpiece and the antickickback fingers make contact with the workpiece. The purpose of the fingers is to dig into the wood in the event the blade pulls the wood backward during cutting.

If you'll be ripping a long or wide workpiece, set up sturdy outfeed support on the right side of the saw and in front, if necessary. Have a long push stick nearby to guide the end of the cut. To make the rip cut, stand on the left side of the saw with your body on the left side of the wood. Never stand behind the end of the board—the saw will shoot it in this direction during kickback. Start the saw and feed the wood slowly along the fence and into the blade. Keep the workpiece pressed firmly against the fence as the cut progresses, and feed with a smooth, even motion. When the end of the workpiece reaches the table, use a push stick to feed it the rest of the way past the blade to complete the cut.

Set a long push stick close by before you begin the cut and make sure there's sturdy outfeed support behind the saw. Begin the rip cut by feeding the workpiece along the fence and slowly into the blade. Stand to the left of the workpiece so your body is clear of it at all times.

Feed the workpiece through the blade with a smooth, steady motion. Keep one edge pressed against the fence throughout the cut.

Use a long push stick to feed the workpiece completely past the blade to finish the cut. Keep your hands clear of the blade at all times.

Install a dado blade on a radial saw with the teeth facing clockwise on the arbor. Distribute the chipper blades uniformly and so the teeth do not touch.

Cutting Dadoes

Radial-arm saws are ideal for cutting dadoes with a dado blade, especially on long or heavy workpieces that would be unwieldy to cut with a table saw. Install the dado blade with the teeth facing clockwise, in the same orientation as a standard blade on the saw. For stacked dado blades, arrange the chippers uniformly around the arbor to help distribute the weight and balance the blade.

To set up a dado cut, raise the saw arm so the height of the blade teeth off the saw table matches the depth of dado you want to cut. Use a combination square or the actual workpiece to help set the blade height, and make the first dado cut on a piece of scrap with the same thickness as your actual workpiece. Line up the blade to a reference line on your workpiece, just as you would a normal crosscut. Pull the blade from its fully retracted position through the fence and workpiece to make the cut. Twist your upper body with your arms locked to pull the blade along. As soon as the blade completes the cut, retract the motor and turn off the saw. Check your test piece for accuracy, and change the dado blade height as necessary to fine-tune the setting. Then

proceed to make the final cuts on your project workpiece. Use a slower feed rate than you do with a standard blade to keep from overwhelming the motor—the dado blade is removing more material with each pass.

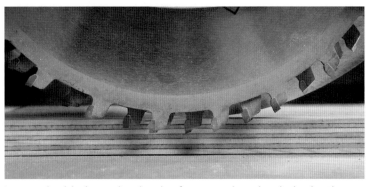

Lower the blade so the depth of cut matches the dado depth you wish to cut. Check your depth setting with a combination square or by making a test cut on scrap.

Workpiece

You'll need to cut a kerf slot through the fence for dadoing. If you do this beforehand, it can make a handy reference for lining up the actual dadoes on the workpiece.

Use a slow, steady feed rate when pulling the motor carriage across the workpiece to make dado cuts. Return the blade to the starting position before setting up the next cut.

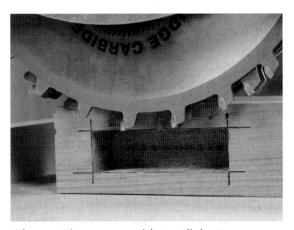

When cutting tenons with a radial-arm saw, use the mortised workpiece to help set the blade depth for trimming the tenon cheeks and shoulders.

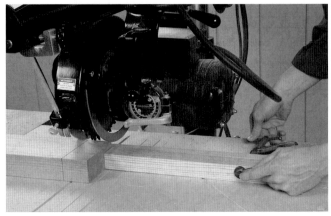

Clamp a stop block to the saw's fence to serve as an index for establishing the tenon shoulder cuts. Line up the far side of the blade so it meets your tenon shoulder layout lines.

With the workpiece pressed against the stop block, make the first cut to form the tenon shoulder.

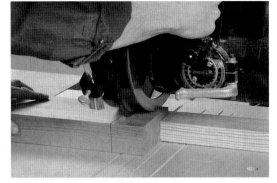

Once the shoulder is cut, slide the workpiece away from the stop block and cut away the rest of the waste in several more passes to create the tenon cheek.

When one side of the tenon is finished, flip the workpiece to the other face and use the stop block again to register the other shoulder cut.

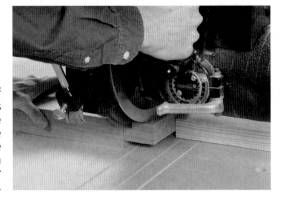

Cutting Tenons With A Dado Blade

Using the basic dadoing technique, it's easy to cut tenons, lap joints or rabbets with a radial-arm saw. For tenons, mark the thickness and location of the tenon shoulders on the workpiece. Raise the blade until it's even with the top shoulder of the tenon, and clamp a stop block to the fence so the blade meets the shoulder on the first cut. Then cut the first cheek and shoulder in a series of side-by-side passes to remove all the waste, starting with the shoulder cut. When the first cheek and shoulder are completed, flip the workpiece over, set it against the stop block again and repeat the process for cutting the other cheek and shoulder. Follow the same process to set up and cut rabbets or lap joints.

If you replace the fence board on your saw with a taller fence, you can even cut the short end cheeks and shoulders of a tenon by standing the workpiece on edge against the tall fence. Raise the blade accordingly and reset the stop block so the short shoulder cuts will line up with the broad shoulder cuts you've already made.

MITER SAW TECHNIQUES

Miter saws cut on the downstroke, against the rotation of the blade rather than with it, as on a radial-arm saw. Making a cut with a miter saw involves pivoting the motor down on the saw arm and plunging it into the workpiece. Since the teeth are cutting downward, the plunging motion helps to press the workpiece against the saw table and fence. Kickbacks are relatively uncommon with a miter saw, and they typically only happen because of defects in the wood or internal stresses that pinch the blade during cutting. Cutting against the blade's rotation also cancels the possibility of the blade climbing up and out of the cut, as can happen on a radial-arm saw. With reasonable care and proper stock preparation, a miter saw is a safe tool to use for even novice woodworkers.

A miter saw can be used without any modification, but for crosscutting long or heavy workpieces, you'll want to add suitable supports on either side of the saw. Clamp the saw down to a large, sturdy workbench, and add blocks of scrap next to the saw to provide temporary workpiece support. A better long-term setup for your miter saw is to build a pair of extension tables as shown below. Extension tables create solid support surfaces, and you can outfit them with numeric scales to create a highly precise crosscutting system. Woodworking project books and magazines often publish plans for building miter saw stations. If a miter saw is a permanent part of your home shop, a miter saw station will help you make the most of the saw's versatility and accuracy.

A pair of extension tables on either side of your miter saw will improve workpiece support. You can also use them with stop blocks for accurate, repetitive crosscutting.

Crosscutting With A Miter Saw

There are no special techniques to learn for making accurate crosscuts

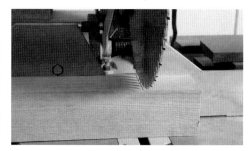

With the saw turned off, line up the edge of the blade teeth with a reference line on the workpiece. Make sure the blade will cut on the waste side of the line.

With the motor in the fully raised position, start the saw and pivot the blade slowly down into the workpiece. When the blade finishes the cut, turn off the saw and wait for the blade to stop spinning before raising it out of the wood.

Clamp a stop block to your extension table to set up repetitive rip cuts. The distance from the closest edge of the blade teeth to the stop block sets the workpiece length.

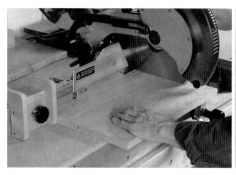 

You can crosscut workpieces wider than the blade's maximum cutting width by making the cut in two passes instead of one. Make the first cut as far as the blade will reach (left). Then flip the workpiece over and make another cut to finish it (right). A clamped stop block keeps both cuts aligned.

with a miter saw. To line up the cut, tilt the saw blade down until it touches the workpiece, and align the blade with your reference line. Raise the blade back to the top of the saw's travel, and hold the workpiece firmly against the saw fence with your left hand. Make sure your hand is clear of the warning marks posted on the saw table or fence. Start the saw and pivot it slowly and smoothly down through the wood to make the cut. When the blade cuts the workpiece in two, release the tool trigger and wait for the blade to stop before retracting it up and out of the cut.

It's possible to make repetitive crosscuts by clamping a stop block to the saw fence or to an extension table next to the saw. The distance from the end of the stop block to the closest edge of the blade teeth determines the length of cut.

Occasionally, you'll need to crosscut workpieces that are wider than the saw's maximum width of cut. In these situations, you have two options to try. If the workpiece is only slightly wider than the cutting capacity of the blade, slip a piece of 1x scrap wood beneath the workpiece on the saw table. Adding a spacer raises the workpiece to expose it to more of the blade's circumference, which may help complete the cut in one pass. Spacers are most effective on thin workpieces where the extra reach that's required isn't significant.

For thicker workpieces, make the crosscut in two passes without adding a spacer. Cut all the way through the workpiece on the first pass, giving the blade plenty of time to penetrate the thick material. If the blade starts to bog down in the cut, slow down your feed rate. Then, flip the workpiece to the other face and carefully line up the kerf from the first cut with the blade. A second pass will complete the crosscut.

Cutting Miters And Bevels

Miter saws excel at making accurate angle cuts. The saw table swivels and locks to any angle you choose, right or left. There are also a group of preset "detents" for locking the blade at common angles like 15°, 22.5°, 31.6° and 45°. To make a typical picture frame–style miter cut, lay the workpiece faceup and against the saw fence. Swivel the table to the angle you need to make and line up the blade with the angled reference mark you've drawn on the workpiece. Hold the wood securely and plunge the blade down and through the workpiece to make the cut.

Another option for cutting miters is to stand the workpiece on edge against the saw fence. This is a common way to orient base molding for cutting scarf joints or outside corners where molding wraps around a wall. Line up the blade the same way as for making flat miter cuts. Make sure the workpiece isn't wider than the saw blade's depth of cut so you can cut through it in one pass without interference from the blade guard or arbor washer.

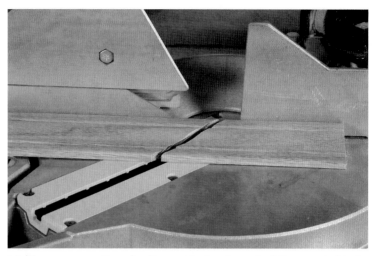

Making a conventional miter cut is simple: swivel the saw table to the desired angle, line up the blade with a reference line on the workpiece and plunge the blade down to make the cut.

By unlocking and tipping the saw arm off of 90°, a miter saw will also make bevel cuts. Follow the same process as for setting up and making flat miter cuts. Line up the blade with the cutting line by lowering the saw blade down until it touches the workpiece. You may need to slide the tall fence extension that comes with many miter saws out of the way so the blade can move through the cut without the guard contacting the fence.

Baseboards and other workpieces can be bevel-cut by standing them on edge against the fence and swiveling the saw table.

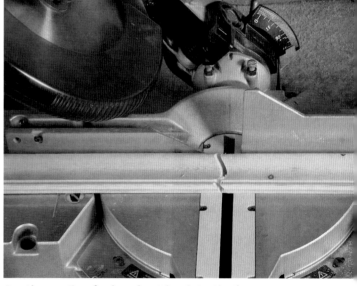

Another option for bevel-cutting is to tip the saw arm to the desired bevel angle and keep the saw table locked at 90°.

Compound miter cuts combine both bevel and miter angles together. They're common when cutting crown molding for trimwork and furniture. Dialing in the precise angles required for a tight joint can be challenging.

Combining miter and bevel settings enables your miter saw to make compound miter cuts as well. Compound miter cuts are necessary for cutting crown and cove moldings to fit around the tops of cabinets and casework or for trimming the intersection of walls and ceilings. Your saw's owner's manual may provide a helpful chart for determining the correct miter and bevel settings to use. Try your setup on test material first to make sure you've got the angle dialed in correctly, then cut the actual molding pieces.

Another approach for making compound cuts in moldings is to set them upside down and backwards against the saw fence and table. Visualize the saw's fence as the wall and the saw's table as the ceiling. In this position, the molding mimics the inverted way it will tip against a cabinet or off of a wall. You'll sometimes hear this referred to as cutting molding in the "sprung" position. From the standpoint of saw setup, cutting molding in the sprung position is easier than laying it flat on the saw table: it isn't necessary to tip the saw to a bevel angle. Simply pivot the saw table and cut the molding as you would a standard flat miter cut.

You can hold the molding against the saw without other clamping aids, but it can be difficult to hold the material steady during cutting. The wider the crown molding and the narrower its support edges, the harder it is to hold precisely. Simple compound miter cutting jigs are available with a stop that holds the molding steady; all you do is hold the jig against the saw table. These jigs are adjustable to suit various widths of crown molding. If you are cutting lots of expensive crown, a jig will be a blessing.

The easiest way to make the compound angle cuts required for crown moldings is to use a jig that holds the moldings in the correct bevel position on the saw.

Avoiding Tearout And Cutting Short Workpieces

The gap between the fence sections on a miter saw is too wide to support workpieces right up to the blade. When the blade passes through the workpiece, the teeth will often splinter the wood where they exit on the back side. Tearout is also common around the throatplate opening where the blade plunges down into the table. The best way to reduce or even eliminate tearout altogether is to back up the workpiece you're cutting with a piece of scrap hardboard or other wood. Set one scrap between the workpiece and fence and a second piece under the workpiece on the saw table. If you are making just one cut, it isn't necessary to fix the scraps in place on the saw. Just hold the workpiece tightly against them during cutting. For repeated cutting, secure the scraps to the saw with strips of double-sided carpet tape. A few pieces of scrap held in the right places will make an impressive difference.

A narrower blade opening eliminates the tearout on the back side of a cut that would otherwise happen with the saw's standard blade and table openings. Notice the cleaner edges produced on the left workpiece using a narrow kerf opening.

Reducing the size of your miter saw's blade and fence is also a convenient improvement when cutting tiny slivers and offcuts. These would otherwise fall into the blade opening.

An excellent way to prevent tearout on a miter saw is to tape scraps of hardboard across the saw table and fence where the blade passes through. Cut through them to create a smaller opening around the blade.

TIP

CHOOSING A MITER SAW BLADE

Most new miter saws come with 24- to 40-tooth general-purpose saw blades. These standard blades are fine for cutting construction lumber, but you'll get a much cleaner cut for woodworking purposes if you switch to a higher tooth count blade. Blades with 60 to 100 teeth counts are ideal for finer crosscutting work. Saw blade manufacturers sell blades engineered specifically for miter saws. These precision blades can be expensive, but you'll never regret paying more for a high quality blade once you see how well it performs.

DRILLING TECHNIQUES

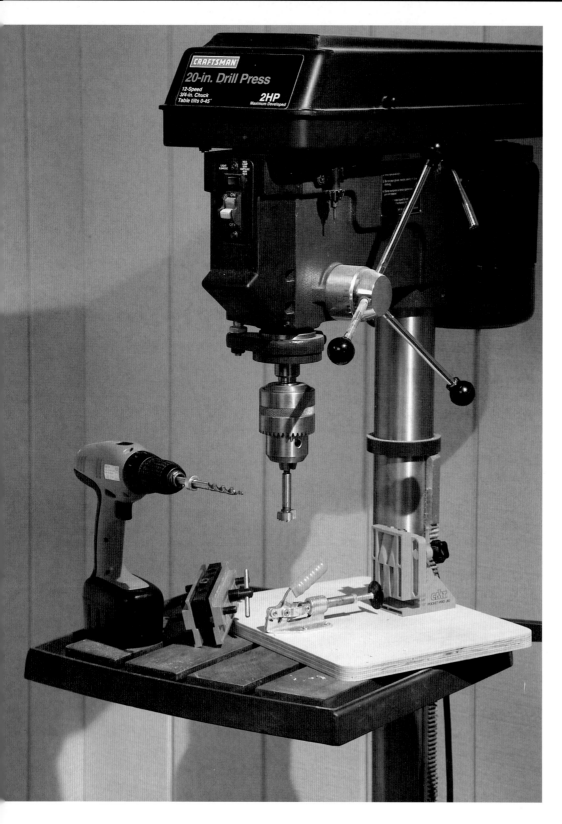

Whether you are counterboring screw holes for wood plugs, drilling holes for a dowel joint or boring the entry hole in the front of a new wood duck house, woodworking involves a fair amount of time spent drilling holes. Most DIYers and aspiring woodworkers are familiar with how to use an ordinary power drill and drill bit for drilling holes. A corded or cordless drill is, of course, the workhorse tool for smaller drilling tasks. It won't be the best choice for drilling perfectly straight, large or stopped holes. In these situations, the best tool for the job is a dedicated drill press. The following section will show you how to use a drill press correctly. We'll also cover a few specialized joints you can make with a handheld drill and a few handy, inexpensive drilling jigs.

Basic Drill Press Drilling Procedure

Drill presses are among the simplest shop machines to use. An enclosed motor on top of the machine spins a vertical shaft inside a moveable column called a quill. A gearing system allows you to move the shaft up and down with a lever to drill holes. Most drill presses have three clusters of stacked pulleys and a pair of drive belts for setting the drilling speed to optimize the cutting action. Large bits, hard materials or metal require slower drilling speeds than small bits in soft wood or plastic. A chart inside the lid of the pulley compartment will help you choose the right speed for the job. To change speeds, you loosen a pair of lock knobs and slide the motor forward to release the belt tension. Slipping the belts among the different pulley sheaves changes the drilling speed. A three-jaw chuck mounted to the bottom of the vertical shaft holds bits securely.

Once you've tightened a drill bit in the chuck and set the machine for the correct drilling speed, place your workpiece on the drill press table. Check the travel of the bit up and down by moving the handle; you want to be sure the bit will pass all the way through the workpiece if you are drilling a "through" hole. If your drill press table has a hole in the center, make sure the bit will plunge down into this hole at the bottom of the stroke and not drill into the table itself. If there's no hole in the table, place a piece of scrap underneath the workpiece. This will also help reduce tearout on the bottom side of the workpiece.

Line up the tip of the bit with the center point of the hole you want to drill. If you need to drill a "stopped" hole that only penetrates partway through the workpiece, your drill press should have a depth stop system to set the bottom limit of the drill stroke. On some drill presses, the stop will consist of a pair of jam

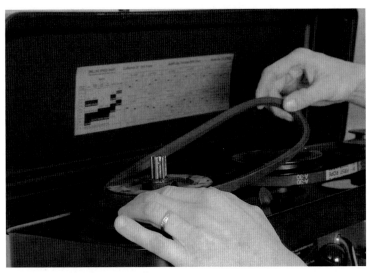

Set the correct drilling speed for the bit size and material type you are drilling by arranging the drive belts correctly on the pulley clusters. Most drill presses will have a belt configuration chart inside the pulley compartment.

nuts on a threaded shaft. The stop may be incorporated into the quill handle as well. Check your owner's manual to learn more about the sys-

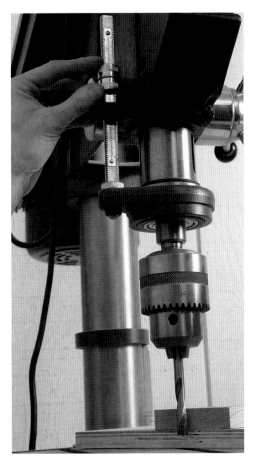

Depth stops on your drill press prevent you from drilling too far or worse— into the metal table! They're most handy for making stopped cuts.

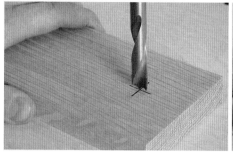

There's no rocket science involved with drilling holes on a drill press. Simply lower the bit and align the tip with the center point of the hole. Raise the chuck, start the machine and lower the bit gradually into the wood to bore the hole. For small holes, you can hold the wood safely without clamping it down.

tem that comes with your drill press. Set the stops accordingly for the hole you are drilling.

If the bit you are using is less than 1 in. or so in diameter or your workpiece is large enough to hold easily on the table, it's safe to simply hold the wood while drilling it. Bore the hole by starting the machine and lowering the bit into the wood. You can drill the hole in one pass if the bit seems to clear the chips adequately. Otherwise, make the hole in a series of plunging cuts to help clear the chips out of the hole and off of the bit.

When you are using large hole cutters or Forstner bits, or for optimal precision, clamp a piece of scrap wood across the drill press table to act as a fence. The fence will prevent the bit from pulling the wood out of your hands and spinning it. A fence also makes it easy to drill a series of perfectly aligned holes along the length of a workpiece. Just slide the workpiece along the fence to make lines of shelf pin holes or to drill a mortise (see page 187).

Fences are easy to set up correctly. Lower the bit until it meets the center point of the hole you plan to drill, and press it lightly into the wood with the drill press turned off. If your depth stop has a jam nut for stopping the chuck in the "down" position, set it to hold the bit in the workpiece. Or, just hold the handle down for the next step. Slide your scrap fence against the back surface of the workpiece, and hold it in place while you raise the bit off the workpiece. Without moving the fence, use a pair of clamps to secure it to the drill press table. Check the fence position by lowering the bit again and see if the bit still lines up correctly.

TIP

TIGHTENING A CHUCK CORRECTLY

Installing a bit in a drill press chuck may seem obvious: stick the chuck key in a hole, hold the bit inside the jaws and tighten the chuck. However, a little trick will help prevent bits from slipping—especially large bits with smooth shafts. After you've tightened the chuck jaws with the key, turn the chuck and try tightening the jaws using the other two chuck holes.

You'll probably find that there's actually some play left. Snugging the jaws up using all three chuck key holes helps distribute the clamping pressure all around the bit for a better grip.

Back workpieces up with a clamped fence when you are drilling with larger bits. Hand pressure alone is not enough to withstand the rotational forces developed by large bits.

Mortising With A Drill Press

A drill press provides a safe and easy means for cutting mortises for mortise and tenon joints. The process involves drilling a series of side-by-side holes along your workpiece to hog out most of the waste. You can use either a Forstner bit or a sharp, brad-point bit to drill mortises. Either choice will shear a clean hole into the wood. Ordinary twist bits tend to tear the wood fibers around the entry hole.

Set up the mortise cut by first laying out its location and proportions on the workpiece. For this application, you'll also need to clamp a fence behind the workpiece to keep the holes perfectly aligned in the mortise area. Use the depth stops to establish the mortise depth. Drill the mortise slightly deeper than the tenon you plan to make for joint. The extra clearance at the bottom of the mortise will give excess glue room to pool without holding the joint open.

Install a clamped fence behind the workpiece. Line up the mortise layout line with the tip of the bit before tightening the fence clamps.

Drill out the waste, starting at one end of the mortise and locating the holes so the edges of each hole touch but do not overlap. Slide the workpiece along the fence to locate each new hole. Work your way along the mortise until you reach the other end. This series of passes will leave crescent-shaped areas of waste in between. Make a second round of passes to drill away this waste. Continue the drilling process until most of the waste is removed.

Complete the mortise by squaring up the ends with a sharp chisel. Clamp the workpiece in a bench vise or to your workbench surface to hold it steady. Hold the chisel vertically and tap it down into the mortise with a mallet. It doesn't take hammer-forced blows to tackle this task; take your time and tap the chisel down gently. Once the ends are squared, shave the side walls of the mortise smooth with a sharp, wide chisel.

Once you've set the depth stops for the correct mortise depth, drill out the waste in a series of side-by-side holes. Make these holes just touch but not overlap.

Drill out the crescent-shaped waste areas between the first round of holes to clean out the mortise area further.

Use the drill press to remove as much waste as possible. A few rounds of passes should produce a fairly clean, smooth-walled mortise.

Shave the walls of the mortise and square up the ends with wide and narrow chisels. Clamp the workpiece in a bench vise for this task.

Cutting Wood Plugs

Tapered wood plugs are easy to make on a drill press with a set of plug cutters. A plug cutter shears away the wood and forms a plug inside a hollow in the center of the cutter. To cut plugs, start with a reasonably large piece of scrap stock. If you hold the scrap firmly against the drill press table, you don't have to clamp it in place or back it up with a fence. However, it's still a good idea to immobilize the wood in one of these ways, especially when you are cutting large plugs. Since plug cutters have no center point, they can chatter or wander a bit when starting to cut. Plunge the cutter into the wood until it nearly bottoms out in the wood, then withdraw the cutter. To remove the plugs, break them out with a screwdriver, or stand the scrap on edge and slice the plugs free with a bandsaw, similar to making a resaw cut.

A doweling jig with a built-in clamping feature makes it easy to create dowel joints with a hand drill.

Drilling A Dowel Joint

Dowel joints are quick and easy to make with a handheld drill and a doweling jig. The one shown here clamps to each member of the joint and automatically centers itself on the workpiece. It comes with a set of removable drill guides in various sizes for boring $1/4$-, $5/16$- or $3/8$-in.-dia. dowel holes.

For dowel joints that connect parts of a frame, usually a pair of dowels spaced evenly across the joint is all that's required. Use more dowels for joining wider drawer parts or for joining sections of a large glued-up panel. To make the joint, hold the parts together and draw a pair of lines across the joint to mark the dowel locations. Thread a drill guide into the doweling jig, and clamp it to each workpiece. Markings on the jig make it easy to align the drill bit with the registration marks you've drawn on the workpiece. Use a piece of tape to "flag" the depth of cut on the drill bit you'll use for boring the dowel holes; make the hole depth in

Cutting plugs with a plug cutter is similar to drilling a conventional hole. The center hollow of the cutter creates the plug. Plug cutters are designed to be used in a drill press, not with a handheld drill.

Break the plugs free with a screwdriver or chisel. Or cut them out by resawing the workpiece on the bandsaw.

each workpiece a little more than half the length of the dowels.

Run the drill at a medium to high speed as you plunge it down into the drill guides to bore each hole. You may need to withdraw the bit a couple of times to clear the wood chips. Depending on the design of your jig, you may need to re-clamp the doweling jig to align and drill the other holes. Once the holes are completed, insert a pair of dowels into one half of the joint without glue, and assemble the joint "dry" to check the alignment of the holes. If the joint fits together properly, pull the pieces apart and use a pair of pliers to carefully remove the dowels. Spread a light coating of glue on the dowels as well as the contact surfaces of the joint parts and clamp it together to complete the joint.

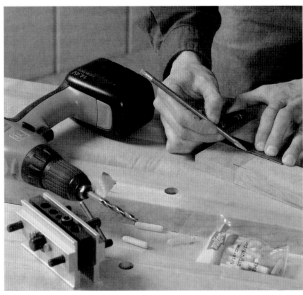

Lay out the dowel locations across both parts of the dowel joint. Use tape to establish the correct drilling depth on the drill bit.

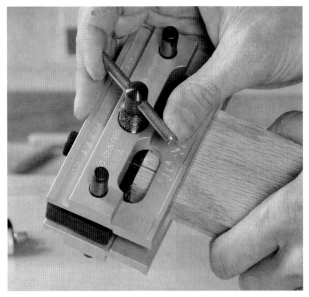

Clamp the doweling jig in place so the jig alignment marks line up with the registration marks you've drawn on the workpiece.

Clamp the workpiece in a bench vise and drill the holes. A bushing in the doweling jig guides the bit accurately.

Once both joint parts are drilled, insert dowels in the holes without glue and slip the joint together to check its fit.

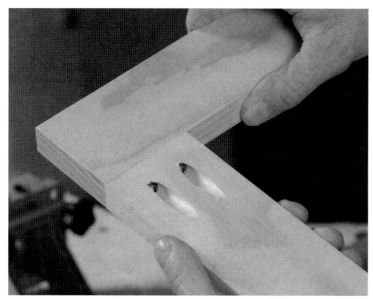

Pocket hole joints are ideal for making frames and joining cabinet parts together. They are quick, incredibly strong and require no glue.

Making A Pocket Hole Joint

Pocket hole joinery is another fast and simple option for building surprisingly strong frame joints. Pocket

hole joints can also be used for making edge-to-edge butt joints, attaching table legs to aprons and fastening tops to cabinets. Regardless of the application, the process for making a pocket hole joint is the same. The jig allows you to drill steep, angled pocket holes into one half of the joint for countersinking the screws that hold the joint together. Auger-tip pocket hole screws cut their own pilot holes in the mating workpiece.

To make these joints, you'll need a pocket hole jig, a specialized stepped drill bit made for drilling pocket holes and panhead, auger tip screws. Pocket hole jigs can usually be purchased as a system that comes with everything you need.

Follow the instructions that come with the jig for setting it to match the thickness of the joint part you'll be drilling. The jig shown below has a material thickness gauge that makes the initial setup easy. You'll also need to set the drilling depth of the bit in the jig to stop the counterbored holes properly. Slip the drill bit into one of the drilling guides and follow the instruction manual to set

Drilling the steeply pitched holes for a pocket hole joint requires a specialized jig and stepped drill bit. You can buy all the necessary components in a pocket hole jig kit.

the correct depth of cut. Clamp a stop collar to the bit to limit the depth of cut.

With the jig and bit set up correctly, plunge the bit down into the jig's drilling guides to bore the countersunk holes. Clear the chips as you drill by pulling the bit out of the guides a few times. Once the holes are cut, clamp the joint parts together and drive a pair of panhead screws down into the holes to attach the parts. Once the screws are tight, the joint is finished. Pocket hole joints are strong enough with screws alone that glue isn't necessary.

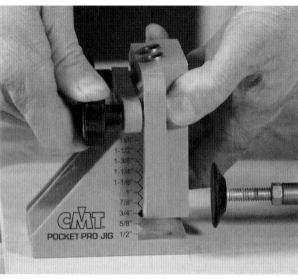

Adjust the jig correctly for the thickness of material you'll be drilling. This model has a rack-toothed gauge to make the process easy.

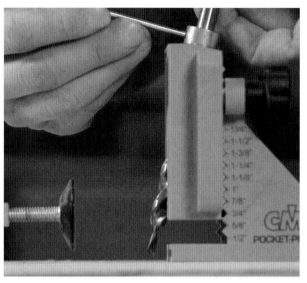

Tighten the drill bit's depth collar to stop the bit at the correct drilling depth. This will be detailed in the owner's manual that comes with your pocket hole jig.

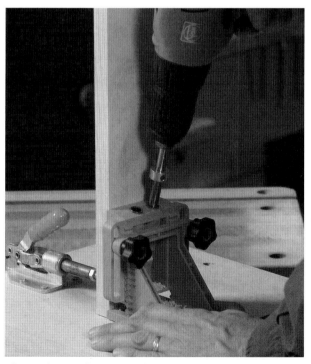

Clamp the workpiece in the jig and bore both angled holes for recessing the pocket screws. Only one of the two joint parts needs to be drilled.

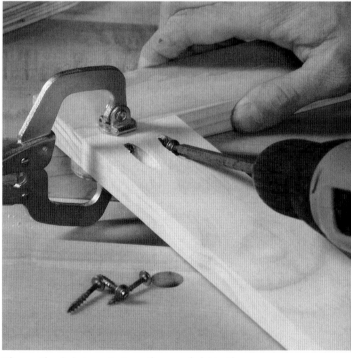

Clamp the joint parts together and drive the connecting screws through the pocket holes and into the undrilled joint part. No glue is required.

Drilling A Counterbored Screw Joint

Screws and glue are a sturdy way to strengthen the common butt joint, and usually you'll want to hide the screw heads so they don't show on the finished project. The simplest option for covering screw heads is to use wood putty, but it usually won't match the surrounding wood, even when it's tinted. Over time the putty can shrink and fall out. Instead of helping the joint blend into the project, poorly matched putty will just call more attention to itself. The better way to hide screw heads is to drill counterbored holes for the screws and install plugs made from the same wood as the rest of the project. Well-matched wood plugs can make the screw locations virtually disappear.

A counterbore drill bit makes the process of drilling counterbored screw holes easy. The bit has an adjustable, tapered collar that cuts the shank hole and the counterbore all at once. To set up the bit, loosen the collar with a small Allen wrench and extend the bit so the bit length plus the tapered portion of the collar are a little shorter than the length of the screws you're installing in the joint. The taper creates a beveled depression for seating the screwhead. Use a medium drilling speed to bore the hole. When drilling, sink the counterbore collar into the wood about $1/4$ in. past the tapered portion. This will create a $1/4$-in.-deep counterbore for inserting the wood plug. It's a good idea to stop the bit once or twice during drilling to check the depth of the counterbore—you don't want to accidentally drill too far.

Drive a screw into each counterbored hole and tighten them down until the joint is snug. Then use a plug cutter in your drill press to create matching wood plugs (see page 188). Leave the plugs longer than necessary. Use a dab of glue to install the wood plugs, pressing the tapered ends into the counterbores. Be careful to line up the wood grain on the plugs with the surrounding grain as best you can. Trim off the excess with a flush-cutting saw, or pare the plugs flat with a sharp chisel.

Set the depth collar on the counterbore bit so the drill bit will make a pilot hole slightly shorter than the length of the screw shank. You can stop the collar when it forms a taper for the screw head or continue drilling even further to create room for a wood plug.

Drive screws into the pilot holes to connect the joint parts. Rub the threads with a little paste wax to make the screws drive more easily.

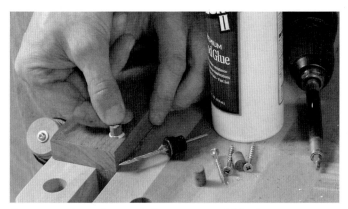

On counterbored screw joints, you can hide the screw heads with wood plugs. Apply a dab of glue in the hole and press the plug in place.

Trim off the excess plug flush with the surrounding surface. A flexible flush-trim saw makes this easy.

BEST DRILL BITS FOR WOODWORKING

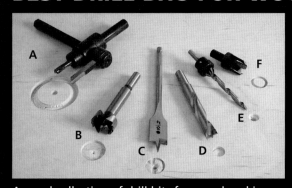

A good collection of drill bits for woodworking include, from left to right: a circle cutter, Forstner bits, spade bits with spur tips, brad point bits, countersink/counterbore bits and plug cutters.

There are a variety of bits to choose from for drilling clean, accurate holes in wood. Here's a brief description of each type:

Circle cutters **(A),** also called fly cutters, consist of a center mandrel that holds an adjustable rod with a chisel-shaped cutter on the end. A twist bit at the center keeps the cutter from wandering and locates the center of the cut. Circle cutters can score holes with clean edges or even make perfect wheel shapes. Change the size of the hole by moving the rod and cutter in or out from the mandrel. For safety's sake, use circle cutters at slow speeds and only in a drill press. Clamp the workpiece down firmly to the drill press table before drilling, and keep your fingers and sleeves clear of the spinning bit.

Forstner bits (B) are excellent choices for drilling large, flat-bottomed holes. They're ideal for drilling mortises with a drill press. A sharpened or sawtooth rim slices a crisp entry hole without creating tearout, and chisel-shaped cutters remove the waste in large chips. Forstner bits are not intended for hand drilling; be sure to use a drill press for best results.

Spade bits (C) For faster cutting, spur-tipped spade bits are another good option for either drill press use or hand drilling. They won't cut an entry hole as cleanly as a Forstner bit, but tearout is generally minimal. Spade bits don't produce a flat-bottomed hole. The spurred variety is better suited for woodworking than spade bits without spurs; save these for carpentry and remodeling jobs.

Brad point bits (D) have a center spur for locating the exact center of a hole, and a pair of sharpened tips score a clean entry hole. They're suitable for both hand drilling or drill press use and are made in diameters up to 1 in. Use these instead of conventional twist bits for general hole drilling tasks.

Countersink/counterbore bits (E) have a conventional or tapered twist bit mounted to a counterbore collar. The collar cuts either a countersink for recessing a screw head or a counterbore for a wood plug, depending on how far you drill into the wood. The collar can be adjusted on the drill bit to suit different screw lengths.

Plug cutters (F) form round wood plugs used to fill counterbored holes. They're usually sold in sets for cutting a range of plug sizes. Each cutter makes one size of wood plug. Plug cutters cannot be used in a hand drill, because they have no center point to prevent the cutter from wandering.

MORTISING MACHINE & BISCUIT JOINER TECHNIQUES

Mortising machines, which are also called hollow-chisel mortisers, are single-purpose tools intended for cutting square-cornered mortises. They function similar to a drill press: a three-jawed chuck inside the machine moves up and down with a side-mounted hand lever. The chuck spins a modified twist bit that fits inside a square chisel. The chisel mounts on a fixed collar that holds it stationary during cutting. When the bit is plunged into the wood, four sharpened tips on the end of the chisel cut the perimeter of the hole, and the center twist bit removes the waste. If you make lots of mortises, there's no faster way to create them than with this efficient, easy-to-operate machine.

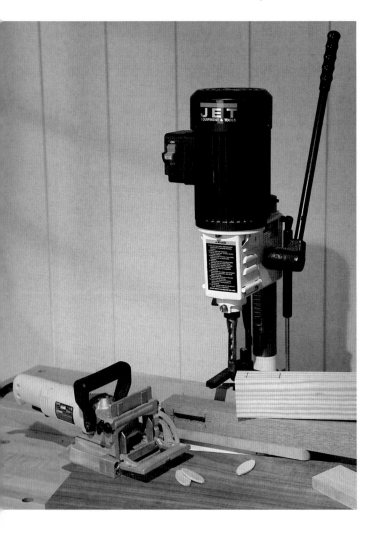

The combined action of drilling and chiseling makes a mortising machine arguably the fastest way to cut mortises.

Mortising machines use hollow chisel bits, which consist of a modified twist bit that fits inside a square chisel with pointed tips. The drill removes most of the waste, while the chisel squares up the cut edges.

Mortise-Cutting Procedure

Setting up and using a mortising machine is a fairly straightforward process. Open the chuck inside the machine and back out the chisel collar screw enough so you can insert the center bit and chisel. Clamp the bit in the chuck and tighten the chisel collar enough to hold both in place for the moment. The next order of business is to create clearance between the end of the bit and the end of the chisel. To do this, loosen and slide the chisel down from its flange collar on the motor head about $1/16$ in. and tighten the chisel enough to hold it in place. Loosen the bit in the chuck and push the bit all the way up until it seats in the end of the chisel. Tighten the drill chuck securely. Loosen the chisel's setscrew again, and push the chisel up against the flange collar. Tighten it enough to hold it in place. This will create a $1/16$-in. space between the bit and the chisel to help clear the wood chips.

Now, lower the handle until the chisel nearly touches the mortiser's table. Slide the fence on the machine forward, and loosen the chisel collar screw. Move the fence until it touches the chisel. Twist the chisel left or right and press the fence against it until both surfaces are flush. Adjusting the chisel parallel with the fence in this way will ensure that the walls of the mortise will be parallel to the edges of the workpiece. Tighten the chisel firmly in its collar, and raise the handle.

Next, lay out your mortise shape on the workpiece, and set it on the mortiser table against the fence. Move the fence in or out until the chisel lines up with the mortise, and lock the fence in place. Your mortising machine will have a depth stop, which usually consists of a rod and clamp. Lower the chisel next to the workpiece to establish the mortise depth, and lock the depth stop rod to stop the chisel here. Test the stop position by moving the chisel up and down. Finally, raise the bit and adjust the mortiser's holddown clamp over the workpiece. The holddown will keep the bit from lifting the work-

Slide the fence and workpiece in or out until the chisel aligns with the mortise layout lines on the workpiece. Tighten the fence's locking lever.

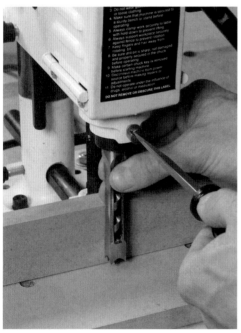

The fence and chisel must be aligned with one another in order to produce mortises that are parallel to the workpiece edges. Slide the fence forward and adjust the chisel flush against it.

Set the depth of cut for the mortise by lowering the chisel until it aligns with a depth layout line on the workpiece. Lock the machine's depth stop rod to hold this setting.

With the fence and chisel settings dialed in, begin to cut the mortise by making a pair of cuts to define the ends. Plunge the bit into the wood slowly and steadily so the bit can eject the chips.

Make additional passes along the mortise, spacing the cuts about one chisel width apart to remove more waste material. Spacing the cuts will keep the chisel from wandering into adjacent cuts.

Finally, drill out the remaining stepped-off areas. Once all the waste has been excavated, make one more round of plunge cuts to clean out any remaining material at the bottom of the mortise.

piece off the table when you retract it. Set the holddown so there's just enough play to slide the workpiece along the fence and table.

With the bit adjusted and the fence properly set and locked, start at one end of the mortise and plunge the chisel slowly into the workpiece. If you feed too quickly, chips may become impacted inside the bit instead of clearing properly. You'll know this is happening if the cutting action seems to decrease or if the chisel stops spitting out chips. Depending on the wood you're using, some amount of clogging may be inevitable. Feed slowly and steadily until the bit reaches the bottom of the cut. If the bit clogs up and starts to smoke, withdraw it and turn off the machine. Remove the impacted wood chips by rotating the bit in reverse by hand. A small screwdriver or scratch awl may help you pick out any remaining chips.

Cut both ends of the mortise first, then continue by making a series of plunge cuts along the length of the mortise. Space these cuts one chisel width apart. If you make them side by side, the chisel can wander out of the cut and possibly bend—the chisels are relatively flexible and delicate. Finish up the mortise with more passes to remove the intermediate waste areas. Once you've hogged out most of the waste, take another round of passes along the length of the mortise to clean up any waste that still may be present at the bottom of the cut.

TIP

LUBRICATING A MORTISING BIT FOR SMOOTHER CUTTING

A periodic light spray of dry lubricant can help keep a mortising chisel cutting smoothly.

One easy way to help your mortising chisels cut more cleanly is to spray them with a light coating of dry lubricant before use. The lubricant will keep resins from sticking and help the bit clear the chips more effectively. Choose a lube made for protecting machine tables that doesn't contain silicone; it can prevent glues and finishes from adhering properly to the wood.

Cutting Biscuit Joints

Biscuit joiners and mortising machines are actually kissing cousins, to some extent. A biscuit joiner essentially cuts an oval-shaped mortise that fits a loose tenon—in this case, shaped liked a football. Biscuit joiners are even easier to use than mortising machines. The tool has a moveable fence that adjusts up and down for locating the biscuit on the thickness of the workpiece. The fence also pivots for cutting slots in workpieces with beveled edges. Biscuit joiners have a circular, carbide-tipped blade that's normally retracted inside the tool. The fence assembly is spring-loaded on the motor housing. To make a biscuit slot, you hold the fence against the workpiece and plunge the blade into it, which compresses the fence springs and exposes the blade. After making a cut, the fence snaps back to the starting position to hide the blade again.

Biscuits used to be made in just three different sizes—#0, #10 and #20. Now, the popularity of biscuit joinery

A biscuit joiner's adjustable depth of cut makes it possible to cut at least three standard sizes of biscuits—#0, #10 and #20.

has opened the doors to many other sizes and types of biscuits. In addition to new micro-sized and oversized biscuits, you can also buy plastic biscuits for outdoor projects, two-part metal biscuits for making knockdown joinery and many other types.

BISCUIT JOINT VARIATIONS

There are numerous ways to configure biscuit joints for different woodworking applications. Really, any style of butt joint can be reinforced with biscuits. Biscuits are primarily used for aligning joints in panel construction. As these photos illustrate, however, you can build face frame corner joints by joining end grain to edge grain. You can also join miter joints for picture frames and bevel or right-angle joints for box corners. You can even install double sets of biscuits to join thick workpieces together. Regardless of the joint style, all you need are two workpieces with surfaces large enough to register against the joiner's fence. Make sure to choose a biscuit size small enough to keep the slots from becoming exposed when the joint is assembled.

Mitered joint.

Right-angle frame joint.

Right-angle box corner joint.

Bevel joint.

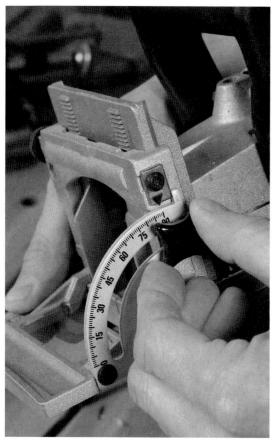

For cutting slots into the edge of a workpiece, adjust the fence to a right angle so the cuts will be parallel to the workpiece faces.

Adjust the fence up or down to position the slots correctly on the thickness of the workpiece. For 1x stock, it's common to center the biscuits on the workpiece thickness.

Regardless of the size or type of biscuit you choose, the technique for setting up the tool and making the cut is basically the same. First, set the fence to 0° so it creates a square corner to register against the workpiece. Adjust the fence up or down to locate the biscuit slot where you want it on the workpiece. For stock thicknesses up to about 1 in. you'll only need one row of biscuits to reinforce the joint. Usual protocol is to center the biscuit on the thickness of the workpiece. Placing biscuits too close to the surface of a workpiece, especially on plywood, can cause them to show through when they swell with glue moisture. It's a problem called telegraphing that's easy to avoid by simply centering the biscuits. You also need to set the depth of cut to match the biscuit size you are using for the joint. Your joiner has a knob that indicates each size of biscuit slot it can cut.

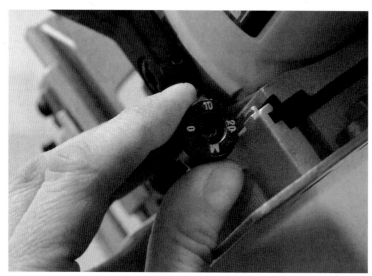

Set the machine's depth of cut index for the size of biscuit you'll be using.

Lay out the biscuit slot locations by setting the joint parts together and drawing short reference lines across the joint. There's no hard-and-fast rule for the number or spacing of biscuits in a joint. Generally, one biscuit every 6 to 12 in. should be sufficient.

To cut the slots, hold the fence of the joiner firmly against the workpiece so the registration mark on the tool lines up with the layout mark for the biscuit. Press the fence down with your left hand, squeeze the trigger with your right hand and plunge the blade all the way into the workpiece. Release the trigger and retract the blade. That's all there is to it. Proceed to cut a slot at each layout mark on both workpieces. When all the slots are cut, slip biscuits into the slots without glue, and check the fit of the joint by sliding the parts together. If any of the biscuit slots seem to hold the joint open, set up the jointer again and re-cut the slot. It may not have been fully cut by the blade on the first pass.

Draw short reference marks across the joint to lay out the biscuit locations. One biscuit every 6 to 12 in. is a typical spacing for panel glue-ups.

To cut each slot, set the joiner against the edge of the workpiece with the fence resting on the board face. Start the machine and push the motor forward to plunge the blade into the edge. Retract the blade before moving on to the next cut.

Once all the slots are cut, dry-assemble the joint with the biscuits in place to check the fit of the biscuits in their slots. The board faces should line up evenly and flush.

199

CUTTING RIGHT-ANGLE JOINTS WITH A BISCUIT JOINER

Biscuit joints offer reasonable shear strength for attaching small, light-duty shelves inside a cabinet. The following photo sequence shows you how to set up the joint cuts. To align the biscuits accurately, adjust the joiner to cut slots that are centered on thickness of the shelf work-piece. Set the joint parts in position and draw a layout mark to indicate where the shelf will meet the cabinet side. Mark the biscuit positions on the shelf only. Then lay the shelf flat on the side panel and clamp them together along the layout line. Cut the shelf biscuit slots first. To cut the mating slots in the cabinet side, stand the biscuit joiner so the base rests against the shelf and the blade faces down against the cabinet side. Line up the registration marks on the tool base with the shelf biscuit slot layout marks, and cut the cabinet slots.

1 Hold the shelf and cabinet side workpieces in position to mark the joint location.

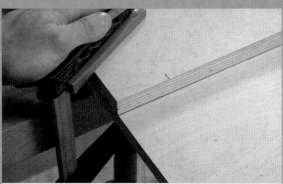

2 Mark the shelf for biscuit locations, then lay it down on the side panel so it lines up with the joint layout line. Clamp the parts together and to a worksurface.

3 Set up the biscuit joiner to cut slots that will be centered on the shelf's thickness. Proceed to cut the shelf slots.

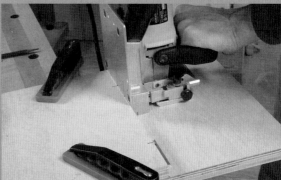

4 Cut the cabinet-side slots by standing the biscuit joiner so the base rests against the shelf. Line up the center reference line on the machine's base with each of the biscuit reference marks on the shelf, and cut the mating slots.

5 The resulting pairs of slots should line up exactly across the joint.

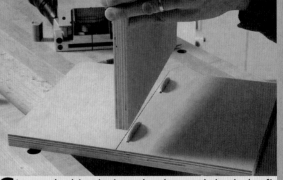

6 Insert the biscuits into dry slots and check the fit of the shelf in the side panel. The shelf should align with the initial layout line on the cabinet side.

ROUTER & ROUTER TABLE TECHNIQUES

Routers are remarkably simple tools that perform an astonishing variety of woodworking techniques. A mid-sized router in the 1- to 2½-hp range and the appropriate router bits are all you need to cut dadoes, grooves, rabbets and dozens of different edge profiles. With a bearing guided straight bit and a shop-made template, your router becomes an accurate part duplicator. It can also trim laminates and veneer, drill holes, make lettering for signs and even cut precise dovetail joints when used with a dovetailing jig.

You can expand the versatility of a router even more by mounting it to a router table. It will effectively turn your portable tool into a stationary machine. Instead of moving the router over the wood, you slide the wood across the table and past the bit. The broad, flat tabletop improves stability when working with small parts. Guiding workpieces against the router table's adjustable fence or starter pin ensures optimal control. With a full-size router mounted in the table, you can raise panels for cabinet doors, mill large profiles for custom molding or make interlocking joints with heavy bits that would be dangerous to use in a handheld router.

Whole books are dedicated to exploring the full range of router capabilities, but space doesn't allow for that here. The following section will introduce you to many of the core capabilities of a router, both in and out of the router table. If you only use a router occasionally on your woodworking or home improvement projects, here's an opportunity to broaden your skills. For a more extensive overview of routers, be sure to read other router books and magazine articles focusing on a variety of router techniques not covered here. A router will surely open new doors of possibility for your projects.

Cutting Dadoes And Grooves

You'll recall that dadoes are three-sided channels cut across the grain of a workpiece, and grooves are similar cuts made along the grain. It's possible to make either type of cut with a handheld router or router table, depending on the size of the workpiece. Handheld routers are the better choice for cutting dadoes across the width of long boards or large panels that would be difficult to maneuver over a router table. A router table, on the other hand, is ideal for milling grooves along a narrow edge or face of a workpiece. It's also easier to cut dadoes and grooves in small workpieces using the router table; the table and fence provide more support, and it's easier to see what you are doing without the workpiece hidden underneath the router. Choose the routing method that best suits the workpiece and task.

Cutting Dadoes Or Grooves With A Straightedge

Cutting dadoes or grooves with a handheld router requires a straightedge that you can clamp securely to the workpiece. The straightedge pro-vides backup support for guiding the router along the cut. You can use a piece of flat-edged scrap wood or sheet material for the straightedge—MDF works well for this purpose. Woodworking catalogs also sell metal straightedges with built-in clamps. Either way, you have to be able to clamp the straightedge without the clamps interfering with the router during the cut, so make sure your scrap straightedge is wide enough to allow plenty of room for clamps.

The fastest way to make dado or groove cuts is to use a straight bit with a diameter that matches the width of the cut you need to make. If you use a narrower bit, you'll have to reset the straightedge after making the first round of cuts to widen the dado or groove. Install the router bit in the collet and tighten it securely.

To position the straightedge correctly on your workpiece, you'll need to first measure the distance between the edge of the router bit and the edge of the router base. This distance is called the offset, and it will determine how far off your layout line to clamp the straightedge. To find the offset, hold the head of a combination square against the router base, and extend the rule until it just touches one of the cutting edges of the bit at the high point of the cutting arc. It isn't necessary to figure out the precise measurement on the rule—its extension from the head does that for you. Lock the rule on the head.

Next, draw the dado or groove location on your workpiece with a pair of reference lines. Use the locked combination square to mark the offset distance you determined for your router and bit. Mark the offset off of one of the two dado or groove layout lines. Here's where to clamp your straightedge to the workpiece. Then set the router base against the straightedge on each end of the cut and check to make sure the bit lines up with your layout lines. Shift the straightedge position if needed to fine-tune the setting.

The distance from the edge of the router base to the closest cutting edge of the bit establishes the offset distance for clamping the straightedge to cut dadoes and grooves.

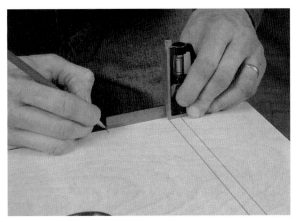

Mark the offset distance next to the dado layout lines. Here's where to locate the straightedge for guiding the router base.

Clamp a flat-edged piece of scrap or metal straightedge in place. Make sure to leave enough room for the router to pass by the clamps.

With the straightedge positioned and clamped, the last step is to set the bit depth for making the cut. If the dado or groove is less than 3/8 in. deep, you can usually cut the full depth in one pass. For deeper dadoes, set the bit to about 1/4 in. deep for the first pass, then reset the router for deeper cuts until you reach the final dado or groove depth.

To rout the dado, the correct feed direction to move the router is from left to right, across the workpiece. It's best to arrange the workpiece on your bench so you can push the router against the straightedge as you feed it across the workpiece. Set the router on the left side of the workpiece and against the straightedge so the bit will spin freely. Start the router, wait for the tool to reach full speed, and feed it smoothly and slowly into the cut. Guide it across the cut, keeping the router base pressed firmly against the straightedge. When the router nears the end of the cut, ease up on your feed pressure and slow the cut down to help minimize tearout when the bit exits the material.

Set the router for a cutting depth of up to 1/4 in. For routing deeper dadoes and grooves, make the cut in several passes, increasing the depth of cut each time.

Rout the dado by feeding the router from left to right across the workpiece. Keep the edge of the router base pressed against the straightedge.

Use a right-to-left feed direction on the router table for cutting dadoes and grooves. Back up narrow workpieces with a piece of square-edged scrap or a miter gauge.

Cutting dadoes on the router table involves making a similar setup. Mark your layout lines on the workpiece, and use the router table fence instead of a clamped straightedge to guide the end or edge of the workpiece. If you're dadoing narrow workpieces, use a large piece of square-edged scrap or your miter gauge to back up the cut. This will keep the workpiece tracking properly along the fence during the cut.

Cutting Edge Grooves On A Router Table

On occasion, you'll need to cut grooves along the edge of a work-

piece for making tongue and groove joints (see page 119) or when you are using splines to join two workpieces edge-to-edge. If the workpiece is narrow, the router table is the right choice for the job. One way to make the cut is to stand the workpiece on edge and use a narrow straight bit to cut the groove. It helps if the bit diameter matches the groove width you want to make or is slightly narrower. Install and tighten the bit, and raise it above the table to set up the cut.

Mark the groove dimensions on the end of your workpiece, and hold it against the router fence next to the bit. Align the bit with the groove layout lines, move the fence flush

Adjust the fence in or out until the bit lines up with the groove layout lines. Lock the fence down securely to the table.

Edge slots for tongue and groove or spline joints are easy to make at the router table.

If an edge groove is 1/4 in. deep or less, you can raise the bit to make the whole cut in one pass. Otherwise, plan to make several passes and raise the bit more each time.

against the workpiece and tighten the fence clamps. Raise or lower the router to set the correct bit height. If the groove is shallower than about $\frac{1}{4}$ in., you can cut it in one pass. For deeper grooves, set the bit for a $\frac{1}{4}$-in. depth of cut first, then make deeper passes by raising the bit to finish the groove.

It's good practice when routing workpieces on edge to clamp a featherboard to the router table. The featherboard will prevent the workpiece from drifting away from the fence and ruining the cut. Once the featherboard is in position, make the groove cut by feeding the workpiece across the router table from right to left. (For most router table operations, the correct feed direction is right to left, against the bit's rotation.) Use a push stick to keep your feed hand safely away from the bit.

Another alternative for cutting edge grooves is to use a slot-cutting bit. This bit extends out from the fence instead of up from the table (see the inset photo below). Set the workpiece facedown and adjust the router up or down so the slot cutter lines up with your groove layout

Before making the groove cut, install a featherboard to keep the workpiece pressed firmly against the fence during cutting. Use a push stick to feed the workpiece along.

lines on the edge of the workpiece. Move the fence in or out to establish the groove depth. Lock the fence and feed the workpiece along the fence from right to left to make the cut.

A slot-cutting bit is ideal for routing edge grooves. Raise the bit to position the groove on the workpiece thickness, and move the fence in or out to set the groove's depth. Feed the cut from right to left.

Cutting Rabbets

A router table offers the best control for cutting rabbets, particularly if workpieces are narrow and you are cutting rabbets on the short ends. You'll use a combination of the fence and the bit height to limit the cut and establish the rabbet proportions. You can use a straight bit or a a piloted rabbeting bit embedded in the router table fence to make rabbets. If you use a straight bit, choose a bit diameter that's wider than the cheek and shoulder dimensions, if you can. This way, you can set the bit partially inside the fence and use the width of the bit to cut most or all of the rabbet tongue or cheek in one setup.

The decision you'll need to make when cutting rabbets this way is whether to orient the workpieces facedown on the table or stand them on end, vertically. For long, narrow workpieces, the facedown approach is safer than trying to guide the workpiece standing up. Back up the workpiece with your miter gauge or a push block. For wider workpieces with dimensions more square than rectangular, you can rout rabbets safely either facedown or standing on end. If the panel is particularly long, install a tall auxiliary fence to your router table fence so there's plenty of vertical support behind the panel to keep it from tipping.

If you're just getting started with woodworking, it helps to mark the actual proportions of the rabbet on your workpiece and use it to help set the bit height and fence position. After you get used to the process of cutting rabbets (and other joinery), you'll probably stop marking workpieces this way and create the proportions by simply measuring off the bit or fence. It's a good idea to always test your setup on scrap wood first to verify the proportions.

Whether you decide to feed workpieces vertically against the fence or facedown, you'll also need to choose how to cut the waste material away most efficiently. There are two options here: You can move the fence away from the bit with each pass but keep the bit height the same. Generally, this method works best for cutting long rabbet tongues with the workpiece facedown on the router table. Set the bit height to cut to the rabbet's cheek, and shift the fence back with each pass until the bit reaches the rabbet's shoulder. Feed the workpiece from right to left across the table as usual. You can also use this method for routing workpieces vertically against the fence, but here you'll set the bit height to cut to the shoulder. Each time you shift the fence back, the bit will cut closer to the cheek.

The other setup option is to fix the fence in place and raise the bit. If the

Adjust the router table fence until the bit intersects the rabbet shoulder line. If the rabbet is large, it may take several passes and fence adjustments for the bit to reach this line.

Raise the bit until it aligns with the rabbet cheek line. If this height is more than about ¼ in., plan to make several passes and raise the bit each time until it cuts to the cheek.

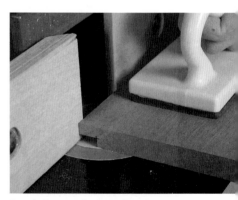

Feed the workpiece from right to left and along the fence to cut the rabbet to shape. Use a slow, steady feed rate to keep from overloading the bit and router.

workpiece is facedown, set the fence so the bit will cut to the shoulder line with the first pass. Raising the bit some with each additional pass eventually forms the cheek. When the workpiece is positioned vertically against the fence, set the fence so the bit cuts to the cheek on the first pass. Raise the bit to work your way to the final shoulder height.

You can also use a piloted rabbeting bit in a handheld router to cut rabbets (see photo at right). It's better to reserve this option for when you're cutting wide workpieces or panels that can provide plenty of support for the router base. Piloted rabbet bits often come with a set of bearings in different diameters so you can use the same bit to cut a range of rabbet sizes. For a small to moderately sized rabbet, you can usually make the full cut in one pass. Just choose the bearing that allows the bit to trim to the shoulder. The distance from the edge of the bearing to the edge of the bit's cutters will determine the length of the cheek and the position of the rabbet shoulder. Use the router's depth of cut to establish the width of the shoulder. Feed the router from left to right, as you would for any other handheld router operation, to make the cut.

You can also cut rabbets with a handheld router and a piloted rabbeting bit. This is a good option for routing workpieces that are too large to manage easily on a router table. Feed from left to right.

Interchangeable bearings allow one rabbeting bit to cut a variety of rabbet proportions.

TIP

MINIMIZING TEAROUT

When cutting rabbets with a handheld router, clamp a piece of scrap wood along the workpiece on the "exit" edge of the cut. Then cut past the edge of the workpiece and into the scrap. This way, the bit can't tear out wood as it breaks through the edge at the end of the cut.

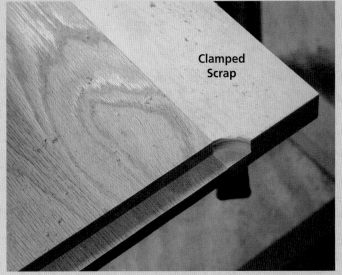

Clamped Scrap

Back up the right corner of a workpiece with a piece of scrap clamped in place to prevent the router from chipping this corner as it exits the workpiece.

Routing Edge Profiles

Cutting decorative profiles along the edges and ends of workpieces is a router's bread and butter. Of all a router's functions, edge profiling is the most common use for the tool. There are several good reasons to add profiles to your projects. First, profiling breaks sharp edges and corners where they could otherwise cause injury. Tabletops, surfaces with sharp-edged laminate and furniture components like chair legs or arm leans are all good candidates for rounded edges and corners. Projects made from splinter-prone materials like oak, cedar and plywood should also have "eased" edges to help preserve the wood and make the project more skin-friendly.

Profiles also form attractive shadow lines, create a sense of depth and turn flat, ordinary edges into surfaces that are interesting to look at and pleasant to touch. On thick parts, profiling works in a reductive way to make parts look lighter and more delicate. Adding a few judicious profiles can enhance even a basic woodworking project or give historical accuracy to a period piece.

You have many choices of bit shapes for cutting edge profiles (see the sidebar on page 212 to see a selection of starter bits to buy). Most profiling bits have a pilot bearing on the tip to guide the bit along the workpiece and keep it from cutting too deeply.

Router tables are ideal for edge profiling. You can shape the outside edges and ends of a workpiece or an inside cutout, and either curved or flat edges are fair game. In fact, for ordinary profiling tasks you may find that a router table is preferable to handheld routing. With the router mounted to the table, you can focus entirely on guiding the wood. Gravity works with, rather than against you as it sometimes does with handheld profiling. The smaller the workpiece, the more you'll appreciate having the router held stationary under the table.

There are a couple scenarios where router tables are less convenient than handheld routers. If you're profiling a large board or panel that's difficult to maneuver by hand, do the profiling with a handheld router instead of on the table. In this situation, a handheld router offers better control. Another case for handheld profiling is when you need to shape the edges of a partially assembled project. If there isn't a smooth, flat surface to move over the table, the only feasible option may be to rout by hand.

A router table fence offers solid backing for routing flat surfaces, so take advantage of it. You may be tempted to use a piloted bit without a fence to rout a flat edge, and just feed the wood in, like you typically do for handheld profiling. The danger comes with starting the cut on the corner or at the end of the workpiece. Without a fence to guide and limit the cut, it's possible for the bit to catch the wood and jerk it out of your hands. Using the fence is definitely the safer approach, and the setup doesn't take much time.

You have two options for setting up profiling cuts on a router table. You can remove the waste by setting the fence in one place and raising the bit a little with each pass, or you can set the bit at one height and move the

Profiling bits add visual interest by creating shape and shadow lines. They also soften sharp edges and reduce the chances of splintering later.

fence back with each pass to expose more of the bit. Either option works well, and you can choose based on personal preference.

However you set up the bit and fence for cutting profiles, it's always advisable to make the profile cuts in several passes rather than one deep pass. The larger the bit or the harder the wood, the more important this becomes. Granted, it takes a little longer to complete the profile this way, but you'll prolong the life of your bits and router as well as leave fewer burn marks or tearout on the wood.

Raising The Bit To Cut Profiles

If you wish to cut a profile by raising the bit incrementally, set the fence so the bit will cut its full profile when fully raised. To do this with a pilot-bearing bit, install and raise the bit so the bearing is above the table. Hold a straightedge against the side of the bearing, and move the fence until the faces line up with the bearing. Lock the fence and lower the router in the table to begin your sequence of cuts. Then raise the bit with each additional pass to remove more wood until you finally cut the full profile. It may take several passes to raise the bit fully and achieve the final cut.

Sometimes the bit won't have a pilot bearing to use as a reference for lining up the fence. In these situations, the center point of the bit becomes what would be the edge of the bearing. Line up the fence with the bit's center point by eye, and lock the fence here.

Moving The Fence To Cut Profiles

If you'd rather move the fence back each time to make the profile instead of moving the bit up and down, just raise the bit to full cutting height. Pull the fence forward and lock it down to expose just a portion of the cutters for the first pass. Then shift the fence back with each successive pass to cut more of the bit's shape. Make these fence shifts about $1/8$ in. at a time to avoid overloading the router or the bit. When the fence reaches the rim of the bit's bearing, you'll be cutting the bit's full profile.

Working With End Grain

When routing across end grain, the "exit" end of the cut is prone to tearout. Use a piece of scrap as a backer board behind the workpiece when routing an end-grain cut on the router table. The backer board will support the fragile corner fibers that might otherwise break away. In cases where you're routing a profile all around the workpiece, rout the end-grain first, then finish up by routing the long-grain profiles. The long-grain cuts will clean up any tearout that occurs on the short-grain cuts.

Line up the rim of the bearing on a profiling bit with the router fence. With this alignment, the bit will cut its full profile when raised to maximum height.

For bits with a large profile, set the bit to a low height to cut just part of the shape with the first left-to-right pass.

Raise the bit higher with each additional pass until the bit cuts nearly the full shape you want. Make a light final pass to remove any ragged edges or burn marks.

Routing Profiles With A Handheld Router

The usual method for routing profiles with a handheld router is to simply guide the router along the

Use a counterclockwise feed direction when routing around the outside edges of a workpiece.

Feed the router clockwise around the inside edges of a cutout area, such as this picture frame.

wood. The bit's pilot bearing registers against the edge or end of the workpiece. The bit's depth of cut controls how much material the router removes with each pass. If you're only trimming off a small amount of material—say 1/4 in. or less—you can set the bit depth to cut away all the waste in one pass. For larger profiles, plan on making the cut in several passes. Increase the depth of cut about 1/8 in. with each pass until the bit cuts the full profile you want. Make sure the bearing will still have a partial edge to ride against on the deepest cut, or the bit won't follow the edge and you'll ruin the cut.

Routing end grain with a handheld router presents the same tearout problems as on the router table. When you are only routing end grain, back up the "exit" end of the cut with a piece of scrap to support the fragile edge fibers. If you are routing all the way around, start the cut midway along a long-grain edge, feed around the end grain, continue around the second long- and end-grain surfaces and finish up on the first long-grain edge. This will automatically clean away any tearout on the end-grain corners.

Proper Feed Direction For Handheld Profiling

One important issue to keep in mind when doing handheld profiling is which direction to feed the router along the cut. Always feed the router against the bit's rotation. For handheld profiling, feed the router counterclockwise around the workpiece when you're routing the outside edges and ends. If you are routing around a cutout inside a workpiece, switch to the opposite feed direction. Feed the router clockwise. You'll know you are feeding the router properly if you feel resistance against the bit when pushing the router along. If the router seems to pull its way along or lurches forward, you are feeding in the wrong direction.

Routing Curved Profiles Against A Starter Pin

When you're profiling along the edge of a curved workpiece with a hand-held router, your grip on the router provides plenty of control for starting the cut safely. The bit's bearing serves as a suitable reference surface. Starting a curved profile cut on a router table presents other control problems. Obviously, the fence won't help support a curved cut, but it's also unsafe to make curved cuts by simply pushing wood into the bit. Depending on your angle of approach, the bit can grab the wood and pull it out of your hands in an instant. The solution for starting curved cuts safely is to install a starter pin near the bit and use it as a fulcrum to pivot the wood into the bit. Most router table insert plates come with a starter pin that presses or screws into holes already drilled in the plate. If your router table's insert plate doesn't come with these provisions, you can drill a hole and install a piece of dowel or short length of steel rod to serve the same purpose.

Install a starter pin near the bit opening on a router table's insert plate for template-routing curved shapes. Most insert plates have holes already drilled for this purpose.

To start a curved cut, insert the starter pin in a hole on the insert plate closest to you. Set the workpiece against the starter pin with the wood clear of the bit. Now, pivot the wood on the starter pin slowly into the spinning bit. It's imperative that the bit and pin are in contact with the same edge of the workpiece. Never allow the workpiece to pass between the pin and the bit, or the

TIP

DISH MATS HELP YOU SKIP THE CLAMPS

When routing freehand, it's important to immobilize the workpiece so it doesn't shift around on your bench as you rout it. On large workpieces, the weight of the part may be all the anchoring you need. Or, clamp the workpiece to your bench. If you are routing a small part, there may be no room for clamps. An inexpensive solution is to use a foam dish mat, available from the kitchen section of any discount or department store. The mat provides just enough "grip" to keep workpieces from moving when you don't want them to. It also makes a great pad for holding things steady when sanding.

Sometimes it isn't easy to clamp a workpiece to secure it for handheld routing. A good alternative is to set the workpiece on a foam dish mat or rubberized routing pad to immobilize it.

Use the starter pin as a fulcrum for beginning the cut. With the workpiece held against the pin, pivot it into the bit.

bit will grab the wood and jerk it out of your hands.

When the wood reaches the bit's pilot bearing and rests against it, begin to feed the workpiece from right to left (or clockwise) as usual, so the bit follows the curve. As long as you keep the wood against the pilot bearing, it no longer needs to touch the starter pin. You'll probably find that feeding the wood along the curve will naturally cause you to swing the wood away from the starter pin anyway. The starter pin only needs to provide a pivot point when engaging the bit in the wood.

Once the template touches the bit's bearing, feed the workpiece clockwise to trim it to final shape.

STARTER SET OF PROFILING BITS

There are dozens of different profiling bits you can buy, but you won't need them all to take care of most profiling needs. Five basic bit shapes will serve you well: chamfers, coves, roundovers, ogees and beads. Chamfers, roundovers and coves are the most common options for easing edges and adding decorative detail. Chamfers convert a square corner into a 45° bevel. Roundovers create a convex quarter-circle, and coves make the mirror image of a roundover—a concave relief. A single chamfering bit is the most versatile of these three shapes, because the same bit can produce both narrow and wide chamfers by simply changing the cutting depth. Roundovers and coves are limited to cutting the size of the shape formed by their radius. You'll need a few sizes of these bits to cover the usual gamut of your project needs. An "S"-shaped ogee bit, a bullnose bit and a beading bit are other typical and appealing profiles to add to your collection.

A good starter set of profiling bits includes (from left to right): a chamfering bit, roundover bits in various sizes, bullnose bit, edge-beading bit, ogee bit and various sizes of cove bits.

When the cut is underway, there's no need to keep the workpiece held against the starter pin. The bit's bearing provides all the support required. Turn the workpiece as needed to complete the cut.

Template Routing

Template routing is an excellent way to turn your router table or handheld router into a part-duplicating machine. The technique for template routing is wonderfully simple: Essentially, you use a rigid pattern made of hardboard, MDF, plastic or wood to guide the router bit for cutting a shape that matches the template. Cut and shape your template carefully: the router will replicate its shape—including every minor blip or bump you don't quite sand away when you make it.

You can use either a handheld router or a router table for template routing. A handheld router works best for duplicating part shapes on workpieces that would be too large to move over the router table. Router tables provide improved support and control for duplicating smaller workpieces that don't offer adequate bearing surface for the router base.

Template routing is primarily a trimming operation. Routers aren't

Attach templates securely to a workpiece before routing them. A couple strips of double-sided carpet tape form a quick, sturdy bond.

meant to be saws. Using your router to cut a workpiece to initial shape places excessive stress on the motor and bit. For template routing, use the template to trace the shape on your workpiece, then cut the workpiece to shape about 1/16 in. outside the layout lines. Or mount the template to the workpiece and saw carefully around

Cut the workpiece to shape so it's slightly larger than the template. You can mount the template beforehand or trace its shape and then stick it on after cutting.

Use a piloted flush-trim bit to trim away the excess so the workpiece matches the template shape. The bearing follows the template edge.

to the workpiece. Any of these options will keep the template from shifting out of position.

Bit And Guide Collar Options For Template Routing

A well-made template is one half the equation for successful template routing. The other element is choosing a bit or guide collar to follow along the template. You can use a straight bit with a bearing mounted at the tip—called a flush-trim bit—or a straight bit with the bearing mounted on the shank—called a pattern bit—for template routing. The bit you choose will depend on whether the template is mounted on top or below the workpiece. On these specialized bits, the bearing and cutter diameters match, so the bit will cut flush with the rim of the bearing. Set the bit depth so the bearing rolls along the template and the cutter trims the full thickness of the workpiece.

Another option is to attach a guide collar to your handheld router and use a straight bit instead of a piloted bit. Guide collars are simply short bushings cast into a flange that fits into a hole in your router's baseplate.

it, leaving about 1/16 in. of waste material to trim off with the router. For curved workpieces, cut the workpiece to rough shape with a jigsaw or on the bandsaw.

It's important to attach a template securely to the workpiece so it doesn't come loose during routing. You can use hot-melt glue, double-sided carpet tape or short brad nails to attach the template temporarily

There are three cutting options for template routing: You can use a handheld router with a straight bit and guide collar (left), a piloted straight bit in the router table (center) or a piloted straight bit in a handheld router.

The collar is held in place with screws or a knurled nut that threads onto the flange from inside the router base. Guide collars are made in various sizes to fit around different straight bits. Collars are usually sold in sets so you can use them with various diameter straight bits. In a template-routing situation, the bushing portion of the collar follows the template instead of a pilot bearing on the bit. The downside to guide collars is that there will always be a bit of offset between the bushing and the bit so it can spin freely. You'll have to take the offset into account on the finished workpiece, because the guide collar will create a workpiece slightly larger than the template. Flush-trim or pattern bits, on the other hand, will follow the template exactly with no offset.

Pay careful attention to the feed direction you use for template-routing on a router table versus using a handheld router. On a router table, feed the outside edges of a workpiece against the bit in a clockwise direction. If you are routing around the interior of a templated workpiece on a router table, feed the workpiece counterclockwise.

You'll need to switch the feed directions for template-routing with a handheld router, because the direction of bit rotation changes when you flip the router right-side up. For routing around the outside edges of the template, feed the router around counterclockwise. Move the router clockwise around the inside edges of a template when the workpiece has a cutout area. Again, you'll know you are headed in the right direction if the router offers resistance as you slide it along. If it tries to pull itself forward, switch directions; you're feeding the wrong way.

Treat the end-grain surfaces of a workpiece carefully when template routing. When possible, rout them first, then finish up with the long-grain edges to remove any tearout at the corners of the end-grain surfaces.

It's also possible to rout templates with a handheld router. Feed the tool counterclockwise to template-rout the outside edges.

A router table and straight bit will cut clean-walled mortises with ease. Cut deep mortises in a series of passes, raising the bit about ¼ in. each time.

Cutting Mortises On A Router Table

Cutting mortises is easy to do with a router table equipped with a straight bit. The cutting procedure is "blind" in the sense that the bit will be embedded in the wood, but you'll mark its whereabouts right on the fence or table so you can set your cutting limits for precise cuts. You'll raise the bit incrementally to cut the

Use a strip of masking tape placed in front of the bit to mark its diameter. Hold a combination square or piece of scrap against the bit to mark the cutting edges.

mortise depth, but the fence will remain locked in the same place for the whole operation.

The first step in setting up a mortise cut is to make reference marks on the router table that indicate where the leading and trailing edges of the bit are. Install a straight bit that matches the width of the mortise you want to cut. Then draw a pair of reference marks on a piece of bright masking tape placed in front of the bit so you can see them easily when moving the workpiece over the bit. Hold a combination square or piece of scrap against the infeed and outfeed cutting edge of the bit to locate each of the two marks on the tape.

With the bit's location marked, lay out the mortise shape on the workpiece, and extend hash marks onto the side of the workpiece you'll see during the cut. The hash marks set the length of the cut so you can start and stop the cut accurately with the bit hidden. Make a second set of hash marks on the end of the workpiece to indicate how far the cut is offset from the fence. Sometimes these marks will be centered on the thickness of

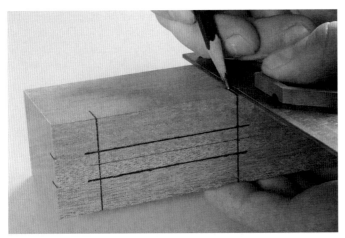

Since mortising on a router table will hide the cut from view, extend reference lines for the width and length of the mortise around to the end and side of the workpiece.

Move the fence and workpiece as needed to line up the bit with the mortise layout lines on the end of the workpiece. Lock the fence securely.

the wood and other times not, depending on where the mortise needs to be. Line the bit up with these marks and lock the fence with the workpiece held against it.

The process of cutting the mortise is simple: Set the bit to a height of about 1/4 in. for the first pass, and lower the wood down onto the spinning bit so the left mortise layout line aligns with the left bit line on the tape. When you do this, it should be a pivoting motion with the rear corner of the wood held against the router table. A stop block clamped to the table or fence can help anchor this corner for even better stability. Press the wood down slowly into the bit, holding the workpiece firmly against the fence.

Once you've made the first plunge cut and the first set of marks align, slide the wood slowly from right to left along the fence until the second set of marks line up. Again, you can clamp a stop block to the fence on the left side to stop this cut, to help minimize errors.

Repeat this process, raising the bit with each pass until you reach your final mortise depth. You'll probably need to blow or dig out impacted wood chips periodically; the mortise slot tends to fill quickly. Or, make a second pass without changing the bit height to clear out the mortise. Another option is to use a spiral upcut bit instead of a conventional straight bit. The spiral cutting flutes on an upcut bit will automatically clear the waste.

Begin the cutting process by lining up the left workpiece and bit reference lines. Start the router and slowly press the workpiece down into the spinning bit. Keep the workpiece held tightly against the fence.

Slide the wood along the fence from right to left until the other mortise layout line aligns with the right bit reference line. Turn off the router and wait for the bit to stop before lifting off the workpiece.

Cutting Cope And Stick Joints

If you check the corner joinery on manufactured cabinet doors, you'll find that most are assembled with cope and stick joints. This joint style is also called a rail and stile joint. Cope and stick joints are easy fare on a router table equipped with a mid-sized to larger router and specialized cope and stick bits. The joint forms a strong interlocking connection with glue alone. It's also efficient: the bits make a decorative profile, a groove that fits a wood or glass panel and a tongue that fills the groove.

Cope and stick router bits are generally manufactured as a matched set, although you can also buy one-piece bits that cut both the cope and stick profiles by changing the bit height. A third style has removable cutters and bearings that can be stacked in both the cope and stick configurations. Regardless, cope and stick bits are fairly expensive to buy.

Notice in the photo of the exploded cabinet door (below) that door frames are made of two components: stiles and rails. The stiles are the vertical members of the frame, and the rails are the top and bottom horizontal members. The rails fit between the stiles. On a cope and stick joint, you use the sticking bit to rout the inside edges of both the stiles and rails. The sticking bit forms a groove to house a wood or glass panel. It also makes a decorative chamfer or ogee shape along the "show" edge to add visual interest to the joint. The coping bit mills a mirror-image profile in the ends of the rails only. It fits exactly into the sticking profiles.

In a two-piece cope and stick bit set, the sticking bit (left) cuts the inner panel slots and profile on both the rails and stiles. The coping bit (right) creates a complementary cut on the ends of the rails only so they mesh with the sticking cuts on the stiles.

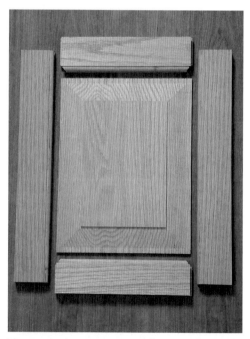

The typical components of a raised panel door include a center panel and a frame made of two horizontal rails and two vertical stiles. Cope and stick bits cut only the door frame joinery.

Cope and stick joints are usually made with two bits, or you can use single-piece bits that cut both halves of the profile by changing the bit height.

The photo sequence on the following pages shows you how to use a cope and stick bit set to cut door joints. When setting up the bits to make the appropriate cuts, keep several tips in mind. First, make your rails and stiles from straight-grained wood, and surface the pieces so they are absolutely flat. Even the slightest amount of warp or mismatch will affect the fit of the joints when you assemble them, and chances are, the final door won't end up flat. You'll also notice that two-piece cope and stick sets cut the profile upside down. This means you'll need to rout the rails and stiles facedown on the router table. You may want to mark the backs of the rails and stiles before routing them to help keep their orientation clear. For best results, run your router at its highest speed when cutting both parts of the joint, and feed the parts through slowly but steadily. The router will remove a significant amount of material. Setting the bit for high speed will allow it to cut away the waste in smaller bites.

Finally, start with rails and stiles that are several inches longer than necessary; you can trim them to final length after making the sticking cuts. This way, you can trim off any tearout that happens on the ends of the parts. It's a good idea to cut a few test pieces on matching scrap before you rout your actual workpieces, in order to get used to the cutting process and how the bits work. Some woodworkers even create a few spare rails and stiles, just in case.

Making The Sticking Cuts

As we've already mentioned, all four door frame parts receive the sticking profile along the inside edge. To set up the sticking cutter, install and tighten the bit securely in your router table. Line up the bit's top bearing with your router table fence, using a rule to align the bearing and fence. Set the correct bit height off of one of the rail or stile workpieces. The sticking bit should be adjusted so the profile portion of the cutters (facing down) will mill the full shape plus a tiny shadow line on the front face. Check that the bit's setting will also leave about 1/8 in. of material along the top edges of the rails and stiles. This "lip" supports the back of the groove for the door panel and rail joints.

After you've installed the sticking bit, adjust the router table fence even with the rim of the bit's top bearing.

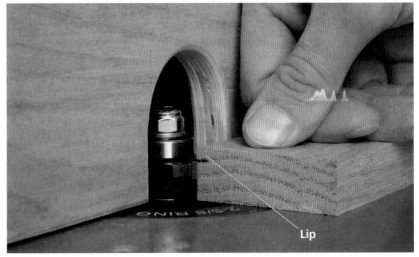

Adjust the bit height so the bottom will cut the full profile plus a tiny shadow line and the top cutter leaves about a 1/8-in.-thick lip.

Install featherboards all around the bit, then make the sticking cuts on both the rails and stiles. A single pass cuts the entire shape; you cannot "sneak up" on these cuts.

Making The Cope Cuts

Recall that the cope cuts are made only on the ends of the rails. Remove the sticking bit from the router table and install the coping bit. Like the sticking bit, it will cope the door rails facedown. Use one of the completed stiles to set the height of the coping bit. Adjust it up or down until the groove on the stile lines up with the center bearing on the coping bit. The profiling and shoulder cutters on this bit should align exactly with the groove walls. Rotate the bit by hand to check the intersection of the cutters with the groove. Then use a rule to adjust the router table fence flush with the bit bearing, just as you did with the sticking bit.

Install a featherboard on the router table to press the rails and stiles firmly against the fence when you make the sticking cuts. Feed the rails and stiles past the bit slowly from right to left to cut the profile. Be sure to use a push stick to keep your fingers clear of the cutter when milling these narrow parts.

Once you've made all four sticking cuts, check the dimensions of your doors against your project drawings and cut the stiles to final length. To determine the length of the rails, take the overall width of the door, subtract the width of two stiles and add the length of two groove cuts made in the stiles. Crosscut the rails to this measurement.

Switch to the coping bit. Use one of the routed rails or stiles to set the bit height. Make sure the cutters line up evenly with the routed workpiece.

It's a good idea to make rails and stiles from overly long stock, then cut them to final length after routing the sticking profile. A clamped stop block and back-up board will ensure precise, clean cuts on the miter saw.

When you rout the first coping profile, back up the flat edge of the rail with a square-edged piece of scrap. Rout across both the rail and the backer board.

Cope the other end of the rail by flipping it around and inserting the sticking profile on the rail into the coped profile of the backer board (see inset photo). This will keep the bit from tearing out the sticking profile during coping.

Since the coping bit will cut across the narrow end grain of the rails, back up the cuts with a large, square-edged piece of scrap material. The scrap will keep workpieces from rocking away from the fence as you push them past the bit. It also reduces tearout. At this stage, rout only one end of each rail with the flat edge of the rail flush against the backup board. Hold the rails down firmly against the table with a push pad or push stick. Push the backup board all the way through the bit as well. You'll use the coped profile on the backup board for routing the other ends of the rails.

With one end of the rails coped, flip them end-for-end on the router table to mill the other ends. This time, turn the backup board so its coped edge faces forward. Slip its coped profile into the sticking edge of the rails, which now face the backup board. The coped edge of the backup board will prevent the bit from tearing out the sticking on the rails as it exits the cut. Mill the two remaining ends of the rails.

TIP

TRIM THE TONGUES TO IMPROVE THE FIT

If the rails and stiles fit together but a bit too tightly, the easiest way to loosen the joints is to take a few shavings off the rail tongues with a shoulder plane. A few swipes should be all that's necessary to improve the fit.

One way to loosen the fit of too-tight door joints is to take a few shavings off the rail tongues with a shoulder plane. This can also help flatten a slightly twisted door frame.

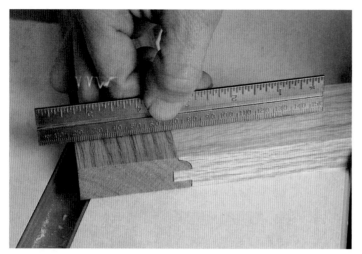

Check the completed door joints for flatness. Flat, square and seasoned door stock will usually produce nice, flat door joints. Any twisting now will likely lead to a twisted door later.

Measure the length of a rail and subtract ⅛ in. to determine the width of the panel required for the door.

Checking The Joints And Determining The Panel Proportions

When all the frame joints are complete, slip the rails and stiles together and check the fit of the parts. The joints should slip together with a slight bit of friction if you've cut them carefully. Now you can calculate the final dimensions of the door's center panel. Make the width of the panel equal to the length of a rail, from tongue to tongue, minus ⅛ in. When you build door panels from solid wood, making them ⅛ in. undersized will give the wood room to expand and contract across the grain with changes in humidity. For glass or plywood panels, it still doesn't hurt to make the panels slightly narrower than necessary to make sure the corner joints will close properly.

To measure panel length, flip the door frame over and measure the distance between the inside flat edges of the rails. Add the length of two panel grooves to this measurement and subtract ⅛ in.

Calculate the panel length by measuring between the back inside edges of the rails, adding the length of two panel grooves and subtracting ⅛ in.

Raising Panels On A Router Table

With the proper bits and a powerful router, it's possible to raise door panels with your router table. However, panel-raising requires extreme caution and should only be done on a sturdy router table. There are two basic styles of panel-raising bits: horizontal and vertical cutters. Horizontal panel-raising bits cut their profiles with the panel laying flat on the router table. These bits are large and heavy, and they demand substantial power from your router. The best routers to use with horizontal bits are those in the 3- to 3.25-rated hp range. Vertical panel-raising bits can be used safely with smaller $1^1/_2$- to $2^1/_2$-hp routers. You stand panels up against the fence with vertical bits to mill them. Both bit styles are manufactured in straight and curved profiles to suit different door styles. Some horizontal bits also have a second "back" cutter on top that trims the back of the panel into a narrow tongue to fit in the door frame grooves.

If you use a horizontal bit to cut panels, be sure to refer to the bit manufacturer's recommendations for setting the correct router speed. Large bits require slower speeds to be used safely. It's also imperative to cut the deep profile shape in a series of shallow passes. Depending on the bit size and the hardness of the lumber, you may need to make more than a dozen passes to complete the job. You may only be able to raise the bit $1/_{16}$ in. or so for each pass to keep from overloading the router. It also helps to connect your router or router table fence to a dust collector for this operation. Raising panels produces piles of shavings in no time.

To set up the cut, install and tighten the panel-raising bit securely and adjust the router to the proper speed. Line up the rim of the bit's bearing with the router table fence using a straightedge, and clamp the

Panel-raising bits cut horizontally or vertically, with the horizontal style requiring a larger, full-sized router in the 3 hp range. Various bevel profiles are available. Some styles also include a "back cutter" that shapes the back edge of the panel.

fence securely in place. Lower the bit until only about $1/_{16}$ in. of its cutters are exposed above the table. If your router table fence has adjustable facings, move them in toward the bit to close the opening around the bit as much as possible.

Adjust the fence on your router table so the rim of the bearing lines up with the fence facings. Open the facings wide enough to clear the cutters.

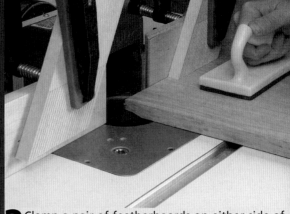

1 Raise the bit just enough to make a light shearing cut on the first pass. You'll need to make many cuts to form the deep, broad bevel profile.

2 Clamp a pair of featherboards on either side of the bit to keep the panel pressed firmly down against the table. Feed the panel from right to left. Cut the end grain first.

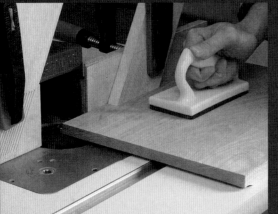

3 After you shape the two ends, rout the long edges. Follow the same end-grain-then-long-grain procedure for the entire routing process.

4 Raise the bit about 1/16 in. to make the second series of passes to remove more waste. Here's how the panel should look after the first few cuts.

5 Continue routing until the ends and edges are slightly thinner than the panel groove in the door rails and stiles (for more on routing the rails and stiles, see page 218).

6 When completed, the panel will have a thin shadow line around the field area. Careful routing should produce a profile that requires little sanding.

Roll up long sleeves and remove your watch before beginning; you don't want anything but wood catching those big cutters. Some router fences have a top guard to help shield you from the bit. This is a good occasion to use it.

Make each round of passes on the end grain first, then the long grain. Feed the panel slowly past the bit, pressing it down firmly against the router table. If the router begins to bog down in the cut, reduce your feed speed. You may have to lower the cutting height if the router labors excessively. Continue making rounds of passes on the end grain, then the long grain. Raise the bit a little with each round until you reduce the panel to the edge thickness you need. Check the fit of the panel in the door frame; continue the milling process until the panel fits easily into its groove and the door frame joints close fully. Make the last round of milling cuts with the bit set just a hair higher to help shear the final surfaces cleanly.

For vertical panel-raising bits, you'll want to install a taller fence facing on your router table, as shown at right. The fence needs to be tall enough to provide a firm backing behind the panel. Create the beveled profile by setting the bit to full height and adjusting the fence backward to expose more of the cutters for each round of passes.

Increase the depth of cut gradually; about 1/16 in. is a good benchmark to use. The smaller your router, the shallower the passes should be. Cut the end grain first, then the long grain to reduce tearout.

When using a vertical style panel-raising bit, make light passes and shift the fence backward rather than changing bit height to advance the cut. Cut end grain first, then the long grain.

Cutting Half-Blind And Through Dovetail Joints

Dovetails are the calling cards of fine craftsmanship. Even non woodworkers look for them on the corners of every drawer. We love these dovetail joints, and for good reason. The angular, repeating symmetry is pleasant to look at, and all those interlocking surfaces create a huge gluing area that makes a rock-solid joint. Half-blind dovetails are the most popular style for drawer joinery. The sides of the drawer are outfitted with the tails of the joint, and these fit into mirror-image pin slots in the ends of the drawer face. Another variation—the through dovetail—has tails that extend all the way through the drawer face so you can see them on the front. You can make both styles of dovetails on a specialized jig, and the joints will take your projects to a higher level of detail and skill.

Dovetail Jigs

There are at least a dozen different models of dovetailing jigs available, with each manufacturer attempting to make an easier, fool-proof design. The fact of the matter is, every jig will challenge you with its own unique learning curve. The most common style of dovetail jig consists of a heavy base with a clamp on top and in front to hold workpieces during routing. Usually, a metal or plastic template fits on the jig to establish the exact spacing of the pin and tail

Both half-blind dovetails (top) and through dovetails (bottom) create an interesting interplay of geometry, color and grain contrast.

Dovetail jigs vary in style, but most consist of a removable, fingered template that fits onto a heavy base. A clamp on top and in front hold workpieces securely.

pattern. For half-blind dovetails, the template will look like a comb, with a series of equally spaced teeth. To make through dovetails, the template may have adjustable parts so you can vary the spacing of the pins and tails. You'll cut the joint parts with either a dovetailing bit or a straight bit, using a guide collar in the router base to follow the template pattern.

Routing A Half-Blind Dovetail

Be sure to carefully read and follow the setup instructions that come with your dovetail jig. Typically, there are numerous adjustments to be made before the jig is ready for use. The manual will probably outline in detail the step-by-step process for making a half-blind dovetail joint using the starter template supplied with the jig. Mount this template on your jig.

Next, install the appropriate guide collar and dovetail bit in your router, and adjust the bit depth to the manual's specifications. Be aware that precision is critical with each step of this process. If the manual says $19/32$ in. for a depth setting, do your best to set this accurately. Each variable in the setup will affect how well the joint fits together in the end.

The best way to ensure an accurate setup is to make test cuts on

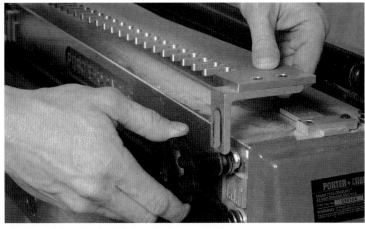

Install the half-blind template that comes with your jig. Mount a straight bit and the proper guide collar in your hanheld router.

scrap material that matches both the width and thickness of your final workpieces. Slip these test parts into the jig. Generally, the drawer face installs on top of the jig, and the drawer side fits vertically in the front clamp, with the board facing the floor. There will be an offset required between these two parts when you fit them in the clamps, so follow the manual carefully. Again, this offset will be a precise distance that must be set exactly.

It's important that the workpieces are absolutely flat, square on the ends and uniformly thick, so a careful job of initial surfacing is impera-

Clamp the joint parts in the jig. If you are making a drawer, usually the drawer face mounts on top and one of the drawer sides clamps in front. It's a good idea to make your first cuts on scraps of test material that match the dimensions of the final workpieces.

Follow the instructions that come with your jig to set the proper offset between the parts as well as other stops and guides. This is usually a fussy—but critical—task.

tive. You should also find out whether your jig requires parts made to a specific width; some jigs won't cut an even pattern on the ends of the joint unless the part width is evenly divisible by a set measurement. Find out if this is true for your dovetail jig. It will save you frustration in the end.

Make final adjustments to the jig before cutting the test parts. Some jigs, like the one shown here, will have adjustable stops that need to be set. Once these are accurately positioned, you can cut joint after joint of the same size without calibrating the jig again.

For the jig shown here, the first cut to make is a "climb" cut that shears away the face grain on the back of the drawer side. Slide the router from right to left to make this cut; you'll notice that it's opposite the usual feed direction for handheld routing.

To shape the matching pins and tails, feed the router in and out of the

Your first cut may actually be a "climb" cut that shears the edge fibers to prevent tearout. Climb cuts have an opposite feed direction from normal handheld routing: right to left.

Now cut the pins and tails to shape by feeding the router in and out of the template fingers. Go over this important cut twice, seating the guide collar fully in the back of each finger slot to make sure you remove all the waste material.

template "fingers" from one end of the joint to the other, working left to right as usual. Make this cut gently to prevent tearout and to help minimize excessive strain on the bit. Before removing the parts from the clamps, be sure you've cut every finger slot carefully; as a preventive measure, go back across the joint a second time with the router to clean up any remaining waste. Even the smallest bit of extra waste can keep the parts from fitting together.

Unclamp and remove the workpieces and inspect the finished joint. Notice how the slotted tails have curved bottoms that fit the curved backs of the pins. It's a clever bit of engineering and a brain-teaser to understand until you see both halves of the joint side by side. If luck is on your side, both ends of the pin board (drawer front) should be evenly sized so the pattern looks balanced from one end to the other. Try to fit the parts together. The pins and slots should mesh with a slight amount of friction and with minimal gaps in between. Don't be surprised if they don't, however. You'll probably need to adjust the bit depth or workpiece positions in the jig slightly to create a tighter or looser-fitting joint. You may also have to make adjustments to create a pattern that begins and ends evenly on the edges of the parts.

If it's back to the drawing board for another round of cuts, slice this attempt off the ends of your test pieces, and make a few more adjustments to your setup. Try to work systematically with each test cut, changing one variable at a time to see how that change affects the outcome. Do your best to keep from getting frustrated. Eventually you'll arrive at the right combination of settings to achieve the perfect joint. Take notes as you go so you can refer to them the next time you need to set up the jig.

Notice how one template and jig setup creates mirror-opposite, interlocking pins and tails for a half-blind dovetail joint.

Don't be surprised if your first test joint doesn't fit together perfectly. You may need to make several test cuts and adjust the jig or bit depth settings to improve the setup. Cut off and save each attempt to help you keep track of the adjustments and results.

A properly made half-blind dovetail should fit together easily by hand without gaps or binding between the parts. Ideally, the outermost edges of the joint should match.

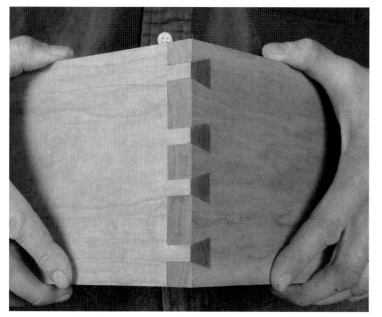

Setting up most dovetail jigs to cut through dovetails is a more challenging proposition than half-blind dovetails. Here, you'll use two different template setups and bits to cut the joint parts, which adds complexity to the routing process.

Routing A Through Dovetail

Through dovetails present similar challenges for setting up and cutting the joints accurately. The position of the jig stops, the bit depth settings and the spacing of the template on the jig all impact the final fit of the pins and tails. Make plenty of extra test stock that matches the width and thickness of your drawer workpieces, and plan on setting aside a few hours to experiment with your setup. Cutting through dovetails will require a good deal of patience and a methodical approach to achieve a perfect fit. Don't expect the first go-around to fit properly, but stick with it and follow your manual carefully. Make one adjustment at a time to help control the setup variables, and take notes as you go.

Notice in the photo sequence on the next few pages that you'll need a different template style for cutting through dovetails than the "comb" pattern used for half-blind dovetails. For this joint, the template consists of a group of moveable guides. The guides can be adjusted to cut equally spaced pins and tails, or you can vary the spacing for a more custom appearance. Follow the instructions that come with your jig to install and adjust the template accordingly.

TIP

CHECK THE LOCATION OF THE DRAWER BOTTOM GROOVE BEFORE YOU CUT IT

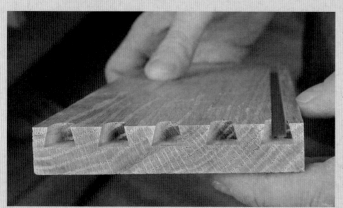

Think carefully about where a drawer bottom groove will intersect the corner joint. You may need to stop the groove short if it will pass through a pin and show from the outside.

When building a drawer with dovetail joints, be careful when you position and cut the groove for the drawer bottom. Try to situate the drawer bottom groove so it lines up with slots in the dovetail joint. This way, you can simply cut the drawer bottom slot all the way across the drawer face without issue. When the groove lines up with the pins instead of the slots, you'll have to stop the groove short of the ends, otherwise you'll cut through the pins, and the groove will show through on the finished joint. There's no good way to fix this mistake; you'll need to make another drawer face and try again.

Cutting through dovetails will require a different template setup than the "comb" style fixed template used for half-blind dovetails. Here, the template consists of moveable guide forks.

One significant difference for cutting through dovetails with the jig shown here is that both halves of the joint are milled using only the front clamp of the jig. Plus, you'll cut the parts one at a time. The drawer sides are routed first, using a guide collar and dovetail bit to create the "tail" side of the joint. Check your dovetail jig owner's manual to be sure the dovetail bit you are using has the correct bevel angles—dovetail bits are made in 7.5°, 9° and 14° styles. If you use the wrong bit angle, the joint won't fit together properly.

You'll see in the photo series that the router is fed only into the forked areas of the guides for cutting the tails. Move the router from left to right across the template to rout the

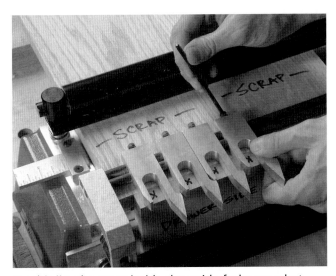

On this jig, the areas inside the guide forks are what need to be removed to create the tails. It helps to mark them with "X"s to avoid confusion during routing.

Install the guide collar and correct dovetail bit for your jig. Set the bit depth to account for the thickness of the template and the drawer face.

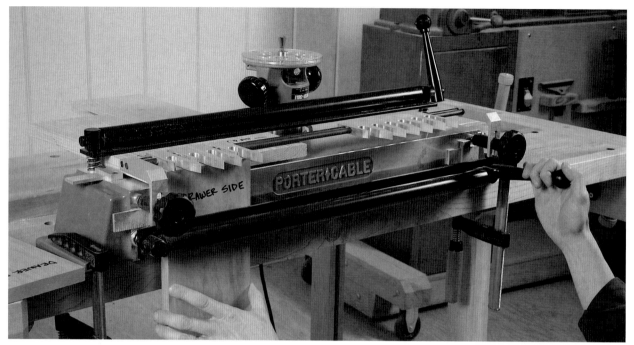

Install the through dovetail template in your jig and follow the instructions in your owner's manual to set the guide fork spacing. Clamp the drawer side board in the jig to prepare for cutting the tails.

tails. The bit will be cutting a larger amount of material away each time, so don't force the cut. Feeding gently and slowly will produce the smoothest cuts. For this jig, a backup board clamped behind the workpiece helps eliminate tearout on the back side of the cuts.

Once the tails are cut, reconfigure the template on the jig, if necessary, and switch to a straight bit for cutting pins on the ends of the drawer face. It may help to mark "X"s in the waste areas so you won't get confused about where to make the pin cuts. Again, a backup board clamped behind the drawer face will help ensure clean pin cuts. If there are spaces on the

Cut the tails by guiding the router inside each fork. These are heavy cuts, so feed the router gently keeping a firm grip on the tool. A scrap backer board protects the jig.

Once the tails are cut on both drawer sides, replace them with the drawer face to make the pin cuts. Reset the jig accordingly; on this jig, the router cuts the pins around one long fork of each guide.

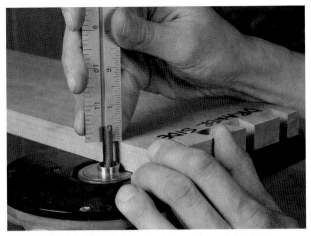

Pins are cut with a guide collar and straight bit instead of a dovetail bit. Set the bit height to account for the drawer side and template thicknesses.

Steer the router from left to right around the long guide forks to mill the pins. Rout the outermost spaces carefully to avoid tearout.

ends of the drawer face, use extra care when routing this material away. The corner grain chips easily, and tearout or chipping will show when the joint is assembled.

When all the pins and tails are cut, fit the pieces together. The parts should slip together fairly easily. If the parts fit but so tightly that you want to reach for the closest mallet, you're not done tweaking your set-up. Same goes for a sloppy, overly loose fit. Either way, the jig or bit

depth needs a bit more fine-tuning. Make your bit and jig adjustments and try another set of test parts. It may take many attempts to achieve that ideal friction fit, but take heart: when you finally rout enough test pieces to get everything dialed in correctly, you'll create a beautiful joint that's worth boasting rights to anyone who appreciates it. Be sure to take notes as you work through the adjustment process so the process goes a bit easier the next time around.

On a drawer made with through dovetails, the drawer face (foreground) receives pin cuts, while the drawer sides (rear) are milled with tail cuts.

GLUING AND CLAMPING TECHNIQUES

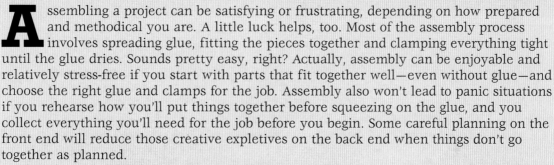

Assembling a project can be satisfying or frustrating, depending on how prepared and methodical you are. A little luck helps, too. Most of the assembly process involves spreading glue, fitting the pieces together and clamping everything tight until the glue dries. Sounds pretty easy, right? Actually, assembly can be enjoyable and relatively stress-free if you start with parts that fit together well—even without glue—and choose the right glue and clamps for the job. Assembly also won't lead to panic situations if you rehearse how you'll put things together before squeezing on the glue, and you collect everything you'll need for the job before you begin. Some careful planning on the front end will reduce those creative expletives on the back end when things don't go together as planned.

This chapter will help improve your assembly techniques in several ways. First, you'll get an introduction to various woodworking adhesives so you can choose correctly for different applications. We'll also review various styles of woodworking clamps that are helpful to have on hand. The right clamps, applied judiciously, will make complicated glue-ups much easier. Of course, not all woodworking joints will stand up to the test of time with glue alone. Learn more about options for reinforcing joints with screws and nails in Chapter Five.

If you've never glued a panel together, you'll learn how to do it here. Panel glue-ups are one of the most common assembly processes you'll undertake when working with solid wood. You'll also learn how to dry-bend wood around a form to make curved parts as well as how to apply plastic laminate. Then, we'll provide a variety of useful assembly tips at the end of the chapter to add to your repertoire. This chapter won't show you how to glue a project together from start to finish; that would only serve limited value. Instead, you'll get the kind of general tips and techniques that you can apply to any project you're building.

One aspect of assembly not covered in this chapter is sanding. Sanding may not seem like part of the assembly process, but generally it helps to sand your project parts before putting them together. It's much easier to sand when all the surfaces of workpieces are still fully accessible. Turn to Chapter Seven if you want to learn more about the sanding process. Give your project parts a thorough smoothing, and they'll be ready for the assembly table.

CHOOSING THE RIGHT GLUE FOR THE JOB

There are more than a dozen different types of woodworking glues, and the choices can seem a little bewildering. The good news is, you don't need to buy them all. A couple glue types will probably suffice for most of your wood-to-wood gluing needs. This is not to say some types of glue are superfluous. Each glue is carefully formulated to achieve specific adhesive properties. If you are a boat builder, for instance, your demands for a water-resistant glue will differ from those of a woodworker who's simply building a deck chair for the patio. After all, the boat won't float if the glue fails. When the need for a specialized gap-filling, waterproof or slow-setting glue arises, it's out there if you know what to buy. For less specific applications, you'll be fine using adhesives that are commonly available from the lumberyard or home center. Here's a short guide to help you pick suitable glues for your project needs.

There are many formulations of glue for woodworking. Choosing the "right" glue for a task depends on factors such as the type of material being glued, complexity of the glue-up, reversibility, drying time, moisture exposure and of course, final joint strength.

GLUE TERMINOLOGY

Here are some helpful definitions for common glue terminology:

Open time: The amount of time you have, under normal temperature and humidity conditions, for spreading glue and assembling the parts before the glue begins to set.

Set time: The amount of time to allow for glue to cure before removing clamps. Set time does not mean that the glue is fully cured. Parts can be gently handled but not machined. Allow at least 24 hours for any adhesive to reach full strength.

Shelf life: Duration between when the glue was manufactured and when it should be tossed out. Shelf life usually decreases as soon as you open the container.

Glue creep: The tendency of cured glue joints to shift or pull apart slightly under extreme stress.

Yellow Carpenter's Glue

Adhesive Type

Aliphatic resin; non-toxic in both wet and cured forms

Applications And Properties

For indoor projects that aren't subjected to extreme humidity or water immersion, the venerable yellow carpenter's glue is an excellent general-purpose adhesive. Use it with confidence for panel gluing and joinery. It has a relatively short open time of 3 to 5 minutes, so work quickly once it's applied. Allow the glue to set for 30 minutes to one hour before removing clamps. Yellow glue has poor gap-filling capabilities and its strength will be compromised in this situation. Do not use it for bonding oily woods such as cocobolo, rosewood or teak. It has poor resistance to glue creep.

Cleanup

Soapy water when wet; acetone, toluene or xylene when cured

Shelf Life

2 years; less if allowed to freeze

Water-Resistant Yellow Glue

Adhesive Type

Cross-linking polyaliphatic; non-toxic in both wet and cured forms

Applications And Properties

Water-resistant yellow glue is a good choice for outdoor projects that occasionally get wet or for interior projects. It has the same open and set times as interior yellow glue. Do not use it as a gap-filler or on oily woods. It has poor resistance to glue creep. Some manufacturers now offer waterproof yellow glue that passes specifications for Type 1 water resistance. It isn't intended for continuous submersion.

Cleanup

Soapy water when wet; acetone, toluene or xylene when cured

Shelf Life

2 to 5 years; shorter if allowed to freeze

White Glue

Adhesive Type

Polyvinyl acetate (PVA); non-toxic in both wet and cured forms

Applications And Properties

As unlikely as it might seem, ordinary white "school" glue can be used effectively for assembling indoor projects. Some woodworkers prefer it to yellow carpenter's glue in certain situations, because PVA has a longer open time of about 10 minutes. Allow it to set for at least 1 hour before unclamping. White glue is a good choice for bonding veneer to substrates or fabric to the backs of slats when making tambour doors. It has poor gap-filling qualities and resistance to glue creep.

Cleanup

Soapy water when wet; acetone, toluene or xylene when cured

Shelf Life

1 year; shorter if allowed to freeze

Polyurethane Glue

Adhesive Type
Polyurethane

Applications And Properties
Polyurethane is an excellent general-purpose adhesive for both indoor and outdoor projects where parts can be clamped together. It is waterproof, freeze/thaw stable and has excellent glue creep resistance. It will bond wood to wood as well as dissimilar materials such as metals, plastics, stone and ceramic. However, it will not bridge gaps, and its strength will be compromised if joint parts are too loose.

Polyurethane has the unusual handling characteristic of forming a thick, sticky foam as it cures. The curing process is activated by moisture, so dampen one surface of the joint with water. Be sure to clamp parts securely to prevent the glue from opening joints as it expands. Open time is approximately 20 minutes, with a set time of about 45 minutes to 1 hour. Wear latex or rubber gloves and old clothes when using poly glue; it will stain skin, and both the foaming and cured glue are difficult to remove from fabric.

Cleanup
Mineral spirits before the glue cures; scrape or sand off excess glue when cured

Shelf Life
6 months to 1 year; shorter once opened

Construction Adhesive

Adhesive Type
Solvent-based polymer; non-toxic once cured

Applications And Properties
Contractors use construction adhesive for bonding subfloors to framing and a variety of other non-structural applications. It dispenses with a caulk gun in a thick bead that does not drip or run. You can also buy smaller quantities in squeeze tubes.

Construction adhesive is a good choice for sandwiching sheet goods together or for gluing joints on exterior projects. It resists water penetration and bonds well to treated lumber. Open time is 15 minutes, and the set time is about one hour. The adhesive reaches maximum strength in seven days. Use nails or screws to reinforce joints that do not interlock. Construction adhesive is freeze/thaw stable and remains flexible after it cures, which can be beneficial for allowing wood to expand and contract.

Cleanup
Mineral spirits before the adhesive cures; scrape off excess adhesive when cured

Shelf Life
Several months if you plug the nozzle

Epoxy

Adhesive Type
Two-part epoxy resin and hardener

Applications And Properties
Epoxy is an ideal adhesive for your most demanding applications. It is waterproof, fills gaps without losing strength and will bond even oily woods together without issue. Epoxy does not creep when cured, so it's a good choice for dry bending or high-stress joints. The working and set time for epoxy will vary, depending on the formulation. You can buy epoxy with open times as short as five minutes or longer than an hour. Generally, the tradeoff for shorter open times is less strength in the final cured form. Using epoxy involves mixing resin and hardener together to activate the curing process. Wear gloves and apply epoxy neatly: the cured adhesive is hard to remove.

Cleanup
Lacquer thinner when still wet; scrape or sand off excess adhesive when cured

Shelf Life
1 to 3 years

Liquid Hide Glue

Adhesive Type
Natural protein emulsion

Applications And Properties
Woodworkers and musical instrument makers have used dry forms of hide for centuries.

Dry hide glue is still available today, but the glue must be heated to liquefy it, and the set time is short. Now, you can buy hide glue in a convenient liquid form that dispenses like ordinary squeeze glue.

Liquid hide glue has an extended open time of 30 minutes—beneficial for carrying out complicated glue-ups—and it sets in about 2 hours. It is ideal for joints that may need to be disassembled later. Just dampen cured hide glue with water and apply heat to break the glue bond. Hide glue offers exceptional strength for interior joinery and it does not creep. It also accepts stains and finishes, which makes it a good choice for applying thin wood veneers: if the adhesive bleeds through wood pores, it won't show up under stain.

Cleanup
Soapy water when wet or dry

Shelf Life
1 year

Contact Cement

Adhesive Type
Water- or solvent-based neoprene

Applications And Properties
Use contact cement when you are applying plastic laminate to a substrate sheet material. The adhesive has a thin, milky consistency and can be applied easily with a foam roller. Roll it onto both surfaces of the joint, allow the adhesive to dry and then join the parts together. Contact cement is made in both solvent-based and water-based formulations. The solvent-based variety is flammable and hazardous to breathe, so wear a cartridge respirator and work in a well-ventilated area. The water-based formulation is non-flammable and much less noxious, so a respirator isn't necessary. Contact cement has an open time of 30 minutes to an hour, and it sets immediately to full strength when the parts come together. Heating the joint with a warm iron or heat gun will reactivate the adhesive if you need to break the bond.

Cleanup
Lacquer thinner for solvent-based; soapy water for water-based

Shelf Life
1 year

Hot-Melt Glue

Adhesive Type
Ethylene Vinyl Acetate

Applications And Properties
Hot-melt glue is a good choice for joining wood parts temporarily, building scaled prototypes or for attaching templates to workpieces when template routing. Hot-melt glue is commonly sold in stick form and dispenses from a heat gun. The glue begins to set as soon as it starts to cool, which takes a minute or less. It can fill gaps but has reduced bond strength in these situations.

Cleanup
Breaks off of non-porous surfaces easily when cured; scrape off excess glue from porous materials

Shelf Life
Indefinite

Instant-Set Glue

Adhesive Type
Cyanoacrylate

Applications And Properties
"Super glue" isn't just handy to keep in the kitchen junk drawer. It also has value as a woodworking adhesive. Use it to bond dissimilar materials to wood, such as magnets on doors, or wherever you need a quick, relatively durable bond on delicate trim work or accents. Wood turners commonly use a mixture of "CA" glue and sawdust to fill cracks and other surface imperfections on turnings. As we all know, instant-set glue has a short open time and reaches full strength immediately.

Cleanup
Scrape off dried glue or use acetone to remove it

Shelf Life
6 months to 1 year; less once opened

Applying And Cleaning Up Glue

The general technique for gluing joints is quite easy. Since you'll probably reach for yellow glue more than other types, we'll use it for the following example. Apply a bead of glue to both parts of the joint and spread the glue out into a thin film that covers the full contact area. Use a paintbrush, a scrap of wood, or even your finger to do this. Aim for a thinner, rather than a thicker, film on both surfaces. Too much glue will simply squeeze out of the joint and be wasted when you apply clamps. Wet glue also acts like a lubricant between two parts making them slippery and harder to clamp.

Press the pieces together so the surfaces meet fully and the joint parts are flush. When applicable, slide the parts back and forth against one another a few times to help drive glue deeper into the wood pores. Apply a few clamps across the joint, and tighten the clamps just enough to close any small gaps that may be present between the parts. Over-tightening the clamps can damage the wood, distort the joint, or force too much glue out of the joint and compromise the bond strength. If it seems to take too much clamping pressure to close a joint, you may have trapped a bit of debris in the seam. Pull the parts open and inspect them. Clean off the glue, if necessary, and check the part fit again. Clamps are not a remedy for fixing workpieces that don't fit together properly.

One way to tell you have a well-glued and clamped joint is when it shows a thin line of glue or tiny glue beads along the seam between the parts. If you have lots of glue pooling on the surface or dripping underneath, you've probably applied too much. Wait a few minutes until the excess glue seeps out of the joint. Recheck the part alignment to see that the joint parts haven't slipped out of alignment during clamping. After about 15 minutes, scrape off the congealed glue with an old wood chisel or sharp putty knife. Try to remove most of the semi-cured glue by careful scraping. Then, wipe up any remaining residue with a water-dampened rag. Don't overdue the wiping; switch to a fresh area of the rag or wring out your sponge with water to prevent smearing glue back onto the wood. Even diluted glue smears can show up later when you stain the wood or apply a finish.

Glue bonds are beneficial for strengthening most wood joints, but not all of them. Be careful to keep glue away from cross-grain joints where one of the two parts must expand and contract. Two examples of this situation are when connecting solid-wood tabletops to the table frame or fitting a solid-wood panel inside a door frame. Tabletops and door panels must be allowed to swell and shrink across the grain as humidity levels change. If you apply glue all along these cross-grain joints, eventually, either the glue joint will break as the wood attempts to move, or the wood will split along the grain.

Choosing Clamps for Woodworking

There are many different clamp styles that can help make assembly easier. You may have heard that old woodworking adage that says you can never have enough clamps, and it seems to be true. Just when you need one more clamp during a glue-up, Murphy's Law takes effect and you'll discover the clamp rack is empty. Clamps can be expensive to buy, but the upside is that they'll last a lifetime if you clean them occasionally and keep them from rusting.

For gluing up wide panels or for general joint assembly, you'll want to own at least a half dozen long pipe or bar clamps. Both styles feature moveable clamp heads that fit onto either a steel bar or a length of ordinary 3/4-in. iron plumbing pipe. One clamp head slides along the bar or pipe for making coarse adjustments; the other clamp head is fixed and has a hand screw mechanism for final tightening. Pipe clamps are particularly versatile, because you can install the clamp heads on pipes of any length.

For clamping shorter assemblies, have a selection of 18- to 36-in. bar clamps on hand. They're easier to handle and apply plenty of clamping pressure. Most styles have a fixed head on the end of the bar and a sliding head on the other. Some have a twist handle for tightening, while others have a squeeze grip. Squeeze-grip style bar clamps have a quick-release lever that loosens the clamp. Bar clamps have a series of spring-loaded slip plates that provide the same quick-release function.

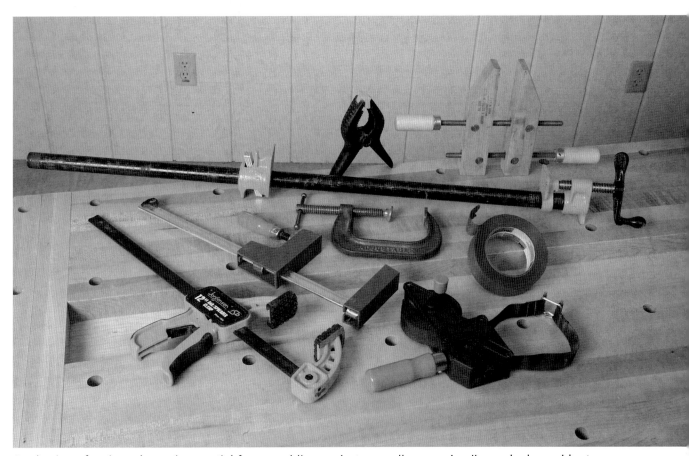

A selection of various clamps is essential for assembling projects as well as securing jigs and edge guides to workpieces. Build a collection of long pipe clamps, shorter bar and quick-grip clamps, C-clamps, spring clamps, woodscrew clamps and band clamps. Even good-quality painter's tape, heavy rubber bands or rope can be used as makeshift clamps.

To clamp small parts or hold jigs in place on router tables and saws, you'll want to own several C-clamps in the 4- to 6-inch size range. Inexpensive metal or plastic spring clamps are also handy to have for low-strength clamping situations. Buy the type with pivoting plastic or rubber-lined jaws. Wood screws, which operate by turning two threaded shafts in opposite directions, are not only effective for closing joints but also do double-duty as makeshift vises to hold parts steady on the drill press.

Band or strap clamps are helpful for pulling mitered joints closed, securing the staves of round cylinders or holding odd-shaped assemblies together, such as chair legs and rails. These clamps have an adjustable strap that cinches up with a ratcheting mechanism. In a pinch, a length of surgical tubing, a piece of rope, or even strips of packing or duct tape can become band clamps.

Clamps don't need much maintenance, but spray a little lubricant on the thread assemblies every so often. Chip dried glue off of clamp heads to keep it from denting workpieces. Scrape dried glue off of clamp bars and pipes as well so the moveable head slides smoothly.

Dry-Fitting And Staging An Assembly

Before slathering glue onto your carefully crafted project parts and clamping them together, plan how you want the assembly process to go. Think about each step, just as you would if you were setting up for a machine operation. In order for parts to go together as you hope, you have to work methodically and neatly but without delay. Once the glue is spread, you'll have a limited time to get everything properly fitted and tightened down.

One way to prevent gluing and clamping headaches is to dry-fit the parts first. Be sure all the joints go together easily without glue. If you have to reach for a mallet to pound things closed, you'll probably have to do it again when you apply glue. Fix those overly tight joints. A "slip fit" with just a hint of friction is generally tight enough for glue to bond properly. There's really no need for brute force in the assembly process.

It's a good idea to stage some glue-ups ahead of others, even if it means that assembling a project takes several days. Better to allow some stages of the glue-up time to dry than try to do too much gluing at once. For particularly complicated glue-ups, write down the order in which you'll glue the parts together at the dry-fit stage, then follow it carefully. Sometimes it helps to label your parts, especially if several pieces look alike but don't assemble interchangeably. Do whatever you can to keep from getting confused and gluing together the wrong pieces.

Rehearsing your assembly is also a good chance to arrange all the hardware and supplies you'll want to have close at hand. Install the clamps on the dry-assembled parts to make sure they'll work properly, then open the clamps a few cranks wider than necessary when you remove them. That way they'll slide right into place without extra fuss. Lay them within arm's reach of the bench. Have a bucket of water and a sponge close by for wiping up squeeze-out and drips as well as to keep your hands clean while you work. Be sure there are paper towels nearby as well. Line your bench top with waxed paper, a sheet of plastic or plastic trash bags to keep the bench clean and to prevent parts from sticking where you don't want them to. If your bench is small and you have lots of parts to glue together, set your supplies on another table next to the bench to reduce the clutter.

Gluing Up A Panel

When gluing up individual boards to make larger panels, some woodworkers use biscuits or dowels to align the joints. However, all you really need for strength is glue. Do a careful job of jointing beforehand to make sure all the panel pieces have flat, smooth edges. Arrange the parts into a panel with a pleasing grain pattern that hides the seams. If the pieces of the panel are wider than about 4 in., alternate the arrangement of the growth rings from piece to piece; it will help keep the panel from warping later on. For panels made with narrower strips, don't worry about the orientation of the growth rings.

Try not to rush the process of gluing up a panel. Glue a few pieces together at a time so you can keep the number of wet glue joints to two or three seams. Don't try to glue up the entire panel at once if it has more than three boards, or you'll probably end up with pieces sliding out of position during clamping and a lot more wet glue to clean up. Then glue those assemblies together to make a larger one. This will also help reduce the anxiety that sometimes goes along with big glue-ups.

To assemble the panel, spread an even coating of glue on the mating surfaces of the pieces, press them together and slide the parts back and forth to help spread the glue. Apply clamps both above and below the panel in an alternating pattern. This will help distribute the clamping pressure evenly. The number of clamps you need is somewhat arbitrary; install enough clamps to close the joints.

Usually, a clamp every 10 in. or so should suffice.

When applying the clamps, the order in which you install them isn't critical. You can start in the middle and work outward or from one end to the other. Try to apply them all with just enough tension to keep them in place, then tighten each one a little at a time so the glue has a chance to seep out. Check the alignment of the joints as you go along; remember, the glue will act like a lubricant until the

When edge-gluing boards to make a panel, apply a thin, even bead of glue to the mating edges of each joint. Spread out the glue to form a thin film—it doesn't take a river of glue to form a sturdy bond.

Rub the glue joints together to help spread the glue, then apply clamps across the joint. Alternate them above and below the panel to help prevent cupping when you tighten the clamps. Apply just enough clamping pressure to close the joints.

excess oozes out. Tighten the clamps reasonably but not with gorilla force. Too much tension will warp the panel.

Once all the clamps are in position and fully tight, check the panel for flatness with a straightedge. Loosen the clamps slightly to correct any distortions you find. When the glue sets up to a rubbery consistency, scrape off the excess. Flip the panel carefully and scrape the bottom face as well. Keep the clamps in place for at least a couple hours to give the glue a chance to set completely.

It's easy to make a curved workpiece by bending flexible strips of wood around a shop-made form. The adhesive strength of the glue laminations holds the strips in shape.

Before the glue sets, check the panel face for flatness with a straightedge. If the panel is cupping or the boards are sliding out of alignment, try loosening the clamps slightly to relieve some of the pressure.

Once the glue dries past the "wet" stage to a rubbery consistency, scrape off the glue beads with a paint scraper or putty knife. Flip the panel over and scrape the bottom face as well.

Dry Bending Around A Form

Dry bending is an easy way to make curved parts from thin strips of wood. It's an excellent technique to use for making curved rockers and arm leans on chairs. The process involves clamping thin strips of pliable wood around a solid form, with a layer of glue between each of the pieces. The glue's adhesive strength will hold the strips in their curved shape when the workpiece is removed from the form.

There are several factors to account for when you are dry bending. First, most wood species will work for dry bending, but the harder the wood, the thinner the strips will have to be. Ash, oak and cherry are ideal for dry bending. Air-dried lumber tends to be more pliable than kiln-dried lumber, but again, even kiln-dried lumber will bend satisfactorily if the strips are thin and the shape of the curve is reasonably gentle. For really tight curves, you may need strips as thin as 1/16 in.

The type of glue you use for dry bending is critical. Glues that tend to creep when cured are poor choices for dry bending. Use polyurethane, hide glue or epoxy for best results. Plastic resin glue is another ideal adhesive, but it's harder to find. Also, be sure you have plenty of clamps to carry out this technique: you'll need to install clamps every 4 to 6 in..

Build your bending form by gluing together layers of MDF or plywood into a stack that you can cut into the curved shape you want. Make the stack tall enough to provide plenty of support for the width of the curved shape you are making. You can build a form that backs up just one side of the bent lamination (as shown in the photo sequence here) or sandwiches both sides. A "sandwich" will apply more even clamping pressure. Cut your form to shape, then drive wood or deck screws through the lamination to reinforce it further. Smooth the curve carefully by filing and sanding: any flat or irregular spots on your form may transfer into the final lamination, so spend time perfecting the form. Then apply several coats of paste wax to all of its surfaces to keep the glued joints from sticking to it.

Rip your strips from a piece of thick stock so the face grain of the original lumber becomes the thin edge of the strips. Plane the strips down to thickness using a slave board in your planer. The final thickness of the strips will depend on the wood you are using and the shape you're making, but 1/8-in. thickness will probably be thin enough.

Dry bending is definitely a process you'll want to carry out first without any glue involved. Assemble your stack of dry strips around the form, starting in the middle of the form and clamping outward to both ends. Tighten the first clamp fully to hold the strips in place, but apply the

Make a bending form by gluing and screwing layers of sheet stock together in the shape you want to make. Fasten the built-up template to a larger base. Spread a generous coating of paste wax all over the form to keep glue from sticking to it.

other clamps gradually, tightening in stages as necessary to bring the strips to shape without breaking them. Use enough clamps to eliminate all gaps between the parts.

When you are comfortable with the clamping process, proceed with the actual glue-up. Spread glue on the strips, slip them into place on the

Slave Board

Rip and plane enough strips of stock to form the required thickness of the bent lamination. Plane the strips down to around 1/8 in. thick, and clamp them in place on the form to see if they are thin enough to bend properly. Use a slave board when planing thin stock like this.

Spead glue onto the laminations to prepare them for clamping. If you use polyurethane glue, wet one surface of each joint with a water-dampened sponge to activate the glue's curing process.

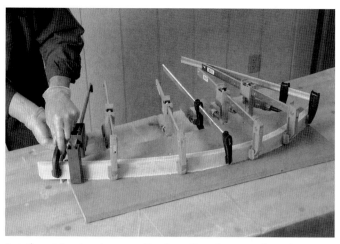

Set the strips in place on the bending form and apply a clamp about every 6 in. Work from the center of the shape outward to the ends. Tighten the clamps gradually to avoid cracking the laminations. Allow the glue to cure completely before unclamping.

form and repeat the clamping procedure you've rehearsed to bend the parts to shape. Leave the clamps in place for 24 hours, even with quick-setting adhesives like polyurethane or epoxy. You want to make sure the glue is fully set and cured before releasing clamping pressure.

One final issue with dry bending is that to some degree, your lamination will "spring back" slightly when you take it out of the form. The amount of springback will depend on a number of variables you can't really control. The best way to determine how much springback to expect is to carry out a fully glued test lamination using the same lumber as the final laminations. Another way to account for springback is to make the shape of the bending form slightly tighter than you ultimately want; give the lamination 1/4 to 1/2 in. of leeway for springback on both ends of the shape.

After you remove the assembly from the form, clean up the foam-covered edges by trimming off the glue on the bandsaw and jointing the final part edges smooth.

Scrape away glue squeeze-out from one edge of the bent lamination, then flatten it on the jointer, if applicable. Provided the glue-up has straight edges, you can joint it just as you would a normal board.

Saw or plane the other edge flat. Here, a resawing "point" fence provides just enough support to rip the curved workpiece easily.

APPLYING PLASTIC LAMINATE

Plastic laminate works as well in the shop as it does in the kitchen. It's an excellent choice for creating smooth, durable and easy-to-clean worksurfaces, jigs and fence facings. Applying plastic laminate is simple: Start with a stable substrate for the laminate. Sheet materials like MDF, particleboard or plywood are the best choices. Use a piece of laminate larger than the substrate so you can trim it flush later. Clean the surfaces of the substrate and the laminate carefully with mineral spirits and compressed air before you begin. Any residue or grit will weaken the adhesive bond, so you want to start with absolutely clean surfaces.

Clean the back of the laminate and the substrate thoroughly with compressed air to remove all traces of debris, then brush or roll contact cement onto both faces. Let the glue dry past the wet stage until it's tacky.

Using contact cement is different than working with other glues. The bond is formed by sticking two cemented surfaces togther after the glue feels dry. Use a foam roller to spread an even coating of cement over the laminate and substrate, then allow the cement to dry beyond the "tacky" stage. Lay strips of wood or dowels over the substrate to act as spacers for positioning the laminate. Spacers are necessary, because contact cement will bond immediately once the laminate touches the substrate. It's difficult to peel laminate off the substrate without breaking it.

Once the laminate is lined up correctly, pull the strips out one at a time, starting from the middle. Press the laminate down as you remove each strip to prevent trapping pockets of air. When all the strips are removed, use a J-roller or piece of 2 x 4 wrapped in a towel to press the laminate down firmly. This will both set the adhesive and drive out any air pockets that might be present. Be careful when rolling near the edges of the substrate to keep from cracking the overhanging laminate. Then, use a piloted straight bit or laminate trimming bit in your handheld router to trim off the excess laminate. The bit will leave a sharp top edge on the laminate; remove the edge with a fine-tooth file.

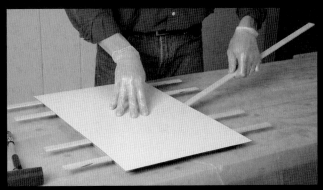

Lay a series of clean wood strips or dowels on the substrate before setting the laminate in place. This will allow you to make adjustments without touching the cemented faces together—the glue bonds instantly. Once the laminate is properly lined up over the substrate, pull out the spacers one at a time starting in the middle.

Roll the laminate down firmly on the substrate to remove air pockets and to promote a strong adhesive bond. Be careful not to press hard near the edges of the brittle laminate, or it will crack.

Trim off the excess laminate using a piloted flush-trim bit or a laminate trimming bit in a handheld router. Feed the router counterclockwise around the workpiece.

Reinforcing Joints With Screws Or Nails

Screws or nails form a mechanical connection that can help reinforce a joint if the glue bond ever fails. The strength of butt or rabbet joints is usually improved with a few fasteners added to it. You may even want to use screws instead of glue to join two parts that may need to be disassembled later on.

Types Of Woodworking Screws

Walk the fastener aisle of your local home center and you'll find lots of options for woodworking screws. For low-strength applications, such as attaching back panels to cabinets, ordinary black drywall screws work well. Switch to heavier-shanked flathead wood screws for general-purpose applications where joints are stressed or load-bearing. They're available in steel, brass or stainless compositions with a variety of chrome, brass or antique finishes. Trimhead screws, designed to attach trim and base moldings to walls, are another good option when you want to hide the screw head as much as possible; the heads are smaller than ordinary screws. You'll also find washer-head screws that work well for attaching thin sheet materials where a tapered head screw could otherwise pull through. For exterior projects, or whenever you are working with treated lumber, be sure to use coated deck screws or stainless-steel screws to prevent the fasteners from corroding. In terms of choosing the right screw length for the application, select a length that will place $2/3$rds of the screw into the threaded side of the joint.

On soft woods, you may be tempted to drive screws without first drilling pilot holes, and sometimes this works without problems. However, the best way to drive screws accurately without splitting the wood is to always drill a pilot hole first. Use a drill bit with a diameter that matches the shank thickness of the screw. When driving screws into particularly hard woods, rub a little beeswax on the threads to help reduce the friction. The screws will zip right into their pilot holes.

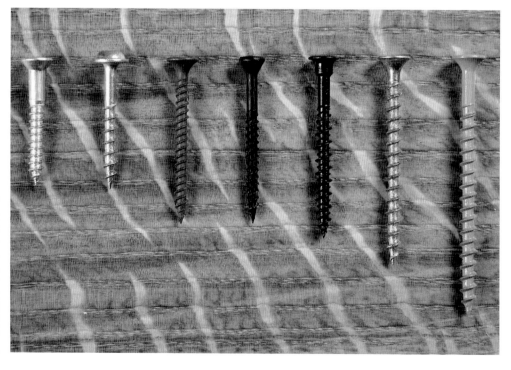

Common screws for woodworking include, from left: flathead, washer-head pocket screw, drywall, trimhead, hi/low thread for composite sheet goods, uncoated deck and coated deck screws for treated lumber.

Nailing With Nail Guns

There's nothing wrong with reaching for a hammer and nailset to drive nails the old-fashioned way, but there are lots of good reasons why air-powered nail guns have taken woodworking by storm. Nail guns are easy to use: place the tip of the gun where you want to drive the nail and squeeze the trigger. You'll never bruise your thumb again. If the gun is set correctly, it will not dent the surrounding wood like a hammer head can, and the gun will set the nail head neatly below the surface. The heads are small and virtually disappear with a little dab of putty.

Pneumatic nail guns are manufactured in a range of sizes and styles. Shown here, from left to right, are: a 16-gauge finish nailer, 18-gauge brad nailer and 16-gauge crown stapler. These three guns will enable you to drive nails from 5/8 in. to 2 in. long as well as heavy staples.

Nail guns are made to drive either fine brad nails or heavier finish nails. Guns are sized by the gauge of nail they drive. Typical nail gauges are 15, 16 and 18; the higher the number, the thinner the nail shank. Specialized "pin nailers" will drive even smaller gauges for attaching tiny moldings. Nail guns will accept a range of nail lengths within a given gauge, from 5/8 to 2 in. long, but most models won't accept all these nail sizes. You can also buy staple guns that drive heavy-duty crown staples for attaching upholstery or thin sheet materials. It isn't necessary to buy one of each gauge of nail gun. For general-purpose woodworking, an 18-gauge brad nailer is an excellent way to start, and it may be the only size you need.

Usually, you'll also have to buy an air compressor to drive a nail gun, although some brad nailers operate off of a rechargeable battery instead of a compressor. A small "pancake" or tank-style air compressor in the 2- to 6-gallon tank size will offer plenty of pressure to drive any brad or finish nailer. Home centers often sell 18-gauge brad nailers, a compressor and all the necessary connectors and air hose in a convenient prepackaged kit.

When nailing solid wood, hold the body of the nail gun perpendicular to the grain pattern. This will help prevent the nails from following the wood grain and splitting through the edge of the board.

TIPS FOR GLUING AND ASSEMBLY

Every project will present you with different gluing and clamping challenges, but a few tips under your belt always help. Here are a few ideas to tuck away the next time you're preparing to assemble a project.

A band clamp provides uniform clamping pressure around multiple joints at once. It's ideal for gluing up frames or irregular objects. Tightening a handle or ratcheting lever pulls the band tight.

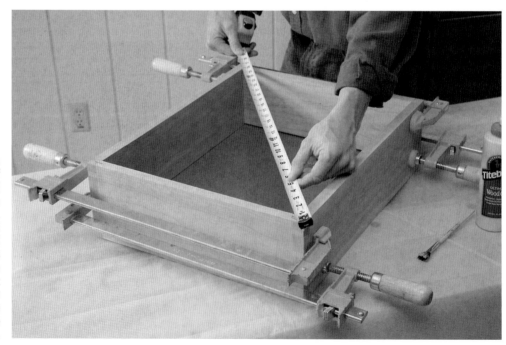

Measure across both diagonals of drawers, frames and boxes when assembling them. Matching diagonal measurements tell you the assembly is square. If the diagonals don't match, install a clamp along the longer diagonal to shorten it.

When using wood plugs to hide screw heads, line up the grain direction of the plug with the surrounding wood grain so it blends in. Use a piece of scrap that has the same grain pattern for the plug stock.

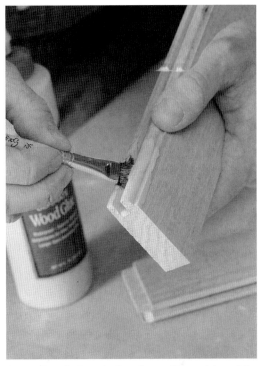

A small artist's paintbrush or disposable acid brushes for soldering make convenient glue applicators. If you clean the brush thoroughly after each use, it should last for years.

A biscuit applicator nozzle installed on a glue bottle makes it easy to apply glue quickly and easily into the biscuit slots.

Strips of painter's tape provide plenty of clamping pressure when gluing solid-wood edging to plywood shelves. Apply the strips every few inches along the length of the shelf edge.

Leave wood edging wider than necessary when gluing it to casework or shelving. Then use a piloted flush-trim bit installed in a trim router to shave off the excess for a perfect fit.

Fluted dowels work better than ordinary, smooth-sided dowels for dowel joints because the flutes allow excess glue to escape. Trapped glue could hold the joint open.

Before you assemble a raised-panel door, stain and finish the panel. This way, bare wood won't be exposed if the panel shrinks during dry winter months.

Even joints that match don't always fit together interchangeably. Assemble the parts dry to find the best fit, then use a system of hash marks to label each joint. Vary the number and spacing of the marks so you won't confuse them during glue-up.

Always assemble a project "dry" before reaching for the glue bottle. A dry run will help you figure out the best assembly and clamping procedure. It will also help you verify that each joint fits together properly.

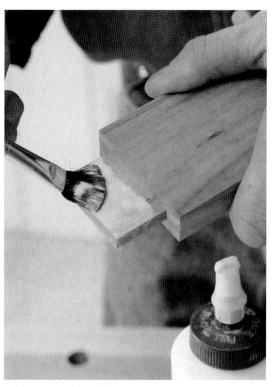

When spreading glue on a tenon, apply the glue to the tenon cheeks but not the shoulders. This way, the glue won't squeeze out onto the surrounding wood when you assemble the joint.

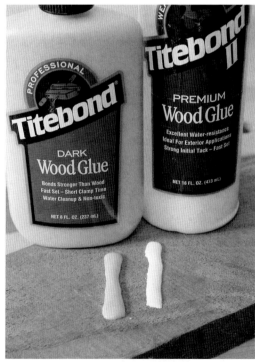

One way to help minimize glue lines on dark woods like walnut is to use a glue tinted for darker woods. However, ordinary white or yellow glue should barely show if a joint is made and assembled carefully.

Panels made from many narrow boards are easier to assemble if you glue them up in several narrower subassemblies first. This reduces the number of wet glue joints you need to contend with. Let the subassemblies dry, then glue them together.

If you use black-pipe clamps, be sure to keep the pipes from contacting wet glue on the wood. Black pipe will leave stains on the wood, which are a hassle to remove.

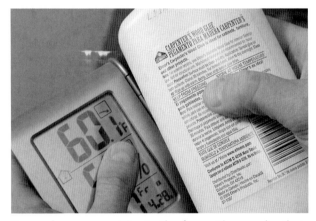

Some glues are sensitive to the freeze/thaw cycles that can occur in an unheated shop. The best way to extend their life is to store them at room temperature.

Polyurethane glue has a shorter shelf life than other glues, and it will eventually cure hard in the bottle. Unless you are building a large project, buy poly glue in the smallest bottle that will serve your needs.

An inexpensive pipe coupling can turn two shorter clamps into a long one when you need it. You'll find couplings sold in the plumbing section of any hardware store or home center.

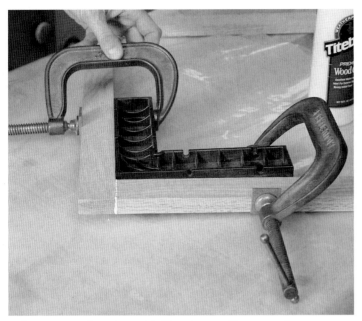

A few corner clamping aids like these will ensure that corners are square during glue-ups. These jigs are especially useful for assembling large cabinets because they also act like a third hand to hold parts in position.

Save those small scraps of leftover hardboard to use as clamp pads. They'll keep metal clamp heads from denting fragile workpieces if you overtighten the clamps.

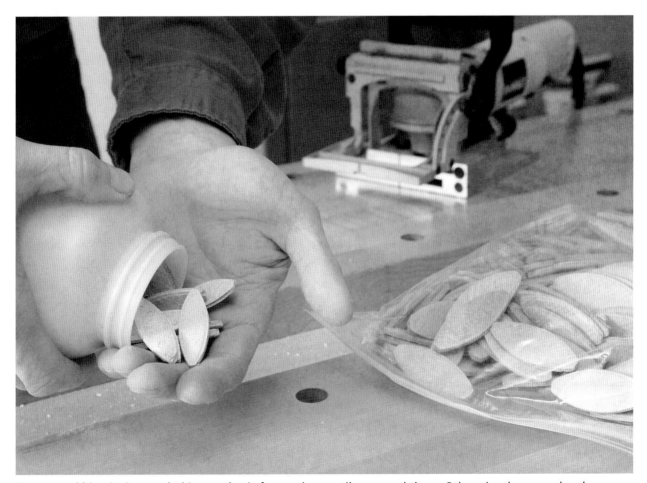

Store wood biscuits in a sealed jar or plastic freezer bag until you need them. Otherwise they can absorb moisture from the air and swell up until they won't fit in their slots.

SEVEN

SANDING AND FINISHING TECHNIQUES

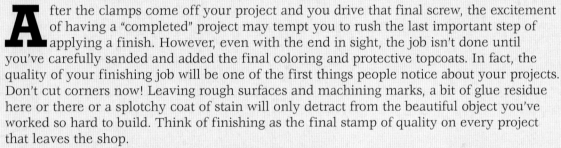

After the clamps come off your project and you drive that final screw, the excitement of having a "completed" project may tempt you to rush the last important step of applying a finish. However, even with the end in sight, the job isn't done until you've carefully sanded and added the final coloring and protective topcoats. In fact, the quality of your finishing job will be one of the first things people notice about your projects. Don't cut corners now! Leaving rough surfaces and machining marks, a bit of glue residue here or there or a splotchy coat of stain will only detract from the beautiful object you've worked so hard to build. Think of finishing as the final stamp of quality on every project that leaves the shop.

There are basically three steps to the finishing process. First, you need to thoroughly sand the surfaces of your project parts smooth to remove all evidence of the machining and assembly stages. Sanding also prepares the wood so finish will adhere properly. Second, you can color the wood to warm its tone, blend in variations of heartwood and sapwood or make the wood match other furniture. Staining can even make ordinary woods mimic more exotic or expensive species. The final stage is to add a topcoat that protects and beautifies the wood. This chapter will show you how to perform all three steps as well as give you an overview of easy-to-apply finish options.

PREPARING WOOD SURFACES BY SANDING

Sanding removes dings, nicks, and swirls or minor burn marks left by saw blades and router bits. It also helps joint parts meet evenly. On a microscopic level, sanding provides "tooth" to the wood, so finishes have something to adhere to. But at its most basic level, sanding abrades wood surfaces so they feel smooth to the touch. Silky-smooth, flawless surfaces are signs of careful craftsmanship. They invite admirers to touch and appreciate your work.

If your project surfaces are easy to reach when assembled, you can wait to sand until just before topcoating. In most situations, however, it's much easier to sand the parts prior to assembly. It's wise to sand doors, drawers, chairs or the apron and leg bases of tables before putting them together. You'll also find it harder to sand the inside back corners of cabinets and other casework, so consider sanding these projects while the pieces are still flat on the bench.

Sandpaper Options And Grits

Sandpaper consists of natural or synthetic grit applied to various types of heavy paper or cloth backing. The three principal grit types are garnet, aluminum oxide and silicon carbide. All three are manufactured in a range of fine to coarse grits, which affect how quickly and smoothly they abrade wood. Garnet is a natural, brown-colored mineral. It tends to wear out more rapidly than the synthetic options, but it is useful for sanding by hand. Don't use it for power sanding because it tends to clog up quickly. Aluminum oxide is a synthetic material with tougher working characteristics than garnet. The particles fracture during use to expose new, sharp cutting edges. Aluminum oxide is applied to backing papers that are suitable for both hand and power sanding. Silicon carbide, the toughest grit type, is also made of synthetic material. Typically you'll find it on fine-grit sandpapers over 150-grit.

Silicon carbide sandpaper is intended for wet sanding finishes between coats or to prepare metal for painting.

Tools For Sanding

The quickest route to sanding is to start with a power sander. Random-orbit sanders are the popular choice and have taken woodworking by storm over the past couple decades. They combine quick abrasion with impressive smoothing characteristics. These sanders use adhesive-backed or hook-and-loop discs with holes in them for dust collection. Random-orbit sanders work effectively because they spin the pad as well as move it in tiny orbital patterns. Switch to a conventional quarter-sheet orbital sander for sanding into corners. The square corners of the sanding pad will reach areas that are inaccessible with a round disc. Orbital sanders don't sand as quickly as random-orbit sanders, but they still are quite effective for final smoothing. There are also many styles of

Most woodworkers start the sanding process with a powered random-orbit or orbital sheet sander, then switch to hand sanding with a block or foam pad to finish up. Always wear a dust respirator to protect your lungs.

powered detail sanders for smoothing contours, spindles or narrow areas.

Whether you consider sanding drudgery or not, the final stage of any good sanding job involves hand sanding. Power sanders simply can't create blemish-free surfaces. There are always a few swirls and or scratch marks left behind by your power sander that can only be removed with sandpaper and some good old-fashioned elbow grease. Use a sanding block rather than holding the sandpaper in your palm. Rubber or wood sanding blocks will ensure that surfaces stay flat as you smooth them. Add a layer of cork to your scrap-wood sanding blocks to provide a bit of "give" to the contact surface. Foam-board insulation also makes excellent sanding blocks for smoothing contoured surfaces. Use a bandsaw, rasp or drum sander to conform it into whatever shape you need.

Whether you are power sanding or sanding by hand, be sure to wear a dust respirator. The ordinary single-band "hospital style" masks don't offer enough filtration. Buy one specifically designed to filter out harmful dust. At the very least, a dust respirator will save you lots of unpleasant nose-blowing and coughing. More importantly, it will protect your health. Wood dust can be an irritant if you have respiratory allergies, and research now indicates that it is also a carcinogen. Even sanding grit particles are hazardous to your lungs if you inhale enough of them.

Choosing Grits

Grit numbers refer to industry standards that regulate the size of the grit particles. As the number increases, the grit size gets smaller. Obviously, low numbers are for heavy stock removal, and high numbers are for finer smoothing. Some manufacturers are making it easier to choose sandpaper by simply categorizing the paper as "fine," "medium" and "coarse."

Try to use the grit numbering system instead of the texture descriptions when choosing which grit to use next. The goal is to start with a grit that's coarse enough to remove the initial machine marks or defects, then sand through each finer grit in sequence. Progressively finer grits of paper remove the more coarse scratch marks left by the grit before it. Skipping grits may leave heavier scratch marks behind. You want to

Sanding is simply a process of creating smaller and smaller scratches on the wood until they become invisible to the naked eye. For best results, follow an orderly progression of grits up to 180 or 220 when you sand, and don't skip grits.

reduce the size of the final scratch marks so they're so tiny that you can't see them under a finish or feel them on the final surface.

For smoothing away imperfections on bare wood, 80-grit paper is the coarsest grit you should ever need to use. Start with this grit if your workpieces have deep scratches or burn marks left by sawing and routing. Once the large blemishes are sanded away, switch to 100-grit paper to remove the abrading left by the 80-grit paper. If your project parts are relatively smooth to begin with and you need to remove just light milling marks or scratches, you can begin with 100-grit paper.

Once you've smoothed away the noticeable imperfections, switch to 120- or 150-grit paper and sand again. You can stop sanding after 180- or 220-grit. The scratches left at this stage won't be noticeable under a wood finish if you do a careful job. Continuing with finer grits can actually burnish the wood surface, which means the wood pores close up and inhibit the adhesion of the finish. Believe it or not, you can actually sand too much.

Sand until the paper loads up and begins to lose it effectiveness. If nothing seems to be happening, try pounding out the paper to unclog it. Switch to a new piece as soon as the grit loses its relative coarseness. Don't be a miser about sandpaper; it's inexpensive, so replace it often. If you make sandpaper the dispensable item in your sanding regimen, you'll sand more effectively and in less time.

Sealing The Grain

Some types of wood such as aspen, pine and mahogany can be difficult to sand. Certain areas of the wood will have fibers that seem to remain "fuzzy," no matter how much you sand them. Once you add a topcoat, the fuzzy areas will end up rough to the touch. Sanding sealers can help remedy the problem. They're basically a formulation of thinned varnish or shellac with other additives that make the sealer easier to sand.

If you're planning to apply water-based varnish, start with a coat of sanding sealer to raise and lock the surface fibers so you can sand them off. Otherwise, the varnish will raise the grain and create a rough surface.

Brushing on a coat of sanding sealer will help lock the wood fibers in place so you can sand them off and produce a smooth surface. It's especially useful as a primer coat under water-based varnish, which will otherwise raise the wood grain. A coat of sanding sealer also helps wood absorb stain more evenly, similar to stain controller (see page 267). Apply sealer just as you would a normal brushed finish before working through the final sanding grits.

Sanding In Four Stages

Sanding has the bad reputation of being a boring, time-consuming chore. It doesn't have to be that way if you start with sufficiently coarse sandpaper, use a power sander and follow this easy, four-step technique. First, sand all the surfaces of a workpiece in one direction, moving the sandpaper at roughly 45° to the long grain. This will help level the overall surface and remove major machining marks. **NOTE:** *Always sand in the general direction of the grain. Sanding perpendicular to the grain will leave scratches that are difficult to remove.* Sand in broad, overlapping strokes, keeping power sanders moving across the workpiece at all times. Let the weight of the sander do the work.

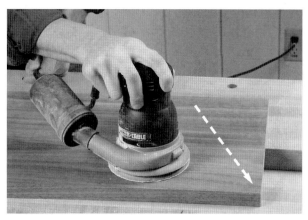

Sand diagonally to the grain first to help level the overall surface and remove the initial machining marks.

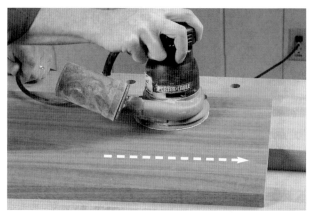

Once the surface is reasonably smooth, keep the same grit but switch to sanding with the grain in long passes.

Bearing down harder on the machine will only increase the chances of leaving deep scratch marks.

Once you've sanded the entire workpiece, switch to the opposite 45° direction and sand the surfaces again. After you've sanded the opposite angle, remove the angled scratch marks by sanding parallel to the grain. Then thoroughly clean off the sanding dust by blowing with compressed air or wiping with a rag dampened with mineral spirits. You don't want residual particles of grit scratching the wood when you're using a finer-grit paper. Switch to the next finer grit paper and sand to all three angles again. Brush or blow off the dust.

To ensure that all power sander scratches are removed, finish up by hand using a sanding block and the same grit as the final power-sanding grit. Sand with the grain only on this last step—skip the angle sanding. Then, continue with 180- or 220-grit paper. You don't have to sand until your arm goes numb; if you've been careful working up through the grits with the power-sanding stage, hand sanding shouldn't take long. Keep switching to fresh paper to speed the process along. When sanding end grain or contoured surfaces, it isn't practical to sand at an angle to the grain. For end grain, your only option may be to sand across the grain. Work gently here, especially with coarse grits, to prevent cutting deep scratches that are tough to remove.

Use a sanding block to remove any power sander scratches. You don't have to sand for a month of Sundays—just enough to remove those last visible scratch marks.

Sweep or blow off all traces of sanding dust before switching to a finer-grit sandpaper. This will prevent any residual grit particles from scratching the surface.

When you're finished sanding, check for sanding scratches by wetting the wood with mineral spirits and shining a light at an angle over the wood. The solvent will highlight any defects (see inset).

Checking For Scratches

After you finish hand sanding, wipe the wood with mineral spirits. Mineral spirits will highlight any scratches that you should touch up without raising the wood grain. Shine a light across your dampened workpiece, and inspect the surface at a low angle while the solvent evaporates. Any scratches you see now will show up later under a stained finish, and the really bad ones are even visible under a clear finish. Make sure to sand these away before proceeding with stain or topcoats.

SMOOTHING BY SCRAPING

Some woodworkers prefer to smooth wood surfaces with a cabinet scraper instead of abrasives. A cabinet scraper is a piece of flexible steel with hook-shaped edge. By flexing the scraper between both hands and holding it at an angle to the wood, you can push or pull the edge over the wood so it cuts like a sharp hand plane. With the correct technique and a keen edge, a scraper will shear off paper-thin shavings and leave a surface that's smooth enough for finishing. It takes practice to get the "hang" of scraping, and you'll also need to learn how to sharpen it properly. Once you get past the learning curve, scraping can be a quiet, dust-free alternative to sanding that's actually enjoyable to do.

A sharp-edged steel scraper will shear off paper-thin wood shavings and leave a glass-smooth surface. It's a quieter, clean-air alternative to sanding.

Fixing Dents And Filling Holes

It doesn't take much to dent bare wood during machining and assembly. One wrong hammer swing, dropping something on a workpiece or tightening a clamp a bit too much is all it takes. Sometimes the little dents don't become evident until the sanding stage when you are paying more attention to surface smoothness. If all the wood in a dent is intact but simply compressed, you can usually steam it out with a household iron. Dampen a piece of cloth with water and lay it over the dent, then apply a hot iron for 10 to 20 seconds or so. The steam will swell the wood fibers and lift out the depression. Be sure to sand these areas carefully when the wood dries and cools. Steaming will raise the wood grain and make it rough.

For filling nail holes or fixing other tiny imperfections, the usual option is wood doughs, putties or fillers. Basically, these products are mixtures of finely ground wood powder and sawdust blended with glue or lacquer.

Although they seem like a convenient solution for making repairs, some putties and fillers don't absorb wood stain the same way the wood does, so the patched area will be noticeable. If you are planning to stain your project, do the staining first, then fill the holes with wood putty tinted to the approximate color of the wood stain. Work carefully to keep the wood putty contained to as small a repair area as possible. If all you need to do is fill nail holes, try colored wax instead of wood filler. Wax sticks are made in various wood finish colors, and you can find them at any home center. Ordinary color crayons in the various brown tones will also work for filling nail holes. Press a small chip of wax into the hole with a fingernail or paint scraper blade and smooth it with your fingertip. Scrape away the excess carefully.

Another option for filling tiny holes is to glue in a splinter of the same wood as the project, and sand it smooth. Do this before staining or topcoating. A wood patch will blend in almost invisibly with the surrounding wood when the finish is applied.

Use a stainable or tinted wood putty to help hide nail heads and other tiny blemishes before finishing. Or, wait until after you've applied the topcoat and fill in the holes with colored wax sticks.

Liquid or gel-based pigment stains are easy to find at a home center. Dye stain, which is available from woodworking suppliers, is sold as a water-soluble powder or premixed with alcohol.

Applying Wood Stain

Stain gives you creative control over how your completed project looks in three ways: First, it allows you to alter the basic color of the wood using a wide range of color tones. If you'd prefer to take the greenish or purple cast out of walnut, a stain provides the means for making the color shift. Second, staining can help blend heartwood and sapwood areas on woods like cherry to even out the inconsistency. Third, stain enhances the natural grain pattern in the wood. This quality can be good or bad, depending on the wood. Quartersawn rays or dramatic figure are highlighted by coloring them. On the other hand, pine and soft maple can look splotchy and uneven when stained, because the wood absorbs stain more deeply in some areas than others.

Types Of Wood Stain

Stain is made of pigments, dyes, or a combination of the two blended with solvents and oil. Pigments are finely-ground particles of colored earth or synthetic chemicals suspended in a liquid. Dyes are made of chemicals called anilines.

Pigment stains color wood by filling the open pores on the surface. The more pigment that gets trapped in the pores, the darker the grain appears. Usually one application of pigment stain fills the pores. Pigment-based stains are more effective in coloring open-grained woods, such as mahogany or oak, rather than denser, closed-grained woods such as hard maple. If the pores are too small to trap the pigment, the color of the wood won't change as much as open-grained woods. The liquid component of pigment-based stains helps the particles of color flow onto the wood easily. A binding agent holds the particles in the pores like glue. Most of the ordinary premixed stains you'll find on the shelves of the hardware store or home center are pigment-based. Some manufacturers mix both pigments and dye into one solution to provide the beneficial characteristics of both materials.

Dye stains work differently than pigment-based stains. Since dyes are molecules of color rather than larger particulates, they absorb into the wood's cells rather than coat the wood. Dyes saturate both open-grained and tight-grained woods relatively evenly. The higher the concentration of dye, the darker the wood color becomes. Dyes can make wood darker than pigments because the coloring action isn't limited by the depth of the surface pores. However, since the dye doesn't concentrate in one area of the wood more than the next, the overall color doesn't have much contrast from open to closed grain areas.

Dye stains are manufactured in both powdered and liquid form. Dye powder is easy to find in woodworking supply catalogs, but you won't find it at the hardware store or home center. The fine powder needs to be mixed with water or denatured alcohol to create the liquid for staining. As long as dye powders have the same solvents, you can mix different colored dyes together to create your own custom colors.

Dye stains sold as premixed liquids have alcohol as their solvent, and they're commonly called "NGR," or non-grain-raising stains. The downside to alcohol dye stain is that it tends to fade more quickly in sunlight than water-based dye stain.

Choosing Between Pigment And Dye Stains

Think about the structure of the wood you are staining before settling on pigment or dye stain. If you want to accentuate those cathedral grain rings on ash or oak, pigment stain is a good choice. On the other hand, if you want a more even contrast and tone, use dye stain. Dye stain is also more effective for blending sapwood than pigment stain, because it's less affected by grain density. Think of dye stain more like a magic marker coloring the wood.

Dyes are also an excellent choice for accentuating highly figured wood. You can use a water-based dye to color the figure, followed by an oil-based pigment stain to color the other areas. The pigment won't absorb into the figure the same way as the dye, so the dye color will show through, "popping" the figure to excellent effect. Using just pigment stain can obscure some of this lovely depth and contrast.

Dye stain offers more flexibility than pigment stain when it comes to changing the intensity and color once you've stained the project. To lighten a too-dark dye stain, wipe the wood with the same solvent you use to mix the dye powder. The solvent reactivates the dye. Blot out the suspended dye with a paper towel. If the color isn't quite what you want, modify it by applying a different color dye right over the first color. More dye will intensify the color and tone. Provided the dyes have matching solvents, the colors will blend to form a new color.

Pigment stains are more difficult to lighten once they are in the wood. The binder seals the pigment in the pores. You can lighten the color of pigment stain while it's still wet by wiping the wood with mineral spirits. However, once the stain dries, the only recourse for removing the color is to sand or strip the wood. You can darken a pigment stain by applying a second coat over the first dry coat and leave the excess on the wood rather than wiping it off. Or, overcoat with a darker-colored pigment stain instead.

Whether you use dye or pigment stain, the best way to evaluate the color and tone is to try the stain on pieces of scrap wood. If your project involves veneered plywood, stain some of that too. Work on large pieces to get a feel for the real work and results you can expect. You can experiment with your application method and tweak the coloring before committing the actual project to it. It will save you the frustration and effort of removing the color afterward.

Options For Controlling Blotching And End-Grain Mismatch

Blotching is one problem with staining wood. Another issue you'll need to address is the tendency of pigment stain to soak in heavily on end grain and make it darker than the face or edge grain. Softer woods like pine are particularly prone to end-grain mismatch. If you don't like this effect, consider pre-treating the wood with stain controller. Stain controller is a blend of thinned varnish or shellac and solvents that help to seal uneven grain and end grain. Brush it on liberally, just as you would a stain, and wipe off the excess. Then immediately follow with stain before the controller dries. The controller will limit how much stain absorbs into the wood.

Another option is to use gel-based stain instead of liquid. Gel stains con-

Stain conditioner, also called stain controller, will help blotch-prone woods like pine absorb stain more evenly. Brush it on immediately before staining.

sist of pigments or dyes suspended in a thick binder with a pudding-like consistency. The thick suspension will not penetrate deeply into the open pores like thinner liquid, so the stain provides more even coverage. Gel stain also makes it easier to stain vertical surfaces because it doesn't drip, splash or run. Simply wipe the gel stain onto the wood with a rag and wipe off the excess.

Notice how the end grain and face grain absorb stain more evenly on the left and center samples treated with wood conditioner or gel stain. Without special treatment, stain will often absorb more heavily on end grain and blotch the face grain, as is evident in the right sample.

Mixing And Applying Stains

Before using a pigment stain, be sure to stir the liquid thoroughly to blend the pigments, binder and solvent together. To mix a dye stain, measure and add the dry powder to the appropriate solvent in a plastic or glass container. Do not use a metal container—it can discolor the dye. Add the powder slowly while stirring to keep it from clumping. For water-based dye, use hot distilled water, and stir the mixture until all the powder is blended into solution. Pour the prepared dye through a disposable paper paint strainer into another container to filter out any undissolved powder. Be sure to prepare enough dye stain to complete your entire project; it will be difficult to duplicate the exact color if you have to mix more midway through the job.

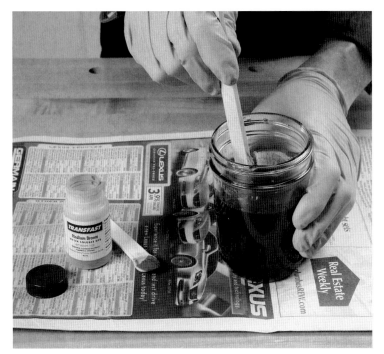

Mix powdered dye stain in a plastic or glass container using warm, distilled water. Stir thoroughly. Add powder until you get the depth of color you want. Try to mix up enough to stain the entire project.

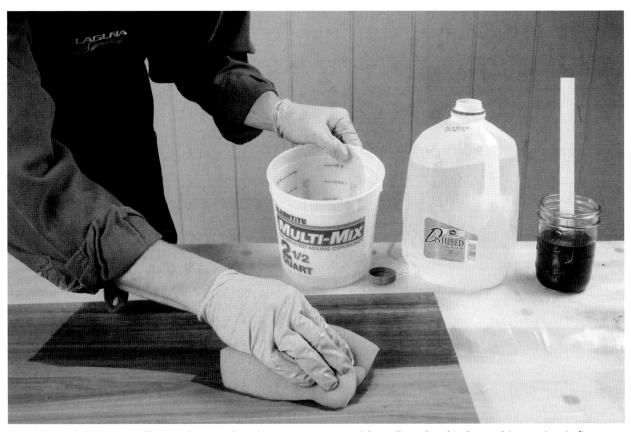

Water-based dye stain will raise the wood grain. One way to avoid sanding the dyed wood is to wipe it first with distilled water, let it dry and lightly sand it. This should eliminate the grain-raising effect when you apply the stain.

Water-based dye stains will raise the wood grain as the fibers swell. You can sand the raised grain flat again, but you'll remove some of the dye color. A better solution is to wipe the wood down first with distilled water and allow it to dry. Lightly sand the raised grain with 220-grit sandpaper to flatten it. Provided you don't sand too much, the grain won't raise again when you apply the stain.

You can spread pigment or dye stain with a clean rag, paint brush or even paper towels. Brushing floods the surface with stain more quickly than wiping, which can help if the stain has a tendency to dry quickly. However, flooding stain near end grain can cause capillary action to pull extra stain into the end grain and cause it to look darker than the face grain. Wiping on stain offers more control of the liquid, and it's a good way to prevent drips, especially if your project has vertical surfaces. It doesn't matter if you apply the stain with or across the grain. Once the stain is on the wood, let it soak in for a few minutes and wipe off the excess with a clean rag. Switch to clean areas of the rag as you wipe the surface dry. Work your way across the surface wiping each stroke nearly dry before moving on to a new wet area. The goal is to achieve an even-colored film of stain without leaving wiping marks behind. Allow the surfaces to dry thoroughly before proceeding with a topcoat of clear finish.

Be sure to stir pigment stain thoroughly to suspend and blend the pigment and binder with the solvents and oil. Your stick should come up clean.

Brush or wipe the bare wood with a liberal coat of stain and give it a few minutes to soak in.

Wipe off excess stain with a clean, lint-free cloth. An old dish towel or T-shirt works well.

CHOOSING AND APPLYING A TOPCOAT

Coating projects with varnish, shellac or lacquer has several important benefits. Topcoats help to slow down the rate of moisture exchange between the wood and the environment. Remember that wood acts like a sponge to moisture, and it's constantly shrinking and swelling. A topcoat has a stabilizing effect so joints stay tighter, the wood warps less and doors and drawers don't swell stuck in their openings. Topcoatings also provide a protective covering from spills, dirt and general wear and tear. Some products have UV inhibitors to prevent colors from fading or finishes from peeling if your project sits in sunlight every day. Finally, a topcoat lends sheen and texture to the wood. Whether you want the wood to have a glossy "wet" look or a low-luster satiny sheen, the topcoat will create the effect.

Regardless of the topcoat you use, it may be tempting to not finish large unseen surfaces such as the bottom face of a tabletop or the inside of a box. However, if you've got finish on one side of a workpiece, always finish the other side too. Remember, bare wood absorbs water vapor. A topcoat will reduce this capability, but the bare side will still absorb water at the usual rate. This sets up different rates of moisture absorption, which can lead to warping. If that tabletop has three coats of varnish on the top side, it should also have three coats on the underside. The quality of those underside coats is really insignificant, but their role as a water barrier is still very important.

Selecting The Finish

There are four basic options for topcoats: wipe-on finishes, varnish, shellac and lacquer. You can find all four types at any hardware store or home center. The big decision you'll need to make is which of the four finishes to choose. Different finishes offer varying degrees of durability, ease of application and reparability. To help you pick the right finish, ask yourself the following questions:

How Will The Project Be Used?

A decorative shelf or mantel clock won't receive as much handling or wear and tear as a tabletop or cabinet door. For heavily used items, you'll want a finish that stands up to abrasion, spills and grime. Think about where your project will be located as well. Will it sit in full sun most of the time, end up in a damp basement or near a heat register? Sunlight, heat, humidity and strong solvents all impact the longevity of a finish. If you have kids or pets, you'll probably want to finish your projects with the toughest coating you can find.

How Much Time And Effort Do You Want To Invest In Finishing?

Applying a finish can be as easy as wiping the product on with a rag. If you only have a limited amount of time and patience for finishing, you may want to avoid certain options that involve grinding and mixing flakes, thinning and adjust-ing ratios or sanding between coats. There are tradeoffs for speed and ease of application; you may not be able to obtain a velvety smooth texture or a dazzling display of grain and figure, but the time you'll save may be worth a less-than-"blue-ribbon" finish.

Where And When Will You Apply The Finish?

Topcoats have different curing characteristics. Polyurethane varnish can dry all day and still feel tacky, while a coat of spray lacquer can be dry to the touch in less than 10 minutes. If your only option for applying the finish is a dusty shop or the driveway, avoid slow-curing varnish. It will catch dust or flower pollen like flypaper. Shellac or lacquer are better choices. By the same token, some finishes have strong-smelling or even flammable solvents. If you are finishing a large project in the middle of the winter, you may want to choose a water-based finish when it isn't practical to open doors and windows. Keep in mind that some finishes are sensitive to humidity. A damp basement in the middle of August is a bad place for brushing lacquer or shellac but less of a concern for wiping on thin varnish.

How Easy Is It To Maintain The Finish?

It's worth considering how much effort it will take to repair or restore a finish if something happens to it down the road. Varnish will give you a tough final coat, but a deep scratch or a peeling coating will be tough to fix. Shellac and lacquer won't provide the same durability as varnish, but you can hide light scratches or minor damage by simply brushing or spraying on another coat. No sanding or other prep work is required.

Wipe-on finishes are quick-drying and easy to apply, but the tradeoff is a thinner, less durable topcoat. This category includes drying oils, blends of oils and varnish or essentially thinned varnish.

Wipe-On Finishes: Fast And Easy But Not As Tough

Among the four categories of topcoats, nothing is easier to apply than wipe-on finishes. If you can dust your house, you can apply a wipe-on finish successfully. All it takes is a rag and some elbow grease. The finish dries quickly, and you'll never have to fuss with drips, sags or messy brushes.

Wipe-on finishes are made from blends of tung, linseed, or other oils with varnish and mineral spirits. Some are simply varnishes thinned with solvent. Wipe-on finishes are sold in many forms, including polyurethane blends, "Scandinavian," "Nordic" or "Danish" oil finishes and varieties of tung oil mixtures. If a product comes in a can and is sold as a "finish," it's probably a thinned var-

nish. Two other options to choose from are purified tung oil or boiled linseed oil, although these two oils take a long time to cure and never cure hard.

Wipe-on finishes apply quickly and easily, but save them for lightly handled or decorative projects. Another attribute of wipe-on finishes is that they produce flat or satiny sheens without also changing the surface texture of the wood. If you don't want your project to look like it's coated with plastic, or if you like the natural look of open pores, a wiping finish is a good choice.

A wiping finish can require occasional maintenance. Depending on how many layers of it you apply and how thin the varnish is to begin with, you may have to add more coats at some point. Sometimes the finish will continue to soak into the wood, and the wood will end up looking dry.

Wiping On A Finish

Pour the finish into a lint-free rag so it's saturated but not dripping, and wipe on the finish until the surface is wet. You can wipe with or across the grain—it doesn't matter. Give the finish a few minutes to soak into the grain, then wipe off the excess with a dry rag and allow the surfaces to dry before recoating. Leaving pools of finish on the wood may seem like a way to build up a thicker coating, but it really just prolongs the amount of time it takes for the finish to cure. You'll get more coats of finish on the wood in less time by wiping thin coats. Since the finish doesn't cure to a film, there's no need to sand between coats.

When you are finished with a rag, be careful to spread it out flat and allow the finish to cure. Once the finish is dry, the rag is safe to toss. Many wipe-on finishes contain boiled linseed oil, which creates heat as it cures. A balled-up rag soaked with wet wipe-on finish can actually catch fire.

Making Your Own Wiping Finish

It's easy to create your own wipe-on finish using oil-based varnish.

There's no easier topcoat to apply than a wiping finish. Just dampen a clean rag with finish and wipe it on. Wipe off the excess.

Simply dilute the full-strength varnish with mineral spirits until it's about the consistency of skim milk. Pour the spirits into the varnish a little at a time and stir the mixture until you get the right ratio. Wipe it on just as you would a premixed finish. You can achieve a thicker film finish by reducing the amount of solvent and still wipe it on with good results.

It's easy to make your own wiping finish: just thin oil-based varnish by a third with mineral spirits. Experiment on scrap to check your results.

Varnish is a tough but slow-drying finish. You can buy it in liquid, gel or aerosol sprays in several sheens. You'll also need to choose between oil- or water-based formulations.

Varnish: Durable But Slow Drying

Varnish is the workhorse consumer finish, and there are plenty of good reasons why. First, varnish forms a tough, protective layer on the wood surface. Most varnishes offer excellent resistance to wear and tear, moisture, most household solvents and alcohol. When fully cured, varnish seals wood pores and helps to reduce wood movement. Another advantage of varnish is that you can buy it formulated to cure to flat, satin, or gloss sheens. This way, you can use varnish to simulate a "close-to-the-wood" finish that doesn't shine, a finish with just a bit of sheen to it, or a highly "wet" looking finish.

Many finishing experts prefer a foam paint pad over a brush for applying water-based varnish. The pad reduces brush strokes.

Varnish is relatively easy to apply with a brush, but it cures slowly. It's not a good choice if you're in a hurry to get that finish applied to a gift project on Christmas Eve or if you do your finishing in a dusty shop.

Varnish is manufactured in three forms: oil-based polyurethane, oil-based alkyd, and water-based acrylic or polyurethane blends. Oil-based polys and alkyds are more durable to water, solvents and heat than water-based products, but the wet varnish has fumy-smelling solvents. Oil-based varnishes take on a yellowish tint as they age, and water-based varnish can leave the wood looking bluish or dull. Polyurethane can crack and peel if it's exposed to direct sunlight.

If you want to varnish a project that will end up in the bathroom, kitchen or outside, choose a "spar" or "marine" varnish. Spar or marine varnish cures to a softer, more flexible finish than ordinary varnishes, but it produces a darker color than ordinary varnish. The softer cure allows the finish to move with the wood as it expands and contracts.

You can also buy varnish with a gel base, similar to gel stains. Gel varnish is convenient for coating contoured or intricate surfaces because you can control the coverage easily without drips and sags. Gel varnish is also excellent for topcoating vertical surfaces. It can be harder to remove globs of gel varnish from inside corners or hard-to-reach areas, so save it for those broad, open areas.

Water-based varnish is more susceptible to damage from solvents, water and heat than oil-based varnish. However, it dries to a tough, clear, scratch-resistant coating that's actually harder than oil-based varnish. Be sure to raise the grain with distilled water and sand off the raised fibers before applying the first coat to keep the varnish from raising the grain. Or start with a coat of sanding sealer. One big advantage to using water-based varnish is that it doesn't smell bad or pose a fire hazard as the solvents evaporate.

Applying Varnish

Varnish doesn't require special blending to get it ready for use. Just stir it up thoroughly. Because varnish cures slowly, especially oil-based varnishes, it's important to work in a clean, dust-free environment. Otherwise, bits of dust in the air will settle on the varnish before it cures and leave tiny rough spots on the surface. Strain water-based varnish through a paper filter before applying it. The low solvent content won't always dissolve bits of solid in the can, and these will end up on the wood unless you filter them out. With either oil- or water-based varnish, don't dip your brush directly into the can. Pour off an amount into a separate container to keep from contaminating the entire can of finish with bits of sanding grit or dust.

Sand lightly between coats of varnish if you have to wait more than 24 hours before recoating. Sanding will help the new finish adhere to the layer beneath it.

Pour water-based varnish through a paint strainer before using it to filter out any particles in the liquid.

Brush on the first coat of varnish using the brushing technique shown in the tint box on page 281. Apply the finish in long strokes, keeping a wet edge and brushing with the grain. Let the first coat cure hard, then lightly sand it with 220-grit paper to remove any dust particles or rough areas. Clean the surfaces thoroughly with a rag dampened with mineral spirits before beginning the next coat.

For most project applications, three coats of varnish are enough to build a durable film finish. If you apply the second and third coats within 24 hours of the first coat, it isn't necessary to sand between coats. The new layers will bond adequately with the semi-cured underlayers. However, if you spread the finishing stage out over several weeks, sand between coats with 320-grit paper. This will help rough up the surface so new layers will bond properly. Varnish isn't like shellac or lacquer, which literally dissolves and fuses to itself.

If you use aerosol varnish instead of brushing it on, spray in light coats, starting off the edge of the workpiece and releasing the applicator after you pass completely by the workpiece. Overlap each stroke to create an even film. Don't spray on more than one coat at a time, or you're bound to get sags.

Shellac makes an excellent wood sealer and a beautiful, repairable topcoat. Home centers sell both liquid and aerosol shellac, but you can also buy it in flake form and mix it yourself.

Shellac: Versatile And Forgiving

Shellac has been used for almost two centuries as a wood finish. Unlike varnish or lacquer, which are made from synthetic chemicals, shellac is a natural substance. It is extracted from cocoon secretions of the lac bug, found in India and Thailand. The secretions are turned into thin sheets and crushed into flakes that look like chips of colored glass. You can buy shellac in flake form and mix it with denatured alcohol to create a liquid finish. It comes in a half dozen different colors ranging from nearly blond to red, with varying shades of yellow and orange in between. Shellac is also sold in liquid and aerosol forms that require no mixing or dissolving. The advantage to flake shellac is that it has a longer shelf life than premixed shellac. If kept dry and in an airtight container, flake shellac will last a couple years, while canned shellac might only last six months after it's opened.

There are lots of good reasons for finishing your projects with shellac. For one, shellac forms an excellent barrier coat over incompatible finishes. For instance, if you apply water-based polyurethane over a water-based dye stain, the varnish will reactivate and smear the stain. A thin layer of shellac over the stain will seal it from the poly. Shellac also encases resins and oils that might

Old shellac will eventually get "gummy" and not cure properly. It's a good idea to write the month and year you first open the can so you can track its age.

bleed through the final topcoat and damage it. Be sure to use the de-waxed varieties of shellac if you apply it as a barrier coat under another finish, otherwise the wax will affect the adhesion of the top-coat. Shellac works as both a standing sealer and stain controller as well.

Shellac makes a wonderful finish all by itself. The amber and red tones it imparts to the wood help to "warm up" pale woods like maple and oak. It also adds depth and clarity to figured wood so those flakes and iridescent areas really sparkle. Shellac is fairly easy to apply by brush if it's thin enough, and the cured topcoat is non-toxic. Once you apply the base layer, another benefit to shellac is that it isn't necessary to sand between coats. Each new coat partial-ly dissolves the layer underneath.

Aside from short shelf life, shellac has a few important shortcomings. It can be damaged by lye, ammonia, alcohol and water. Those pesky white rings you see on antique fur-niture are telltale signs of water-damaged shellac. Shellac also won't stand up to intense heat. Don't use it to finish trivets or steam radiator covers! On the upside, a shellac fin-ish is easier to repair than varnish; just sand the damaged area lightly to remove scratches or dings, and apply a fresh coat of shellac over the damage.

Mixing Flake Shellac

The process of mixing shellac with denatured alcohol is called "cutting." A "2 lb." cut of shellac means a ratio of two pounds of flake shellac mixed with one gallon of denatured alcohol. You don't need to mix shellac in huge batches like this. Just reduce the quantities while maintaining the ratio. A 2-lb. cut is ideal for general brushing purposes. For smaller proj-ects, you can achieve a 2-lb. cut by mixing 4 ounces of shellac flakes (about 1/2 cup of flakes) with 1 pint of denatured alcohol. Use a plastic or glass container for mixing shellac to keep the metal from reacting and dis-

About 1/2 cup of shellac flakes in 1 quart of alcohol will create a 2-lb. cut of mixed shellac—a good ratio for brushing. Thinner cuts will brush well too.

coloring the shellac. If you buy liquid shellac, it's usually a 3-lb. cut. Follow the instructions on the can to thin it to a 2-lb. cut.

To mix shellac more quickly, start by grinding the flakes in a coffee grinder or pulverize them in a plas-tic bag with a soft mallet. Pour the flakes into the alcohol a little at a time and stir thoroughly. Depending on the freshness of the flakes, it may take several hours for the flakes to completely dissolve. Then, filter the mixture through a paint strainer into another clean container to remove any small bits of flake that don't dissolve.

An old coffee grinder will turn shellac flakes into a fine powder that will dissolve more quickly in alcohol.

Brushing Shellac

The trick to brushing shellac successfully is to start with a thin, fresh mixture and don't be too picky. Use a good-quality synthetic or natural bristle brush and load it with a fairly heavy amount of shellac. Use the brushing sequence shown on page 281 to start in from the edge, then flow out the finish in long, smooth strokes. As soon as the brush starts to run out of finish, replenish it so you keep a wet edge throughout. Because alcohol flashes off quickly, you don't have much time between brush strokes. Avoid the urge to "tip off" the finish; you'll only smudge the partially cured shellac and introduce brush marks or overlapping lines.

The first coat will serve as a primer coat over the wood. Once it fully cures, which takes about an hour, you may need to sand lightly with 320-grit paper to remove any fuzz or dust nibs. After the base coat is smooth and clean, you should be able to apply additional coats without sanding between them. Remember, the finish dissolves itself and blends right in to build a thicker layer.

Apply aerosol shellac the same way you would spray varnish. Spray on thin, overlapping coats and allow each coat to fully cure before adding another coat. Spray shellac will require many coats to build to a solid film. Be especially careful when rubbing it out (see page 282) to avoid cutting through the thin film.

Apply shellac only when the humidity is low. Extra moisture in the air or on the wood can end up under the finish and cause it to look cloudy. This condition is called blushing. Sometimes blushing will fade away on its own as the wood and air dry out. Or, you can try to draw it out by wiping the surface with denatured alcohol. The best way to avoid it is to save your shellac finishing for the drier fall and winter months.

Cleanup And Storage

Store any shellac you don't use in an airtight container, and date it so you can monitor its shelf life. One way to check for freshness is to pour a drop on a piece of glass and let it cure. If you can dent it with a fingernail after a few days' time, the finish is past its usable life. There's no need to clean the bristles of a shellac brush between uses. Just soak it in denatured alcohol to soften the stiff bristles, and it'll be ready for use again. Dedicate a brush specifically for shellac if it's a finish you end up using often, and store it stiff until you need it.

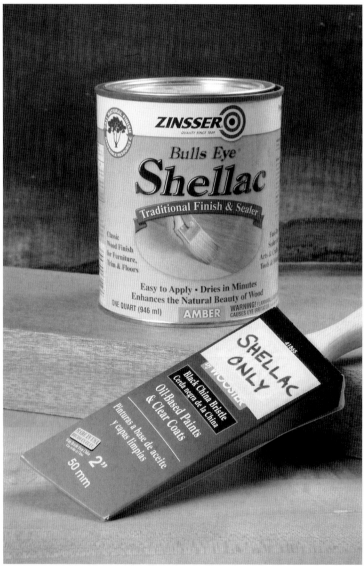

Dedicate one brush for shellac only. When you're finished using it, wring the bristles out and let them dry stiff. Next time you need the brush, just soak the bristles in denatured alcohol to soften them again for use.

Lacquer: Fast And Smooth But Hazardous

Lacquer was originally formulated in the 1920s to replace shellac. It's a complex combination of nitrocellulose, resins and plasticizers that allow it to cure quickly and resist heat, water, solvents and alkalis better than shellac. Lacquer will also cure to a harder finish than shellac, but it still isn't as tough as full-strength varnish. Another benefit to using lacquer is that, like shellac, each new coat partially dissolves the layer beneath it to form a uniform layer. With practice and the right combination of humidity and application technique, you can achieve a crystal-clear, smooth finish in a fraction of the time it would take for varnish to cure. Lacquer also makes an effective barrier coat over other finishes.

Of the four do-it-yourself finishing options shown here, lacquer can be the most difficult to apply successfully. Professional finishers usually spray lacquer with adjustable spray

Lacquer dries quickly and provides a reasonably durable finish. You can apply it by brush or aerosol spray, but most professional woodworkers use specialized air sprayers for best results.

guns under carefully controlled conditions. Adding retarders and thinners can help extend the curing time, but this is only practical with specialized spray equipment. Rapid curing can make lacquer hard to apply without the finish curing too quickly to flow out evenly. Another drawback

CHOOSING BRUSHES FOR FINISHING

The best way to achieve smooth, flawless brushed finishes is to start with a good quality brush. Expect to pay from $10 to $20 for a decent brush and $50 or more for a top-quality brush. Either natural or synthetic bristles will work well for applying oil-based varnish, shellac or lacquer. Do not use natural bristles with water-based stain or varnish or the bristles will tangle and swell. The best-shaped brushes for finishing are those with bristles that are cut to a beveled edge. Blunt, flat-edged brushes tend to leave more brush marks and will spread the finish unevenly. Look for brushes with the bristle tips "flagged" into tiny splits. The flagged tips leave fewer brush marks. Disposable foam brushes are a good option for applying water-based stains and finishes, but stronger solvent finishes can dissolve the foam.

A top-quality finish begins with a good brush. A high-quality synthetic bristle brush (left) will work for most topcoats. Use natural bristle brushes (center) for oil-based finishes only. An inexpensive foam brush (right) works well for staining, painting or applying water-based varnish.

The solvents in lacquer are both flammable and toxic to breathe. Wear a cartridge respirator and work in a well-ventilated area.

to lacquer is that it contains thinners that are flammable and hazardous to your health. Breathing the fumes will cause headaches, nausea and even kidney or liver damage over time. If the smell of nail polish bothers you, you won't like lacquer. It smells similar, only much stronger.

Brushing Or Spraying Lacquer

Unless you have access to a spray gun and an explosion-proof finishing room, your options for applying lacquer are brushing or aerosol-spray. Brushing lacquer is formulated with solvents that evaporate more slowly so you can spread it out before it starts to cure. Apply brushing lacquer with a high-quality synthetic or natural bristle brush the same way you would shellac. Condition your brush first by dipping it in lacquer thinner. Start a few inches in from the edge of the workpiece and brush to the near edge (see brushing technique, page 281). Then go back to the starting point and flow out the rest of the finish to the other end in a quick, smooth stroke. Do not go back over the wet finish again to smooth it, or you'll introduce brush marks. Let the lacquer even itself out.

Lightly sand the first coat of finish with 220-grit sandpaper or a fine-grit foam sanding pad after it cures for an hour or so. This will remove any fibers that may have risen up as well as dust nibs or other debris. From here on, you don't need to sand between coats. As each coat dissolves the underlying coat, it should level itself out.

Lacquer is also susceptible to blushing if you apply it during humid summer months. You can leave any blushing as is and see if the moisture escapes on its own when the humidity drops. Or, wipe the finish with a light coat of lacquer thinner to help release the trapped moisture.

To spray aerosol lacquer, apply it in long, overlapping strokes, starting off the edge of the workpiece and moving past it before releasing the trigger. Keep each coat light to avoid drips and sags.

Whether you apply lacquer by brushing or spraying, wear a cartridge-style respirator to prevent breathing the harmful fumes. Brush or spray it outside on a dry day, or open plenty of windows in the shop to vent the heavy fumes. Do not spray lacquer in the house if you can help it; even one can of aerosol will produce enough fumes to spread to every room and give people headaches. Never apply it in the basement when you are running natural gas appliances like water heaters or the furnace.

BRUSHING ON A FINISH

Brushing on a finish may seem like one of those activities that requires no special technique, but a few tips can really help. The first step toward a good finish is to condition your brush by dipping it up to the metal ferrule in the same solvent you'll use to clean it later. Conditioning the brush helps the finish load onto the brush evenly and makes the bristles easier to clean. Use mineral spirits for varnish, denatured alcohol for shellac and lacquer thinner for lacquer. Squeeze or press out the solvent so the bristles are damp but not dripping.

Before dipping your brush in any topcoat, "charge" the bristles by soaking them up to the ferrule in the solvent for that finish. This will help the finish load properly and also speed up the brush-cleaning process later.

Dip your brush into the finish and press the bristles against the edge of the container to unload the excess. Start by brushing about three inches in from the edge of the workpiece out to the closest end, with the grain. Starting inward and brushing outward unloads the thick finish where it can't run or drip. Then spread out the thick finish, brushing in long strokes to the other end. Finish up by brushing the edges and ends of the workpiece. Look closely for drips and keep the finish thin in these areas.

To brush on a finish, start a few inches in and brush out to the end. This deposits the excess finish on the flat area and not on an edge where it will drip. Apply these short strokes all along the end.

Next, start from the short strokes and brush more finish out to the opposite end in long, smooth strokes. Try to keep a wet edge as you work your way across the surface.

Finish the edges last. Don't load the brush heavily or you'll get drips.

If you're brushing varnish, it's okay to overlap strokes without concern because you can level off any ridges or brush marks before the varnish begins to cure. Just drag the tips of the bristles over the surface in long strokes to "tip off" the finish. This will also help to pop small bubbles that may be present. When brushing shellac or lacquer, try to load the brush with enough finish to make one full stroke to the other end without stopping. Do not tip off shellac or lacquer; these finishes will tend to level themselves out on their own as the top layer dissolves the layer beneath it. Tipping off will just introduce brush lines.

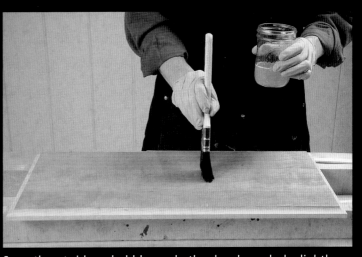

Smooth out ridges, bubbles and other brush marks by lightly "tipping off" the finish with the brush held vertically to the surface. This only works with varnish; shellac and lacquer dry too quickly.

Rubbing out a finish accomplishes two things: it polishes away any minor blemishes and allows you to create the final sheen you're after. Rubbing compound or other lubricated abrasives will build different levels of sheen.

Rubbing Out And Polishing

Brushing or spraying on a finish will leave a reasonably smooth surface, but usually you'll still find little imperfections here and there. An easy way to take your finish to a higher level of velvety smoothness is to rub it with fine abrasives. Rubbing out a finish also allows you to adjust the final surface sheen. You can create a matte, satin or glossy surface depending on which combination of abrasive and lubricant you use. Only finishes that cure to a hard film are good candidates for rubbing out. Wipe-on finishes generally cure too soft to be rubbed out. Oil- and water-based varnishes, shellac and lacquer all rub out well. It's important to start with a thick film finish. If you sprayed the finish on as an aerosol, it should be six to eight coats thick. For brushed finishes, three coats should be sufficient. If the topcoat is too thin, you run the risk of rubbing right through it.

Allow the finish plenty of time to cure completely before rubbing it out. Give shellac and lacquer a week, and allow at least two weeks or more for oil-based varnish. One way to tell if you've waited long enough is to smell the finish up close. If you can still detect a solvent smell, it's still curing. Don't rub it out until all the solvent smell is gone.

Start the rubbing process with 600-grit wet/dry sandpaper lubricated with mineral spirits. Flow on the mineral spirits and rub lightly. The goal here is to abrade the surface just enough to level off any high spots. If you want a matte finish that doesn't reflect light, this stage is all you need to do. To achieve a satiny finish with a bit more sheen, switch to a gray or white synthetic abrasive pad or #0000 steel wool. Lubricate the surface with Murphy's Oil Soap™, ordinary soapy water or paste wax thinned 50% with mineral spirits. For a glossy, mirror sheen, use automotive rubbing compound applied with a clean cotton cloth.

Treat the rubbing out process just like moving from coarse to fine sandpapers: work up the sheen in stages. Whatever level of sheen you choose, you can make it slippery smooth and add a bit of protection by finishing up with a coat of furniture paste wax and a thorough buffing. Spread the wax on in a thin coat, just as you would wax a car. Let the wax dry until it's hazy, then buff it off.

Give your finish a velvety smoothness and superior shine by completing the job with a coat of paste wax.

INDEX

P

Tape measure
measuring basics, 106–107
Taper cuts
bandsaw, 165
defined, 126
table saw, 139–140
tapering jig, 139–140
tooling options, 127
Tapering jig, 139–140
Tearout, 83–84
miter saw, 183
router and minimizing, 207
wetting wood to reduce, 92
Template routing, 213–215
Templates
making, 116
Tenon cuts
radial-arm saw, 178
table saw
dado blade, 155–156
rule of thirds, 154
standard blade, 152–155
tenoning jigs, 153
Thick stock
rip cut
table saw, 137
Thin stock
rip cut
table saw, 138
Through dovetail, 230–233
Tongue and groove joints
description and application
of, 119
table saw, 150–151
tooling options, 119
Tools. *See also* specific tools
tune-up, 25–77
bandsaw, 39–46
benchtop planer, 47–51
caring for cast iron, 28
cleaning blades and bits, 73
drill press, 58–59
frequency of, 26
jointer, 52–57
miter saw, 66–68

new tools, 26
radial-arm saw, 60–65
router table, 69–73
sharpening chisels and plane
irons, 74–77
table saw, 29–38
tools for, 27–28
Topcoat
choosing brushes for, 279
function of, 270
lacquer, 279–280
rubbing out and polishing, 282
selecting finish, 271
shellac, 276–278
tips for brushing on finish, 281
varnish, 274–275
wipe-on finishes, 272–273
Trammel points
drawing circles, 113
Tune-up, 25–77
bandsaw, 39–46
benchtop planer, 47–51
caring for cast iron, 28
cleaning blades and bits, 73
drill press, 58–59
frequency of, 26
jointer, 52–57
miter saw, 66–68
new tools, 26
radial-arm saw, 60–65
router table, 69–73
sharpening chisels and plane
irons, 74–77
table saw, 29–38
tools for, 27–28
Twist
defined, 80–81
remedying, 87–88

U

Urban lumber, 13

V

Varnish
applying, 275
characteristics of, 274
selecting finish, 271
Veneer
core for, 17–18
selecting, 17
types of face, 17

W

Wane, 90
Waney edges
rip cut
table saw, 136
Water-resistant yellow glue, 237
WD-40, 28
Wet sharpeners, 74, 75
White glue, 237
Wipe-on finish
characteristics of, 272
making own, 273
selecting finish, 271
wiping on, 273
Wood plugs
drill press, 188
Woodworking screws, 248
Woodworking stores, 9–11

Y

Yellow carpenter's glue, 237

Z

Zero-clearance throatplate
making, 134